Helmut Meier

'Malleable at the European Will'

British Discourse on Slavery (1784–1824) and the Image of Africans

Helmut Meier

'MALLEABLE AT THE EUROPEAN WILL'

British Discourse on Slavery (1784–1824) and the Image of Africans

ibidem-Verlag
Stuttgart

Bibliografische Information der Deutschen Nationalbibliothek
Die Deutsche Nationalbibliothek verzeichnet diese Publikation in der Deutschen Nationalbibliografie; detaillierte bibliografische Daten sind im Internet über http://dnb.d-nb.de abrufbar.

Bibliographic information published by the Deutsche Nationalbibliothek
Die Deutsche Nationalbibliothek lists this publication in the Deutsche Nationalbibliografie; detailed bibliographic data are available in the Internet at http://dnb.d-nb.de.

Cover picture: Group of African (?) men, women and children captured in order to become slaves. Lithograph, ca. 1880. Source: Wikimedia Commons. © Wellcome Library no. 578847i. Licensed under CC BY 4.0 (s. https://creativecommons.org/licenses/by/4.0/deed.en).

∞

Gedruckt auf alterungsbeständigem, säurefreien Papier
Printed on acid-free paper

ISBN-13: 978-3-8382-1273-9

© *ibidem*-Verlag
Stuttgart 2019

Alle Rechte vorbehalten

Das Werk einschließlich aller seiner Teile ist urheberrechtlich geschützt. Jede Verwertung außerhalb der engen Grenzen des Urheberrechtsgesetzes ist ohne Zustimmung des Verlages unzulässig und strafbar. Dies gilt insbesondere für Vervielfältigungen, Übersetzungen, Mikroverfilmungen und elektronische Speicherformen sowie die Einspeicherung und Verarbeitung in elektronischen Systemen.

All rights reserved. No part of this publication may be reproduced, stored in or introduced into a retrieval system, or transmitted, in any form, or by any means (electronic, mechanical, photocopying, recording or otherwise) without the prior written permission of the publisher. Any person who does any unauthorized act in relation to this publication may be liable to criminal prosecution and civil claims for damages.

Printed in the EU

Table of Contents

1 **Introduction** 11
2 **Methodology** 15
    2.1   CDA 15
    2.2   Post-Colonial Reading and Concepts 20
    2.3   Post-humanism and Agamben 22
    2.4   ~~Race~~ 24
    2.5   QDA Software 25
            2.5.1   *Codes* 28
            2.5.2   *Memos* 31
            2.5.3   *Retrieval* 32
    2.6   Corpus Linguistics 33
3 **Historical Context, Key Events and Discursive Events** 37
    3.1   Introduction 37
    3.2   The "Original State of Mankind" 38
    3.3   Biblical Events 40
    3.4   Greco-Roman Antiquity 42
            3.4.1   *Authority of the Ancients* 42
            3.4.2   *Slaves in Antiquity* 47
                   3.4.2.1 Greek Slaves 48
                   3.4.2.2 Roman Slaves 50
            3.4.3   *Decline and Fall of the Roman Empire* 51
    3.5   Middle Ages and Feudalism 55
    3.6   Orient versus Occident 59
            3.6.1   *Islam as the Ultimate Other* 59
            3.6.2   *Arabic Slave Trade* 61
            3.6.3   *Islamic Influence in Africa as "Some Feeble Light"* ... 62

3.7		Modernity and the Atlantic System 66
	3.7.1	*African History* 66
	3.7.2	*Slave Trade and Abolition* 69
	3.7.3	*British History* 79
	3.7.4	*The American Revolution* 82
	3.7.5	*History of the Caribbean Islands* 85
	3.7.6	*Larger Historical Context —* *British and European History* 89
3.8		Conclusion 92

4 The Discourse on Slavery 95

4.1	Corpus-based Appreciation of the Discourse as a Whole 95
	4.1.1 *The Ten Most Frequent Nouns* 96
	4.1.2 *Thematic Selection from the 150 Most Frequent Nouns* 97
4.2	James Ramsay's *Essay* (1784) 103
	4.2.1 *James Ramsay — Biography and self-representation in the text* 103
	4.2.2 *Synopsis and Argumentative Aims of the Essay* .. 105
	4.2.3 *Ideology* 111
4.3	Anonymous: *An Answer to James Ramsay's Essay* (1784) 116
	4.3.1 *"Some Gentlemen of St. Christopher"* 116
	4.3.2 *Synopsis and Arguments* 118
	4.3.3 *Ideology* 123
4.4	James Tobin's *Cursory Remarks* (1785) 126
	4.4.1 *James Tobin — Biography and Self-representation in the Text* 126
	4.4.2 *Synopsis and Argumentative Aim* 127
	4.4.3 *Ideology* 132

4.5	Thomas Clarkson's *Essay* (1786/88)		134
	4.5.1	Thomas Clarkson — Biography and Self-representation in his Texts	134
	4.5.2	Synopsis and Argumentative Aim	137
	4.5.3	Ideology	141
4.6	Gilbert Francklyn's *Letters* (1789)		148
	4.6.1	Gilbert Francklyn	148
	4.6.2	Synopsis and Argumentative Aims	150
	4.6.3	Ideology	156
4.7	Anonymous: *Observations* (1790)		162
	4.7.1	The Anonymous Author	162
	4.7.2	Synopsis and Argument of *Observations*	163
	4.7.3	Ideology	166
4.8	Clarkson's *Letters* (1790)		169
	4.8.1	Synopsis and Argument of the *Letters*	169
	4.8.2	Ideology	173
4.9	Anonymous: *Fugitive Thoughts* (1792)		178
	4.9.1	The Anonymous Author	178
	4.9.2	Synopsis and Argument	179
	4.9.3	Ideology	184
4.10	"Mercator": *Letters* (1807)		187
	4.10.1	Biographical Note	187
	4.10.2	Synopsis and Argument of the *Letters*	188
	4.10.3	Ideology	191
4.11	Wilberforce: *Letter* (1807)		193
	4.11.1	William Wilberforce	193
	4.11.2	Synopsis and Argument of the *Letter*	196
	4.11.3	Ideology	202
4.12	Wilberforce: *Appeal* (1823)		207
	4.12.1	Synopsis and Argument of *Appeal*	207
	4.12.2	Ideology	211

	4.13 Bridges: *Voice* (1823)	214
	4.13.1 George Wilson Bridges	214
	4.13.2 Synopsis and Argument	217
	4.13.3 Ideology	221
	4.14 Clarkson: *Thoughts* (1823)	222
	4.14.1 Argument and Synopsis of *Thoughts*	222
	4.14.2 Ideology	227
	4.15 Hampden: *Commentary on Clarkson* (1824)	231
	4.15.1 Biographical Note	231
	4.15.2 Synopsis and Argument	232
	4.15.3 Ideology	236
	4.16 Heyrick: *Immediate Abolition* (1824)	238
	4.16.1 Elizabeth Heyrick	238
	4.16.2 Synopsis and Argument	241
	4.16.3 Ideology	243
	4.17 Conclusion	247
5	**The Image of Africans**	**251**
	5.1 Vocabulary for Africans—A Quantitative Approach	251
	5.1.1 Nouns	251
	5.1.2 Pronouns	255
	5.1.3 Adjectives	260
	5.2 Africans in Africa—Qualitative Analysis	261
	5.2.1 Knowing Africa	261
	5.2.2 Anti-slavery: Corrupted Harmony	263
	5.2.3 Pro-slavery: *Locus Horribilis*	273
	5.2.4 Conclusion	276
	5.3 Africans as Slaves	277
	5.3.1 Quashi: The Character of the Slave	279
	5.3.2 The Body of the Enslaved	282
	5.3.3 Wretches	293

	5.4	Managing the African— Humanity, Rebellion and Reform 296
		5.4.1 *The Africans' Humanity*.. 296
		5.4.2 *Suicide or Death*... 303
		5.4.3 *Rebellion* 305
	5.5	Africans in Terms of Gender—African Women........... 307
	5.6	Africans in Terms of ~~Race~~.. 312
		5.6.1 *Whiteness, Light, Darkness, Blackness*................. 315
		5.6.2 *Anti-slavery* 322
		5.6.3 *Pro-slavery* 333
6	**Conclusion** **341**

Bibliography.. **347**

    Abbreviations 347

    Primary Sources.. 347

    Secondary Sources. 352

1 Introduction

The British anti-slavery movement has been the object of historical scrutiny ever since abolitionist Thomas Clarkson published *The History of the Rise, Progress, and Accomplishment of the Abolition of the African Slave Trade by the British Parliament* (1808). It was Eric Williams' seminal work, *Capitalism and Slavery* (1944), that gave rise to a more critical view of British anti-slavery, drawing attention to the connections between this (seemingly) humanitarian project and the rise of capitalism. This set the tone for an extensive scholarly discussion among historians that has continued well into the present day. The present thesis focuses on argumentative texts that were written in the British debate on slavery. My approach is mainly informed by an interest in the quite distinct image of Africans that can be found in these texts. I feel that, despite over 50 years of scholarly debate, the image of Africans as the actual objects of the discourse of slavery has not been dealt with in sufficient detail and that too little attention has been paid to a close textual analysis of the enormous body of argumentative texts on slavery. Therefore, the present thesis focuses on a corpus of fifteen pro- and anti-slavery texts written between 1784 and 1824, in order to arrive at a thorough evaluation of the image of Africans and to contextualise the British anti-slavery debate within larger traditions of thought. As the image of Africans in these texts only manifests itself between the lines within the larger context of the pro- and anti-slavery argument it is necessary to appreciate the latter before arriving at an assessment of the first. The substantial amount of text has made necessary the use of qualitative data analysis software (MaxQda) in order to code significant passages of texts according to a set of criteria in a first step in order to be able to retrieve and analyse them later. Thus, at any time, my analysis is backed by thematic cross sections through my entire working corpus.

Seven anti-slavery texts have been selected around certain key events: the start of the public discussion of the topic in the form of various essays and pamphlets in the years after the American Revolutionary War (1783) and the trial in 1783 that followed the *Zong* incident; the first intensive discussions of the topic in the British Parliament (1788–1793); the final passing of the Abolition Bill by the British Parliament in 1807; and, finally, the rekindling of the discussion of slavery in the British Empire from the foundation of the Antislavery Society in 1823 until the passing of the Emancipation Bill in 1833. James Ramsay, Thomas Clarkson and William Wilberforce are perhaps the most widely known anti-slavery authors. Therefore a selection of texts by these three authors forms the core of my text corpus. Elizabeth Heyrick's text, being the only argumentative essay written by a female author, has been included for reasons of gender variance and because this author is especially outspoken in her rejection of slavery. In my selection of pro-slavery texts, responses to the anti-slavery ones have been preferred.

Quite early in my research, it emerged that the image of Africans in these texts can only be understood if it is seen as part of a larger discourse and larger traditions and patterns of European thought. The texts will therefore be subjected to a critical discourse analysis, which is informed by a post-colonial reading and a critical approach to humanism linked to post-humanist theory. My approach to CDA is indebted to Siegfried Jäger, who proposes an analysis of the overall societal discourse at a given time by understanding texts as "discourse fragments" (cf. Jäger, *Diskursanalyse* 188ff). Jäger describes texts as both the work of individual authors and also part of a larger discourse (cf. Jäger, *Diskursanalyse* 173); therefore, he proposes that "a relatively small amount of qualitative data suffices to [fully capture] the qualitative range of what can be said and how it is said in one or more discourse strands" (Jäger, *Aspects* 51).

Post-colonial reading techniques, informed by such concepts as centre/margin, universalism, race, ethnicity, essentialism, globalisation, hegemony, mimicry and othering are the second pillar of my methodological approach. In particular, its profound critique of the European Enlightenment as one of the means for gaining global hegemony makes post-colonial theory suitable for an analysis of the British discourse on slavery.

On a technical level, my analysis makes use of qualitative data analysis software and concordance software. The first allows one to link text passages to a number of thematic codes, which makes it possible to retrieve thematic selections of text across a corpus of work. The latter can provide concordance lists, keywords and other elements of corpus linguistics as "checks and balances" (Mautner 122f) to back up the results of a critical discourse analysis.

An analysis of the historical dimension of a discourse in the form of "discursive events" (Jäger and Mayer, *Aspects* 48f) forms a first step of the analysis. These are such events as appear "on the discourse planes of politics and the media, extensively and for a prolonged period of time [and] they influence the development of the discourse" (ibid.). This part of my work, however, does not aim to give a comprehensive overview of the history of the British anti-slavery movement, but rather looks at which historical events are repeatedly referred to by authors and how they influence the discourse.

After that, the work provides a detailed analysis of the fifteen discourse fragments. Biographical notes on the authors and their self-representation in the texts are followed by a synopsis of the texts' main arguments. The distinct image of Africans in the discourse on slavery reflected the discursive needs of a British society which was going through rapid transformations during what Eric Hobsbawm aptly described as "the Age of Revolution". Africa and the West Indies were increasingly becoming a laboratory in which social theories were put into practice (Drescher, *Experiment* 7) and the discussion of slavery was at heart a discussion of the acceptable means of coercing a labour force. The discussion of each discourse fragment is, therefore, concluded by an ideological analysis that looks at how authors conceptualise humans both as individuals and as members of society and how they negotiate the relationship between individual freedom and societal control.

The final part of this thesis contains an analysis of the image of Africans in the discourse on slavery. After a corpus-based appreciation of the key nouns and pronouns used in referring to Africans by both pro-and anti-slavery texts, the representations of Africans will be studied according to the following parameters: Africans in Africa, Africans as slaves, Africans in terms of race, Africans in terms of gender, and Africans between rebellion and as objects of European reform.

2 Methodology

2.1 CDA

Two main approaches characterise my textual analysis. On a technical level, my tools for textual analysis are provided by Critical Discourse Analysis (CDA). Teun van Dijk describes CDA as "discourse analysis with an attitude. It focuses on social problems, especially on the role of discourse, in the production and reproduction of power abuse and domination" (van Dijk, *Multidisciplinary CDA* 96). Wodak and Meyer stress that "CDA researchers have to be aware that their own work is driven by social, economic and political motives like any other academic work and that they are not in any privileged position" (Wodak, *Methods* 7). My critical approach is mostly driven by a post-colonial perspective on 18th-century British texts on slavery as products of a colonial or imperial centre.

Turley writes that in order to be successful in their struggle, the abolitionists had to come to terms with a contemporary British culture that offered them only a limited number of forms and channels through which to effect change (Turley 3). An ideology's way to hegemony can be seen as a process of negotiation of what is widely acceptable. According to Siegfried Jäger, "the power of discourse lies in the fact that [it delineates] a range of 'positive' statements, which are sayable" (Jäger, *Aspects* 37). Analysing this process offers insights into the ideology of society at large (cf. Gramsci 325). Gaining general acceptance thus is a historical process determined by cultural, economic and social factors and interests.

Key Events

Norman Fairclough stresses that discourse, as a whole, is historical (cf. van Dijk, *Critical Discourse Analysis* 353). Thus, it will also be of importance to analyse how far pro- and anti-slavery writers drew on historical traditions and examples to support their arguments and also to try to show the sources and the history of their ideas. Texts will be placed in their historical context and related to key dates such as 1772 (the Somerset Case), 1887 (the Committee for the Abolition of Slavery was founded), 1807 (the abolition of the slave trade), 1815 (the Congress of Vienna); 1833 (the Slavery Abolition Act). Those dates can serve as nodes in which several synchronic cross-sections through the discourse show what could be thought, said and written at certain times, and highlight changes and developments. Other historical references will also be analysed in order to arrive at an overall appraisal of both key events and the role of history in the discourse on slavery.

Siegfried Jäger's Concept of Discourse Analysis

On a technical level, my analysis is probably most indebted to Siegfried Jäger's approach to discourse analysis. Jäger describes his methodology of analysing discourses as a Foucauldian one and characterises it as being centred on four basic questions:

> What is valid knowledge at a certain place and time?
> How does this knowledge arise and how is it passed on?
> What functions does it have for constituting subjects?
> What consequences does it have for the overall shaping and development of society? (Jäger, *Aspects* 34)

In his substantial introduction to discourse analysis, Jäger proposes methods for analysing overall societal discourse by analysing journalistic texts in terms of what he calls "discourse fragments" (cf. Jäger, *Diskursanalyse* 188ff). He defines these fragments as "a text or part of a text that deals with a particular topic" (Jäger, *Aspects* 47). Obviously, this kind of approach recommends itself to an analysis of texts on the topic of slavery.

Jäger draws on Leontiev's activity theory and describes texts as the result of a more or less complex individual activity or of a more or less complex individual thinking process. Texts are produced in order to be communicated to others or oneself by authors who draw on their knowledge, follow a motive or need, have a specific aim, usually regard the conditions of reception and obey rhetorical and stylistic conventions (cf. Jäger, *Diskursanalyse* 22, 118). Thus, discourse fragments are both works of individual authors and also part of a larger discourse (cf. Jäger, *Diskursanalyse* 173).

Because of this, Jäger points out that "a relatively small amount of qualitative data suffices to" fully capture "the qualitative range of what can be said and how it is said in one or more discourse strands" (Jäger, *Aspects* 51). He suggests that the analysis is complete once "arguments begin to repeat themselves" (Jäger, *Aspects* 51).

This notion has informed the selection of sources for the present work. Although not strictly synchronic, texts were produced around three key periods. The first group of texts, from 1784 to 1792, represent the first massive public discussion of the issue of the slave trade. Two further texts were written in 1807, which was the year of the actual abolition of the slave trade. The remaining four texts originated in 1823/24, which are the years that saw a re-emergence of the discussion about colonial slavery in the form of the emancipation debate[1]. The selection of texts around these three key periods will also allow for an appraisal of the overall discourse of slavery as well as certain diachronic observations on how the image of Africans changed.

Another aspect of Jäger's approach, which informs my analysis, is the concept of collective symbols. He describes these as,

---

[1] In this thesis, the term 'abolition' always refers to the abolition of the slave trade by the Slave Trade Act of 1807, whereas 'emancipation' is used for the actual ending of slavery in the British Empire by the Slavery Abolition Act of 1833.

'cultural stereotypes', also called 'topoi' which are handed down and used collectively. They are known to all members of a society. They provide the repertoire of images from which we construct a picture of reality for ourselves. (Jäger, Aspects 47f)

It is obvious that an appraisal of such symbols ought to be part of an analysis of the image of Africans. In addition to that, Jäger also points to the importance of analysing vocabulary (especially the nouns and pronouns) of a text (cf. Jäger, *Aspects* 55).

Class Interest

With respect to the discourse of slavery, Hall's concept of discourse adds the dimension of class interest. Hall emphasises that it would be simplistic to reduce discourse to statements that mirror the interests of a particular class; however, "they are part of the way power circulates and is contested" (Hall, *West* 295). This is highly relevant, since the whole scholarly debate about British abolitionism has very much hinged on the question of class interest ever since the historian Eric Williams, in his seminal work, *Capitalism and Slavery,* first questioned the rhetoric of "national triumphalism" (cf. Drescher, *Experiment* 4), which had up to then characterised historical interpretations of British abolitionism in Clarkson's tradition. Williams "argued that it was economic interest, not any moral claims by the abolitionists that brought slavery to an end" (Bender 1). Williams' *Capitalism and Slavery* was followed by an ongoing debate among scholars such as David Brion Davis (cf. *Progress, Revolution*), Thomas Haskell (cf. *Sensibility 1 + 2*) and Seymour Drescher (cf. *Experiment, Capitalism*), to name just a few, about the nature of the connection between abolitionism and the rise of both capitalism and the British Empire.

Davis and Haskell led an especially fruitful debate about the influence of class interest on the debate of abolition. In his essay "Abolitionism and Ideological Hegemony", Davis describes the abolition cause as "an increasingly attractive opportunity to demonstrate their commitment to decency and justice [for] both national and local ruling elites" (805) and argues that "the antislavery movement mirrored the needs and tensions of a society increasingly absorbed with problems of labour discipline" (806). Both Davis and Drescher see a certain link between anti-slavery and imperialism. Davis writes that while "Negro slavery was an intrinsic part of European expansion" (Davis, *Progress* 357), "anti-slavery encouraged more direct intervention [and] helped to justify the subjection of entire peoples to colonial rule, supposedly for the good of their future civilization" (Davis, *Progress* 363). In *Antislavery and Capitalism*, Drescher calls anti-slavery "a legitimiser of imperialism before and after the fact" (165). He raises the issue of race in his article, *The Ending of the Slave Trade and the Evolution of European Scientific Racism*, when he states that:

> .. early abolitionists linked negative characteristics so causally and so completely to the African slave trade and to colonial slavery that they could assure their contemporaries of a more rapid civilising of blacks than of any other 'backward' people on the globe (420)

Since the issue of slavery is very much concerned with control, a main scholarly interest in the British anti-slavery movement is its influence on such modern phenomena as the hegemony of the concept of wage labour. It has been argued that the fact that European wage labour could successfully be contrasted to colonial slavery in the discourse about the abolition of slavery was crucial for the triumph of the former over the latter. During the discussion of slavery, the public in Europe became increasingly confronted with and concerned about Africa and its inhabitants. Therefore, many of the stereotypes and images about the 'dark continent' that are still prevalent today have their origin in the abolitionist discourse.

History has shown that the anti-slavery movement by no means removed domination and control from the relationship of employers and employees. Even a very cursory glance at the 19th century shows that wage labour did not lead to the liberation of

British workers, let alone of the plantation workers in the West Indies. Also, on a bigger scale, the domination of Africa by Europe continued. Anti-slavery even provided the ideology for successfully colonising the continent. Therefore, both in the individual relationship between the plantation owner in the West Indies and his workers and in the relationship between European colonisers and Africa, issues of power and domination are of crucial importance.

The topic of slavery is obviously very much concerned with labour. It has to be noted that both sides show an enormous concern with the issue of labour discipline. Since neither the pro- nor the anti-slavery writers wanted to abolish the West Indian plantation system, they both had to devise ways to keep the workforce in its place. In this context, the power relations that each side wanted to maintain or create, and their respective concepts of man, will be made explicit and analysed.

What creates the significance of discourse fragments is the author who chooses from existing discourses. Thus, critical discourse analysis assumes a highly flexible and changeable connection between single discourse fragments and the discourse of a society as a whole. Especially for argumentative texts, it is not so much the author who invents new language but rather that he chooses from pre-existing channels to get across his point.

2.2 Post-Colonial Reading and Concepts

Of course, as the latter part of the preceding chapter suggests, a reading of British anti-slavery discourse can never be complete without a post-colonial dimension. Post-colonial reading techniques informed by such concepts as centre/margin, universalism, race, ethnicity, essentialism, globalisation, hegemony, mimicry and othering are the second pillar of my methodological approach. Although post-colonial concepts are used anachronistically when applied to 18th and 19th-century discourse on slavery, the fact that abolitionism was a major encounter between metropolitan British culture, Africa and Africans justifies their use. In particular, those concepts describing the relationship of metropolis and margin will be useful. On the other hand, investigating the discourse that is often seen as being one of the origins (cf. Drescher, *Capitalism* 165) of modern Euro-African relations can be one way of approaching a critique of contemporary cosmopolitanism.

In this respect, I am especially thinking of the idea of universalism in a globalised world. Post-colonial studies seem to be critical of universalistic notions of 'the human condition' (cf. Ashcroft, *Concepts* 216f). The discourse on slavery offers us a channel to re-evaluate the concept. On a superficial level, the abolitionists promoted a universalistic image, maintaining that all mankind was essentially equal, most famously in asking the question if Africans were not men and brothers.[2] However, it would be simplistic to assume that anti-slavery texts promoted the idea of one humanity whereas pro-slavery writers were racists. For example, it has been argued (cf. Kitson 11) that the anti-slavery side relied more heavily on arguments of racial equality to combat the arguments of their opponents, thus upholding the concept. What I suggest is that the abolitionist discourse attempted to establish a universal, non-race based conception of mankind in order to universalise the control mechanisms of emerging capitalism while, at the same time, installing, in a very subtle way, social categories of otherness which were applicable to both Africans and domestic workers and aimed at universalising the concept of wage labour.

In this respect, enlightenment seems to play an important role in the discourse (cf. Drescher, *Experiment* 5) as a means of establishing otherness/difference, as well as for gaining power over the non-enlightened part of humanity. Foucault has remarked on the

---

[2] See, for example, 'Am I Not a Man and a Brother?', *Picture History* (accessed on 26 Feb 2009, http://www.picturehistory.com/product/id/632)

"blackmail" of enlightenment constituting "a privileged domain for analysis" and links "the progress of truth and the history of liberty" (Rabinow 43). Furthermore, he states, taking Kant's famous dictum *sapere aude* into account, that a certain imperative forms an essential part of enlightenment (ibid.); the ideological connection to 'the white man's burden' (cf. Ashcroft, *Concepts* 181) suggests itself. In this way, an analysis of the construction of Africa as Europe's 'Other' will offer insights into what was considered to constitute European identity at the time. Enlightenment seems to have been an important part of it.

Thus enlightenment, besides its undoubtedly positive intentions, introduced a division of mankind into a civilised part and a yet-to-be-civilised part, which has survived and shaped the relationships between the so-called first and third worlds until the present day. The argumentative structure of anti-slavery texts might well have laid the foundation for this dichotomy within a European context. It will be attempted to show in how far anti-slavery authors divide their audiences into a civilised, humanitarian and noble anti-slavery part and a pro-slavery counterpart lacking all those qualities. While every reader is invited to join the civilised part of mankind by opposing slavery or the slave trade, the actual African remains an object that is written about but is usually not addressed directly.

2.3 Post-humanism and Agamben

Two further concepts inform my analytic approach: Giorgio Agamben's seminal work on the relation between the modern state and the modern subject in *Homo Sacer* and, more generally, the ideas of post-humanist thought.

Agamben conceptualises the Western state around the fundamental dichotomy between what he calls *zoe* (bare life) and *bios* (political existence) (8). The eponymous figure of the *homo sacer* stems from archaic Roman law. Expelled from political existence as a citizen, the *homo sacer* is reduced to a bare life which "may be killed" (8). Agamben sees modern democracy as a process of "vindication and liberation of zoe, and .... is constantly trying to transform its own bare life into a way of life" (9). He sees the primeval political bond as that of the ban and argues that the Roman *homo sacer* has a brother in "the bandit and the outlaw [in] Germanic and Scandinavian antiquity" (104), which is linked to the image of the *"wargus, vargr,* the wolf and, in the religious sense, the sacred wolf" (104). The word *wargus* shares an etymological root with the modern English term, 'wretch'. The OED still cites the obsolete meaning of the term as, "One driven out of or away from his native country; a banished person; an exile" (OED, 'wretch'). In the present work, I will show that anti-slavery authors, in particular, portray Africans as wretches. Apart from attempting to arouse the readers' compassion for the 'wretched' situation of the suffering African, the representation of Africans as human wretches also served a European utopian vision of improvement and reform. The fundamental stance against slavery was that it was an unfair exclusion of African wretches from the rank of full humans. It is to this position that anti-slavery writers wanted to restore the wretched objects of their texts.

As I have already pointed out above, post-colonial thought is critical of the notion of a universal human condition. This critique is taken a step further by post-humanist theorists. Rosi Braidotti, for example, states: "[a]s a civilizational ideal, Humanism fuelled the imperial destinies of nineteenth-century Germany, France and, supremely, Great Britain" (Braidotti 15). She argues that "the human of Humanism" became instrumental in "practises of exclusion and discrimination ... by transposing a specific mode of being human into a generalized standard" (26). Thus, Braidotti is also critical of "Enlightenment-based secular Humanism" (46) and sees herself as indebted to post-colonial theory for developing the "insight into the notion that ideals of reason, secular tolerance, equality under the Law and democratic rule, need not be, and indeed historically have not been mutually exclusive with European practices of violent domination" (46). Braidotti holds the concept of binary distinctions responsible for practices of exclusion and stresses the urgency of reasserting "the concept of difference as both central and non-essentialistic .... acknowledging the ties that bind us to multiple others in a vital web of complex interrelation" (100). The discourse on slavery constructs the otherness of slaves precisely along such binary distinctions. The claim for African humanity very much resembles what Braidotti calls the "compensatory humanism" (76) that informs the present-day discourse on animal rights. She calls the mere extension of an existing binary distinction to "extend to animals the principle of moral and legal equality ... inherently flawed" (79), as it both confirms the binary distinction as such and denies specificity.

2.4 ~~Race~~

Since the subject of this work is the image of black Africans in texts on slavery, I am faced with a dilemma about which term to use to describe the actual objects of the discourse. Edward Said wrote that an image has the main function of simplifying the complexity of reality. I am aware that the people who are referred to in the texts that form the basis of this thesis have as complex socio-cultural backgrounds as anybody in the world, possibly even more so. The general term 'Africans' will, therefore, be used to refer not only to the people of Africa but also to the general image created by European authors of the very diverse group of individuals who became victims of West Indian slavery. Because of this and for reasons of convenience I will use the term 'Africans' for any general reference to the people whose image I will analyse, even though they might actually be Afro-Caribbeans. At a later point in the present work, I will discuss the problematic fact that writers primarily refer to Africans in the plural and as males. I am aware that the present text probably does so too, because it primarily deals with texts written from the colonial centre.

A second dilemma arises in connection with the concept of 'race'. It is my firm conviction that the application of this concept to the human species has caused incredible injustices and suffering and that it ought, therefore, to be rejected; however, the idea of race is very much present in all primary texts and its application to African slaves, and the development it underwent during the span of the roughly 30 years from which the primary texts originate, is a central element of this work. Since I both reject and need the concept, the best solution seems to be the one suggested by Jacques Derrida, namely to place the concept under erasure, crossing out the word 'race' each time I have to use it. Gayatri Spivak explained this technique as follows: "Since the word is inaccurate, it is crossed out. Since it is necessary it remains legible." (Barker, *Cultural Studies* 100).

2.5 QDA Software

Working with texts from the late eighteenth and early nineteenth century can both be a fascinating and tedious work. It is fascinating to come across text passages that are highly relevant and revealing for the research topic, because they are like a window on the European past and its patterns of thought. However, the work can also be quite tiresome at times when the researcher has to work through long-winded chapters that often bear little relevance to one's area of interest. Particularly when not working with works of literature but with argumentative essays, tracts, pamphlets or letters, this poses a problem and makes it necessary to find ways to keep records both of the overall structure and those passages of one's text that are of relevance for one's research question.

In his work on critical discourse analysis, Siegfried Jäger (236 ff) suggests the preparation and structuring of the textual data, one is working with, as a first step of analysis and stresses the importance of keeping track of whatever ideas occur while doing this. For this qualitative data analysis (QDA), the software offers invaluable help. This sort of software was originally designed for the social sciences in order to help with the qualitative analysis of data such as interview transcripts. In the course of my research, I found that preparing and transcribing texts using QDA software can also be of great assistance in this specific type of discourse analysis. There are two main advantages to this. Firstly, the use of QDA software helps to structure texts and keep track of one's ideas and significant text passages as a first step of analysis. Secondly, once the text is digitalised, methods of corpus linguistics can be used as 'checks and balances' (cf. Mautner 122ff) to back up the results of one's analysis.

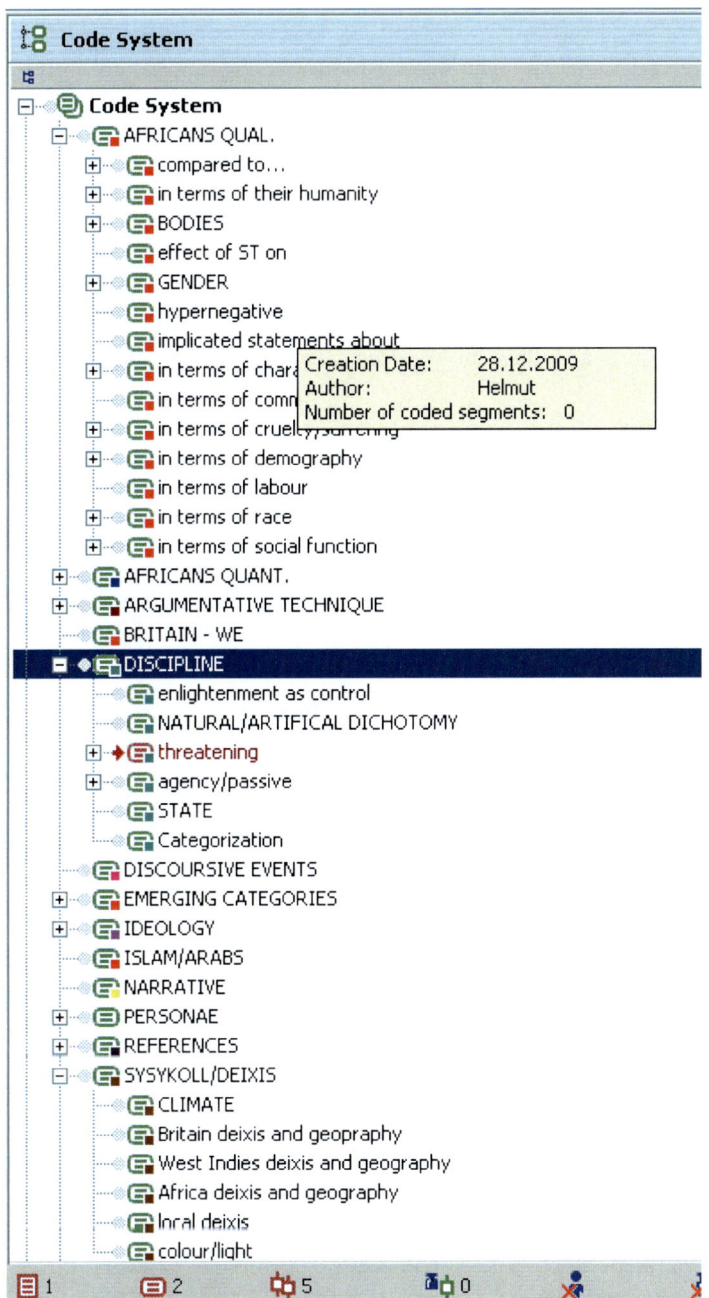

Fig. 1: Code System

The software that has been used in the examples below are various versions of MAX QDA. Its basic function is to link text passages with 'Codes' and 'Memos', thus structuring a text and linking it with the researcher's ideas about it.

2.5.1 Codes

Codes are thematic categories according to which a text is structured and excerpts are ordered. The length of their titles is limited to 64 characters and they are ordered in a hierarchical structure (cf. below).

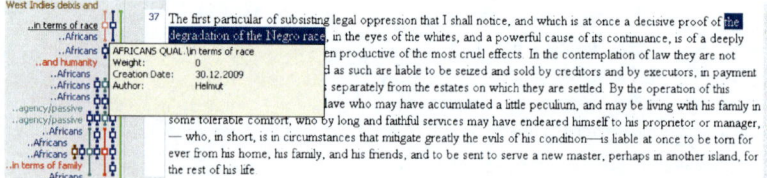

Fig. 2:   Coded Text

The illustration shows an example how the phrase "the degradation of the Negro race" has been coded with the code "AFRICANS QUAL.\in terms of race". Once the text is prepared in this way, the QDA software enables the researcher to query and also to quantify all the passages in which Africans have been written about in terms of race.

Altogether, out of a text corpus of 15 pro- and anti-slavery texts with a total number of over 480,000 words, more than 44,000 sequences have been thematically coded. While many of these categories proved to be minor ones or limited to single texts, some themes repeatedly appeared in different discourse fragments. These were the ones which developed into valid parameters of analysis for the overall discourse on slavery. This process corresponds to what Siegfried Jäger pointed out in relation to the repetition of patterns once the analysis of a discourse nears its end (cf. Jäger, *Aspects* 51). Below is a selection of those codes which became central parameters of my analysis. Codes are hierarchically organised like the filing system of a computer. Thus, the backslash symbol signifies a jump in the hierarchical level.

AFRICANS QUANT.\Africans

For a quantitative analysis of the representation of Africans, the central category is AFRICANS QUANT.\Africans. In all the texts, passages directly referring to Africans have been coded with this code, resulting in a total of 13,882 segments. In order to make possible an analysis of pronouns and collocations, whole phrases have been linked to this code, for example, "their slaves" (CE x) or "the manumission of slaves" (CE x).

AFRICANS QUAL.

For a more qualitative analysis of the representation of Africans in these texts, I have introduced a second group of codes called "AFRICANS QUAL.". This consists of a total of 3,432 segments, which are organised into a number of sub-categories, of which the following are the most important ones:

> AFRICANS QUAL.\in terms of bodies (553 segments)
> AFRICANS QUAL.\in terms of race/species (131 segments)
> AFRICANS QUAL.\in terms of suffering and cruel treatment (411 segments)
> AFRICANS QUAL.\in terms of threat/insurrection (71 segments)
> AFRICANS QUAL.\in terms of character, qualities and civilisation (355 segments)
> AFRICANS QUAL.\in terms of humanity (422 segments)
> AFRICANS QUAL.\in terms of gender (582 segments)
> AFRICANS QUAL.\in terms of comparison to... (276 segments)

One can see how these categories can be conveniently used to come up with thematic cross sections through the discourse for an analysis of the image of Africans in various texts.

DISCOURSE

This group of codes contains categories which describe more general textual features, such as:

DISCOURSE\LANGUAGE (136 segments) – the whole corpus of passages in six languages apart from English, among which Latin and French feature most prominently.

DISCOURSE\DISCURSIVE EVENTS (702 segments) – these are segments which refer to historical events. They will be dealt with in a separate part of the work.

DISCOURSE\DISCURSIVE EVENTS (935 segments) – under this header, all quotes taken from other authors have been collected. This has proved to be immensely useful for both qualitative and quantitative analysis since pro-slavery authors in particular often quote extensively from their anti-slavery counterparts. The most frequent references in this category are James Ramsay (216 times), Thomas Clarkson (102 times), the Bible (38 times) and William Wilberforce (39 times).

SYSYKOLL/IMAGERY

SYSYKOLL/IMAGERY (1,420 segments)

This is a collection of text passages that have been considered as offering insights into the collective symbols and images which are used by the texts.

IDEOLOGY

IDEOLOGY (4,798 segments)

These segments and various subcategories are a collection statements which offer insights into the author's basic ideological assumptions. The category features the following prominent subcategories:

IDEOLOGY\LIBERTY (447 segments)
IDEOLOGY\RELIGION (61 segments)
IDEOLOGY\HISTORY (622 segments)
IDEOLOGY\HEGEMONY (283 segments)
IDEOLOGY\NATURE (628 segments)
IDEOLOGY\CONCEPTION OF HUMAN (2,357 segments)
IDEOLOGY\POWER/DISCIPLINE (689 segments)

The last-mentioned category deals with strategies in which texts constitute power relations by various means, such as categorisation, constructing threats and contrasting colonial centre and margin.

IDENTITY

A last major category is that of IDENTITY (4,333 segments), which comprises such passages in which authors construct identity both via SAMENESS (2,901 segments) and OTHERNESS (1,370 segments).

2.5.2 Memos

Memos provide a space for additional thoughts and can both be linked to codes (thematic categories) and text passages. Figure 3 shows how a memo, opened in the window on the left, was linked to a specific passage text, which is marked blue on the right, and also to a set of codes, which are indicated by the red arrow. The memo then can be retrieved according to the codes it has been linked with and is also visualised on the right side of the text by the little yellow square, which is circled in red.

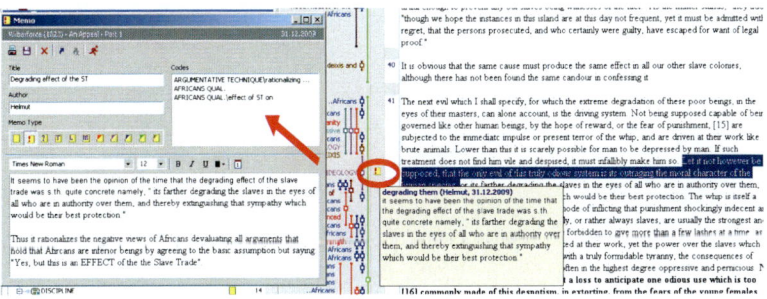

Fig. 3: Memos

The result of preparing texts in this way is a digital and highly annotated corpus, which is structured according to predefined criteria (i.e. codes) and complemented by first attempts at interpretation in the form of memos.

2.5.3 Retrieval

Once the texts have been processed in this way, QDA software enables one to create complex queries for text retrieval. Figure 4 shows how a query has been created for text passages coded as both "AFRICANS QUANT.\Africans" and "DISCIPLINE\threatening" (indicated by the red arrow) and how the programme lists the five passages of text that have been found according to these criteria, which appear on the right. This retrieval is possible either for all texts in the corpus or for any selection, such as only anti-slavery texts or only pro-slavery texts.

An additional feature is that the memos that have been written during the preparation of the text can be retrieved according to one's codes.

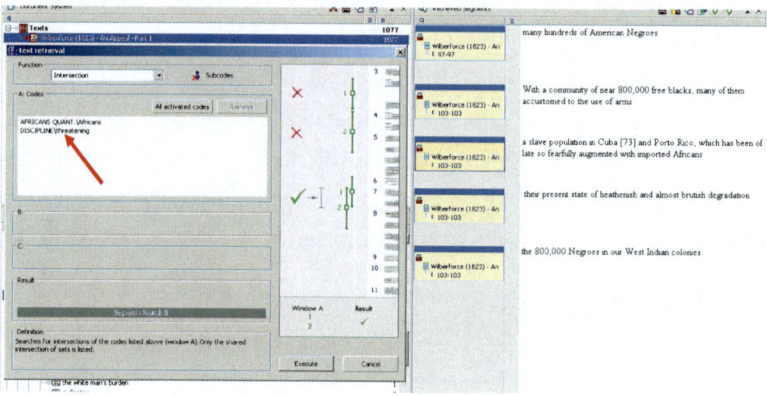

Fig. 4:   Retrieval

2.6 Corpus Linguistics

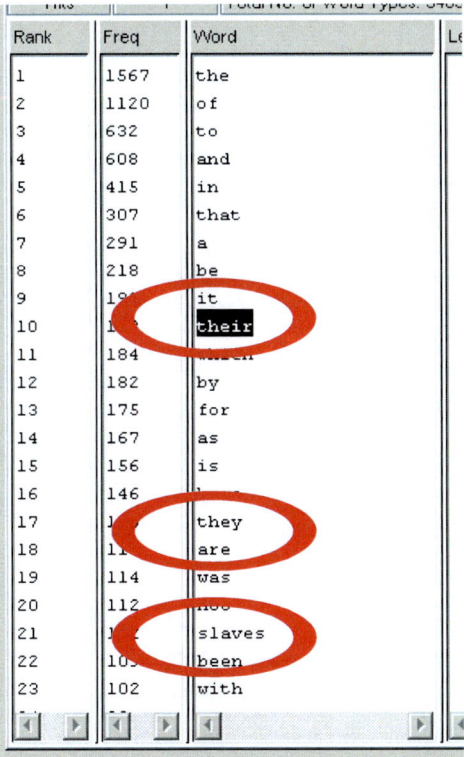

Fig. 5: Worldlist

In order to do all of this, it is vital that the researcher digitalises the text they are working on. So far, the most effective way to do this has been found to be on a paragraph by paragraph basis, digitalising and simultaneously coding one paragraph of text at a time and writing memos if further explanation is needed or thoughts occur. The result of this first close analysis and preparation of texts is a digital and highly annotated version structured according to pre-defined criteria (i.e. codes).

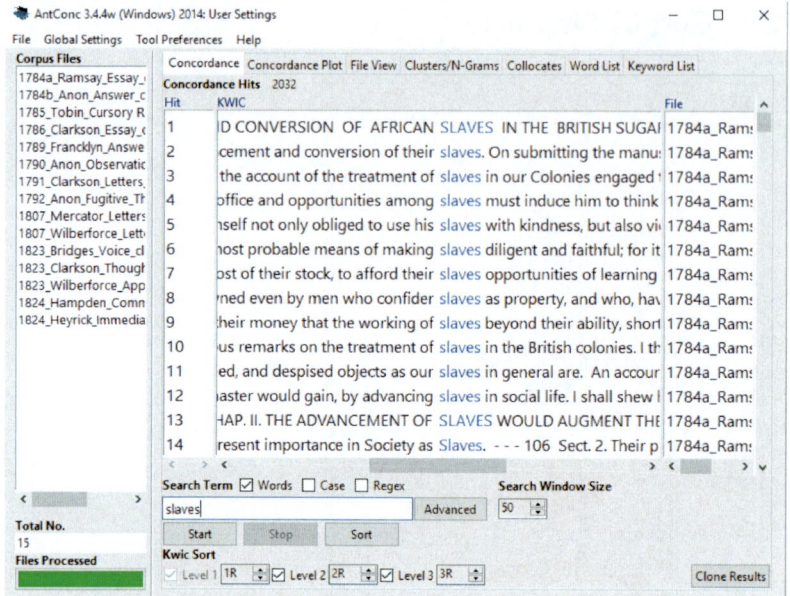

Fig. 6:   Concordance Query – KWIC

Being in the possession of digital versions of texts then puts the researcher in the position of being able to apply methods of corpus linguistics to the primary sources to provide further "both qualitative and quantitative perspectives on …. textual data" (Mautner 123). In this respect mainly, the creation of word lists and lists of collocations (in this case with AntConc3.2.1) can offer valuable insights into the field of research and help reduce researcher bias (ibid). Figure 5 shows the word list of a 1,823-word text by William Wilberforce. Jäger (182f) stresses the importance of collecting and classifying all nouns and pronouns of a text as a crucial element of critical discourse analysis.

MAXQDA, the software that has been used for coding the texts, can provide basic corpus linguistic queries. On the one hand, these are wordlists showing the various word types of a text along with their respective frequencies, which can then be edited in order to show only nouns or pronouns. On the other hand, MAXQDA also offers a query after keywords with an output in the form of

KWIC (keyword in context) lines. These can offer a quick overview of the context in which a certain word most frequently appears in one or more texts, which is convenient for thematic searches.

Statistical facts such as "their" being the most frequent pronoun in text, followed by "they", or that "slaves" is the most frequently used noun can offer critical insights into the ideological structure underlying a text, even more so when considering that due to the pre-coding of all texts, I am now in the position of doing such an analysis only based on segments coded "AFRICANS".

Another very promising perspective of corpus linguistic elements for a critical discourse analysis is querying for collocations of certain words. As MAXQDA does not offer this feature as a function, I have used a freeware concordance software called AntConc. The figure below shows a collocation list for the word "slaves" in the same text by Wilberforce sorted by frequency. Investigating the linguistic environments in which, for example, terms signifying "Africans" frequently occur, of course offers further insights for my research topic, "the European image of Africans".

3 Historical Context, Key Events and Discursive Events

3.1 Introduction

The aim of this chapter is not to give a comprehensive historical overview of British abolition and emancipation. Rather, I wish to set out the historical events that ought to be considered 'key' to the discourse on slavery because they structure and determine this discourse. I will analyse how authors use historical events, historical analogies and historical persons to support their arguments. The idea of the 'discursive event', as suggested by Siegfried Jäger (Jäger and Mayer, *Aspects* 48f), and outlined above, will be the central concept of this part of my work. Jäger and Mayer describe discursive events as such events as appear "on the discourse planes of politics and the media, extensively and for a prolonged period of time [and] they influence the development of the discourse" (48). However, it would be beyond the scope of the present work to catalogue all historical events in a comprehensive number of texts on slavery. What I have attempted to do for my analysis is collect as many instances of historical references in my text corpus as possible, putting them in chronological order and cross checking the rest of the corpus for further references to the same event using a lexical search in order to unearth the historical frame of reference. Thus, the present chapter is my attempt to construct from this data a history of the world from the perspective of late 18th and early 19th-century British discourse on slavery. Furthermore, I will try to establish the differences between the historical analyses of pro- and anti-slavery authors.

3.2 The "Original State of Mankind"

Where is one to start tracing the historical references of a discourse? In the case of the discourse on slavery, historical references go back to the very beginnings of humankind. In a discussion of the fundamental concepts of human freedom and society, referring to the 'original situation of man' is, of course, a powerful ideological tool for establishing hegemonic norms of what is 'natural' and, thus, just. The state of nature was a central concern to many philosophers of the Enlightenment. Two famous examples are, of course, the "solitary, poor, nasty, brutish, and short" lives of early humans in Hobbes' *Leviathan* (Hobbes, *Leviathan* 62) as opposed to the more romantic view of Jean-Jacques Rousseau, who postulated that "nothing is more mild and gentle than man in his primitive state" in his *Discourse on Inequality* (Rousseau, *Inequality* 223).

The version of early human history, which Clarkson outlines in his 1786 *Essay*, bears a striking resemblance to what Rousseau proposes. Clarkson suggests three stages of society: "a first state of dissociation and independence" (56f), "a state of independent society" (59) and, finally, a "state of subordinate society" (60). Clarkson writes of the first stage that:

> It appears that mankind were originally free, and that they possessed an equal right to the soil and produce of the earth. . . . Hence then there was no rank, no distinction, no superiour. Every man wandered where he chose, changing his residence, as a spot attracted his fancy, or suited his convenience, uncontrouled by his neighbour, unconnected with any but his family. . . . Such was the first situation of mankind; a state of dissociation and independence. (CE 56f)

Rousseau envisions an equally idyllic first situation of the human, seeing "him satisfying his hunger at the first oak, and slaking his thirst at the first brook, in his way; finding his bed at the foot of the same tree" (Rousseau, *Inequality* 169). Rousseau's description too has a distinctly positive tinge when he holds that "Accoustomed from their infancy to the inclemencies of weather, and the rigour of the seasons ... mankind would acquire a robust and almost unalterable temperament of body" (Rousseau, *Inequality* 170). One need only look at the high prestige which 'organic' products enjoy in the contemporary discourse on health and nutrition to see that the argument of connecting the state of nature with a healthy body has retained its validity in various discourses of the 21st century.

It is hardly surprising that pro-slavery author Gilbert Francklyn draws a more Hobbesian picture of the original situation of man in his answer to Clarkson,

> Notwithstanding the elegance of his verse, what does the description by Ovid, of this boasted state of dissociation and independence of mankind, in the Golden Age, amount to, but that they lived without government or laws, without labour, and without the knowledge of any of the arts of society, upon the spontaneous productions of the earth, ... now and then, were lucky enough to find an honeycomb in a hollow tree, which we may naturally imagine was a luxury, for which they would bite and scratch one another. (FA 97f)

Despite the unquestionably idyllic elements of the first situation, Clarkson suggests that soon humankind must have entered the second state of independent society because

> In this dissociated state it is impossible that men could have long continued. The dangers to which they must have frequently been exposed, by the attacks of fierce and rapacious beasts, by the predatory attempts of their own species, and by the disputes of contiguous and independent families; these, together with their inability to defend, themselves, on many such occasions, must have incited them to unite. (CE 57f)

Clarkson gives several actual historical examples of independent societies, "This was the exact situation of the Getæ and Scythians, of the Lybians and Goetulians of the Italian Aborigines, and of the Huns and Alans" (58f). What these examples have in common is that they are all peoples who lived on the fringes of the Roman Empire and at one point were in armed conflict with it. These "barbarous nations of antiquity" (CE 14), can be seen as representations of Otherness in the Roman Empire, which will be dealt with below.

In Clarkson's text, they are contrasted with societies living in the third stage of mankind, in which

> Agriculture would furnish them with that subsistence and support, which the earth, from the rapid increase of its inhabitants, had become unable spontaneously to produce. An assignation of property would not only enforce an application, but excite an emulation, to labour; and government would at once afford a security to the acquisitions of the industrious, and heal the intestine disorders of the community, by the introduction of laws. (CE 59f)

Thus mankind entered "a third situation . . . a state of subordinate society" (CE 60). To sum up, Clarkson's historical model is a teleological one, which posits universal stages that all human societies go through. The claim of knowing the goal of human history puts an enormous amount of discursive power in the hands of a colonial centre, defining the metropolitan subjects as "the most free, enlightened, and happy people that ever existed upon earth" (WL 42). The chapter after the next one will show how this position is maintained by claiming a Greco-Roman ancestry of European civilisation. This historical model, therefore, implies strategic power relations. Secondly, Clarkson writes of subordinate society that

> . . . empire then could never have been gained at first by compulsion, so it could only have been obtained by consent; and as men were then going to make an important sacrifice, for the sake of their mutual happiness, so he alone could have obtained it, (not whose ambition had greatly distinguished him from the rest) but in whose wisdom, justice, prudence, and virtue, the whole community could confide. (CE 62.)

The idea of the social contract, which this passage implies, forms an important part of the narrative of legitimacy that modern states tell their subjects.

3.3 Biblical Events

The texts originating from the 18th century, in particular, use the Bible as a historical source in a quite literal sense, taking biblical stories as historical fact. Interestingly, if one considers what Siegfried

Jäger writes about discursive events, the historicity of such events does not seem to really matter much in terms of analysis. Jäger cites the difference between the two reactor accidents of Harrisburg and Chernobyl. Although the two events were quite similar in terms of what actually happened, the first one did not become a discursive event, since it was successfully kept under cover, while the latter received extensive media coverage and "influenced global politics" (Jäger, *Methods* 49). If taken to its conclusion, the argument of course also works the other way round, in that events which possibly never happened, such as the biblical story of the Exodus, can certainly become discursive events if they receive sufficient media attention. David Brion Davis also stresses the tangible effects of biblical narratives for the discourse on slavery when he points out that

> ... from the time of the Mosaic Exodus, slavery and redemption have been extremely powerful paradigms involving the ultimate question for both individual and collective life: the passage from present misery and degradation to a land of Canaan. (Davis, *Hegemony* 168)

Due to the distinctive way in which authors deal with scriptural evidence as historical facts texts, these references to biblical stories are best dealt with as discursive events. Let me just sum up a few biblical events which influenced the discourse on slavery no matter what their actual historicity.

One narrative which received widespread attention in the discourse on slavery was the curse of Ham. The very nature of this curse—"Cursed be Canaan; a servant of servants shall he be unto his brethren" (Genesis 9:25)—accounts for its relevance for a discussion of human servitude. A further passage from the Bible is referred to by Thomas Clarkson when he discusses a theory as to whether the Africans' blackness might be the mark of Cain (Genesis 4:15), which he refutes by stating that "If then the scriptures are true, it is evident that the posterity of Cain were extinguished in the flood" (CE 179). The Exodus is a third biblical event which is frequently used in the discourse on slavery. The narrative of the Jews' emergence from Egyptian bondage of course resonated with the overall concept of personal freedom found in the age of Enlightenment, as has also become evident from Davis' quote above.

The use of the Bible in the texts is at times definitely charged in terms of global power relations. James Ramsay, the former surgeon and Anglican minister, writes about why it was God's plan to divide humans up into different nations.

> By giving man one simple origin, by bestowing on him a common nature, a foundation was laid for the ultimate re-union of mankind, as well now in improved social life as in futurity; a re-union intended to take place in time under the then-promised connecting head of the creation, and particularly rendered practicable in a unity of laws, government, and worship, by this universal equality established among the various families; which keeps the way open for the equal and gradual improvement of their common nature. (RE 207)

Despite the author's claim for a universal equality, the utopia of an ultimate reunion of mankind "in a unity of laws, government and worship" as part of a universal improvement of human nature has a distinct Eurocentric tinge, especially when expressed by an Anglican minister.

3.4 Greco-Roman Antiquity

3.4.1 Authority of the Ancients

Particularly in the period of the Enlightenment, the heritage of classical antiquity was an important authority. This becomes apparent, for example, when Thomas Clarkson refers to the unfortunate fact that as far as slavery is concerned, we "must expect no light from antiquity to guide us on our way; for history gives us no account of persons in those times similarly situated with the slaves in the British colonies at the present day" (CT 16). Despite his disappointment in the specific case in question, the passage implicitly shows the existence of a concept of 'light from antiquity', which could provide authoritative answers to all kinds of questions. The mere fact that it was a competition held at Cambridge for the best Latin dissertation which prompted Clarkson to write his *Essay* gives evidence to the academic importance attributed to Greco-Roman antiquity. Many of the texts that form the basis for the present work feature Latin mottoes and even more contain original Latin and Greek quotes (Latin being considered unnecessary to translate).³ Authors also used etymological considerations about the Greek and Roman terms for slaves and servants. Such as Francklyn's discussion of Hebrew and Greek terminology.

> The name of a Slave in Hebrew, as has been before remarked is Obed. That of a hired servant, is Shekir. In Greek the Slave is called doulos; a hired servant [greek illegible] or [greek illegible]. In Latin a slave is servus, a hired servant mercenaries. (FA 53 fn)

This shows how classical antiquity was used for tracing the origin of modern concepts and how, ever since the Renaissance, the very conception of the modern human has been influenced by an orientation back to antiquity.

Wilberforce describes the universal progress "of human civilization from the very earliest time" (WL 74) at length according to the following steps. In accordance with the Bible, Wilberforce sees Mesopotamia as "the original seat of the human race" (74). He acknowledges the deluge as an historical event, which was survived only by a "single family" (74). One hundred years after that "happened the dispersion of nations, and confusion of tongues; when different races of men, like streams from one common fountain, diverged in various directions to people the whole earth" (74). From then on, Wilberforce describes human history as a continuous passing on of what he repeatedly describes as "the seeds of civilization" (WL 76, 83 and *Appeal* 64). The author sees "Assyria and Egypt [as] the first nations which attained to any great heights of

---

3   Altogether, the text corpus contains 55 Latin and 12 Greek quotations.

social improvement" (74). Describing Egypt, he refers to "the mildness of its climate, and its singular fertility [to have] naturally attracted inhabitants, who, of course, brought along with them the arts of their native land" (74f). It then was "the Phoenicians, a colony from Egypt" by whom "the first rudiments of civilization, above all, the art of alphabetical writing were conveyed to Greece, the various inhabitants of which were then in a far ruder state than most of the African nations in the present day" (75): Wilberforce finishes his narrative as follows:

> About 150 years before Christ, Greece was subdued by the Romans, who thence derived their civilization and knowledge. By the extension of the Roman arms over almost the whole of Europe, the seeds of civilization were first sown in our northern regions, till then immersed in darkness and barbarism; and they sprung up and flourished during the order and security which, previous to the irruption of the northern swarms, prevailed for some centuries throughout the Roman empire. Such was the state of Europe. (WL 75)

This narrative of a single source of civilisation or culture, despite its advocacy for fundamental human equality, of course also laid the foundation for the Eurocentrism of the various imperial projects. Since southern Africa "was separated from the [Roman] provinces bordering on the Mediterranean by an immense sea of sandy desert, near nine hundred miles from north to south" (WL 77), Wilberforce explicitly asks: "how or whence was civilization to find its way into the interior of Africa?" (WL 78) apart from "the feeble light of Mahometanism" (WL 31), which will be referred to in more detail below.

Wilberforce creates a highly interesting case of 'what-if' history. He starts by stating, "Let the case be put, that the interior of Africa had been made by the Almighty the cradle of the world" (WL 80). In the ensuing narrative, he re-traces the major periods of European history from Mesopotamia to the Roman Empire, merely substituting the one geographical setting for another. In conclusion, he asks the question, "Might not some African philosopher, proud of his superior accomplishments, have made it a question, whether those wretched whites, the very outcasts of nature, who were banished to the cold regions of the north, were capable of civilization?" (WL 81). This narrative, of course, gains its power from the unexpectedness of the surprise of the reader with this kind of notion. Despite the superficial semblance of relativising historical inevitability, Wilberforce soon indirectly reminds his readers of what is 'historical fact' when he stresses the importance of Greco-Roman heritage,

> Had not our island therefore been conquered by the Romans, who lodged in the soil the seeds of civilization which sprung up afterwards, when circumstances favoured their growth; and had the neighbouring provinces on the continent, from which otherwise the rays of knowledge might have enlightened us, remained also unsubdued; what reason is there to suppose that we, any more than the inhabitants of any other savage country, should now be a civilized nation? . . . In what state was Britain herself, when first visited by the Romans? More barbarous than many of the African kingdoms in the present day (WL 83f)

The texts attribute universal validity to a specifically British historical narrative about Roman civilisation. Furthermore, one has to consider the military nature of the Roman conquest/acculturation. Thus, Wilberforce's narrative very much makes the concept of empire the means of socio-cultural progress.

One cannot but notice a certain cynicism in suggesting that the 'Almighty' might well have chosen Africa for the cradle of mankind (as indeed 'He' did) merely to re-affirm the exceptionality of the British/European case and the African's ultimate Otherness. Homi Bahbha holds that that "mimicry must continually produce its slippage, its excess, its difference" (Bhabha, *Mimicry* 126). By affirming both Africans' factual lack of Greco-Roman heritage and the theoretical possibility of an alternative course of history, the text does very much create colonial subjects, who are a "reformed, recognizable Other, as a subject of difference that is almost the same but not quite" (Bhabha, *Culture* 122). Wilberforce uses the ancients as a frame of reference for his appraisal of African societies. Considering Mungo Park's examples of the Africans' "almost universal benevolence, gentleness, and hospitality; of their courage, ..." (WL 66), Wilberforce concludes that these instances are "scarcely inferior to any thing which is recorded in Greek or Roman story" (WL 67). To use Bhabha's phrasing, the text obviously produces Africans who are 'almost not inferior, but not quite not'.

Both of these examples propose a highly Eurocentric model of the history of human civilisation in that they make the ability to trace a society's heritage back to Greco-Roman antiquity a sine qua non of attaining "any height of civilization" (WL 55).

Of course, it was not only the anti-slavery side that referred to the ancients as an authority; pro-slavery writers used allusions to antiquity to add weight to their arguments. The anonymous "Gentleman of Basseterre" contrasts James Ramsay's intentions to what they seem to perceive as an example of good practice from antiquity:

> The Legislators of Antiquity endeavoured to introduce and establish their laws by mildness, by reason, and by shewing their esteem and regard for the community they wished to reform; and by proving from their own example, that there was no difficulty for their fellow citizens, as there was no disinclination in themselves, to pursue those measures they wished to see universally adopted. (AA 4)

Authors also see the Roman legal tradition as an authority, which had to be dealt with in their arguments. Clarkson feels compelled to refute the ancient concept of the right of capture (CE 84f) on the grounds that "The voice of nature is against it. It is not lawful to kill, but on necessity. Had there been a necessity, where had the wretched captive survived to be broken with chains and servitude?" (CE 86). In *Thoughts*, Clarkson follows a different legal argumentation from antiquity, namely "the old Roman law, which taught that all slaves were to be considered as cattle" (CT 9). Apart from the obvious counter-argument of claiming the Africans' humanity, Clarkson also takes up a different line of argument when he censors the planters, saying, "It is then upon this, the old Roman law, and not upon any English law, that the planters found their right to the services of such as are born in slavery" (CT 9).

3.4.2 Slaves in Antiquity

For the discourse on slavery, the role of ancient Greece and Rome was of course an ambivalent one since both were slave-holding societies, which allowed pro-slavery writers to claim: "The Antiquity, Universality, and Lawfulness of Slavery, ever having been one of the States and Conditions of Mankind" (FA iii).

James Ramsay laments "how miserable the condition of slaves in general was among the ancients" (RE 27) and Clarkson spends a whole ten pages of his essay to build his case that the slaves of the ancients were not inferior by nature. He deconstructs Aristotle's belief that "the Greeks, from the superiority of their capacities, had a natural right to dominion, and that the rest of the world, from the inferiority of their own, were to be considered and treated as the irrational part of the creation" (CE 25). He refutes "these cruel sentiments of the ancients" (CE 25) concerning their slaves by attributing the Greeks' disparaging attitude towards "those, whom they termed barbarians' (CE 25) to "the combined effects of the treatment and commerce, and, on the other, from vanity and pride" (CE 26). He is anxious to point out that it was "the commerce [of slaves], by classing them originally with brutes, and the consequent treatment, by cramping their abilities, and hindering them from becoming conspicuous" which gave slaves "at a very early period, the most unfavourable appearance" (CE 23).

Despite Clarkson's efforts to prove the humanity of the ancient slaves, there seems to have been widespread agreement among pro- and anti-slavery authors that slavery among the ancients was conceptually different from the West Indian system. The main reason for this being that, "... the Slaves among the ancients were in general of the same complexion, features, and form, with their masters, ... These masters were aware their situation was one, into which they themselves might be reduced by the fortune of war: . . ." (WL 129f). James Tobin agrees, since, "as it has never been pretended, that the slaves either of the Jews, Greeks, or Romans of old, or the European and Asiatic slaves of modern times, were, or are, any way inferior to their masters, except in strength, policy, or good fortune." (TC 141). Thomas Clarkson summarises the issue when he writes:

> There were no particular nations in those times, like the Africans, expressly set apart for slavery by the rest of the world, so as to have a stigma put upon them on that account, nor did a difference of the colour of the skin constitute always, as it now does, a most marked distinction between the master and the slave, so as to increase this stigma and to perpetuate antipathies between them. (CT 16)

In other words, there seems to have been widespread agreement that race was far less an issue for ancient slavery than it was in the Caribbean. In addition to claiming the non-racial nature of slavery in Antiquity, Clarkson and other authors also stress that,

> We [I] may observe, . . . that their [i.e. slaves in Antiquity] situation was in many instances similar to that of our own servants. There was an express contract between the parties; they could, most of them, demand their discharge, if they were ill used by their respective masters; and they were treated therefore with more humanity than those, whom we usually distinguish in our language by the appellation of Slaves. (CE 4)

3.4.2.1 Greek Slaves

Generally speaking, authors seem to agree that slaves in ancient Athens were treated best. Ramsay, for example, admits that the ancients did not have "the light of revelation to direct their conduct," (*Essay* 21); however, he praises the Athenians, who, according to him, had "advanced human nature much nearer to perfection than any other nation" (RE 21). Ramsay writes about their treatment of slaves:

> ... they were indulgent, easy, and kind to their slaves, when compared with their neighbours. And well this condescension became a people, who, by mere force of genius, advanced human nature much nearer to perfection than any other nation. That their good sense did not, in every particular, carry them to that equality of behaviour towards their slaves, which humanity might expect, or benevolence suggest, ... the life of a slave at Athens was much happier than that of a freeman in any other Grecian state. (RE 21)

Ramsay generally praises the legal security that slaves enjoyed in Athens, mentioning such examples as their claim to protection in the temple of Theseus in case of ill-treatment by their masters (21f) and the fact that slavery was a contract in Athens and the slaves "might demand [their freedom] of their master for a determined price" (RE 22).

Ramsay's argument was of course all too easily picked up on and turned around by his opponents, who responded: "We can very easily suppose, that that wise nation established the most prudent regulations and improved society by the most salutary laws, and We are certain, that happiness is far from being confined to universal freedom ..." (AA 52). The implicit conclusion was that an equally wise nation, such as the Britons, would be equally able to protect its slaves without extending universal freedom to all. James Tobin also uses the ancient Athenians to make his argument for the West India planters, "If this [i.e. rewarding the service and fidelity of the slave with freedom] is produced as a striking mark of polished humanity, it very frequently occurs in the West India islands" (TC 12).

Ancient Greece, however, is not portrayed as a single political unit and the classical dichotomy between the *poleis* of Athens and Sparta is drawn upon by James Ramsay, who comments on the Spartans' backwardness:

> ... among the polished Greeks, the Spartans were a nation of savages: their language, like that of other savages, broken, yet expressive; their knowledge confined to war, but to the part of a mere soldier; for they were once so absolutely without a citizen fit to command their army, that they were obliged to employ a lame Athenian fidler as a general. (RE 29f)

Ramsay's evaluation of the situation of the Helots is a surprisingly ambivalent one. He writes of them that,

> ... the Spartans, who, through a wantonly cruel policy, were continually harrassing, ill treating, oppressing, nay, to keep their hands accustomed to blood, butchering their slaves, were held in constant alarms by them, and often were brought into extreme danger, by their desperate attempts to regain their liberty. Yet the condition of slaves among the Spartans, from the circumstance of their being generally the property of the public, and attached to the soil, more readily admitted of universal relaxation and indulgence, than it did among the Athenians, where they were chiefly private property. (RE 24)

3.4.2.2 Roman Slaves

In general, the texts seem to agree that the slaves in the Roman Empire were not treated as kindly as in Athens. As I have shown above, however, the distinction between master and slave is not described in terms of race, but rather as an effect of Rome's military conquests. Thus, the slavery in ancient Rome was linked to the rise and fall of the empire. Ramsay sees the increasingly worse treatment of slaves in the Roman Empire as a sign of the Romans' moral corruption:

> In the infant state of Rome, slaves worked, and lived with their masters, without much distinction of rank or usage. But in proportion as luxury increased among the Romans, the condition of their slaves sunk gradually down to the lowest degree of wretchedness and misery. And indeed such representations as the statue of the dying gladiator, which exhibits the life of a brave useful man sacrificed, not to the safety of his country, but to the barbarous whim of, perhaps, the most worthless set of men that ever were assembled together in one place; ... must fill every reflecting man with such abhorrence of, and indignation at the conduct of the Romans, in the character of masters, in their advanced state of empire, as must prove them unworthy of being drawn into example, except to be execrated for their conduct. (RE 25)

However, Ramsay does not seem to have a conceptual problem with slavery as such and advocates an imperial policy as a solution for domestic social inequality as long as it does "set not one man paramount over another" (RE 52). He devotes a whole chapter of his *Essay* to Fletcher of Saltoun's 1698 plan to make virtual slaves out of vagrant Scottish Highlanders. Fletcher sees the slavery in ancient Rome as something rather positive, since "the ancients had no poor cast loose on the public [and] could, without possessing much other wealth, undertake, with their slaves, great public and private works" (RE 40).

Ramsay refers to the struggle of orders in Rome in a similar context when he asks,

> What were the early seditions at Rome, but struggles between wealth and poverty, till war and distant conquest had enriched or drawn off the oppressed starving multitude? Indeed, where was there room left for public beggars, when the poor were slaves, and had only their own master to whom to cry for help? (RE 48).

This kind of historical analysis makes one, indeed, wonder why this author problematises colonial slavery to such a degree while he portrays restricting the liberty of domestic beggars as a legitimate form of state intervention.

3.4.3 Decline and Fall of the Roman Empire

The concept of the Roman Empire is touched upon in many of the texts. It somehow seems to serve as a prototype for the concept of empire. It is certainly no coincidence that Edward Gibbon had published his highly successful *History of the Decline and Fall of the Roman Empire* between 1776 and 1789. Gibbon's theory that it was a gradual loss of civic virtue (cf. Pocock 287ff) that had brought about the decline of that other empire must have resonated all the more strongly with the readers of a metropolitan Britain which was in the process of losing 14 colonies in the American revolution.

The texts reflect Rome becoming the foremost Mediterranean power through references to events such as the Punic Wars (CE 89f, 130) and the Battle of Corinth (WL 76). Against the background of the Roman conquest of Greece, Wilberforce develops a model of socio-cultural exchange. In accordance with what can still be found in history textbooks today, the Greeks are very much portrayed as a positive cultural influence. Wilberforce writes of it: "About 150 years before Christ, Greece was subdued by the Romans, who thence derived their civilization and knowledge" (WL 76). The underlying model of cultural exchange is highly relevant in the colonial context. Wilberforce again refers to the idea of one nation being improved by the conquest of a more civilised one when he compares the Roman and Islamic expansion. He points out that "the Mahometans ... became civilized by the nations they subdued, as Rome had been before by her conquest of Greece" (WL 78f). The author clearly distinguishes between two types of conquest: If a 'superior civilisation' conquers an 'inferior' one and vice versa. The Roman conquest of Greece is certainly seen as the latter kind and, accordingly, the conquerors were positively influenced by the conquered.

Two arguments from Gibbon's *Decline and Fall* were strongly deliberated on in particular by Ramsay, Clarkson and Wilberforce and their pro-slavery counterparts. Firstly, Ramsay is anxious to refute that "the abolition of slavery and Paganism, by edict, in the time of Constantine, brought on the ruin of the Roman Empire" (RE 29 fn). Ramsay stresses:

> That empire had begun to nod to its fall, long before this change could have produced any effect. The universal degeneracy of manners, the contempt of religion, the prevalence of Epicurean notions, the disregard of national character, the effeminacy of the soldiers, their loss of discipline, the instability of the government, and the natural course of human grandeur, are sufficient to account for the downfall of that fabric, under the rude shock of surrounding savages. (RE 29 fn)

This certainly reflects Gibbon's theory that it was loss of civic virtue which led to the downfall of the Roman Empire (Pocock 287ff). According to Pocock, Edward Gibbon holds the loss of republican civic virtue responsible for the downfall of the mighty Roman Empire in his *Decline and Fall of the Roman Empire*. The authors of the abolition debate would probably have been familiar with Gibbon's famous work, which was published in what Pocock calls the "uneasy years between the American and French revolutions" (287). Roman virtue had originally rested land ownership, which "gave the individual arms and independence, liberty and virtue" (292). The Roman Republic's virtue was the reason why it acquired an empire, which, in turn, destroyed the republic by success and excess. The decline of republican virtue was the natural result of the "rise of commerce . . . as formerly free arms-bearing citizens had become content to pay mercenaries to defend them and absolute monarchs to govern them, the better to enjoy the wealth, leisure, and cultivation which commerce made possible" (292). Gibbon did not advocate a return to this kind of primitive agrarian virtue, but held that the positive effects of commerce and culture clearly outweighed the loss and hoped that capitalism in Smith's sense would convert "man's love of himself . . . into love of his fellow social beings" (292). However, the "ancient image of virtue was never overthrown or abandoned" (292) and, therefore, all theories of human progress somehow carried "the negative implication that progress was at the same time decay, that culture entailed some loss of freedom and virtue" (292f). In the context of imminent downfall, it was easy for the abolitionists to compare the practice of slavery with the Romans indulging their amusements, thus styling abolition as an act saving the British Empire from its decline.

Clarkson also comments on the loss of civic virtue in the Roman empire when he compares the King of Dahomey with the Roman emperors

> The prince, as if he imitated some of the Roman Emperors, gives largesses to his people on certain days. These largesses consist of cowries, and article of European merchandize, which, as I have stated before, passes for money in some parts of the country. He is often so prodigal on these occasions, as to feel himself in want. (CE88 40)

An interesting analogy suggests itself: Originally the "inundation northern nations" put an end to the moral corruption. The official agenda of the imperial projects of the European colonisers claimed to be doing the same thing.

Wilberforce constructs the rise and fall of nations as around a certain fateful inevitability when he writes:

> But he who has looked with any care into the page of history, will acknowledge, that when nations are prepared for their fall, human instruments will not be wanting to effect it; and, lest man, vain man, so apt to overrate the powers and achievements of human agents, should ascribe the subjugation of the Romans to the consummate policy and powers of a Julius Caesar, their slavery shall be (350) completed by the unwarlike Augustus, and shall remain entire under the hateful tyranny of Tiberius, and throughout all the varieties of their successive masters. (WL 349f)

Ramsay refers to the peoples' migration as "the rude shock of surrounding savages". The image of the savage in this expression is an interesting one. The savages are definitely 'Others' and they are a threat to the empire, which generally seems to be seen as something positive by the author, while its downfall is something negative (the very term Middle Ages is an interruption between the ancients and the moderns). Ramsay further writes about the period of migrations:

> The inundation of the northern nations, that broke into the Roman Empire, and the feudal tenures that were introduced by it, gave rise to a new species of slavery in Europe, the remains of which are yet to be found, particularly in Denmark and Poland. (RE 29f)

Clarkson writes that,

> [..] all those nations which assisted in overturning the Roman Empire, though many and various, adopted the same measures; for we find it a general maxim in their polity, that whoever should fall into their hands as a prisoner of war, should immediately be reduced to the condition of a slave. (CE 8)
> and
> it [i.e. the custom of slavery] spread through the Grecian and Roman world; was in use among the barbarous nations, which overturned the Roman empire; and was practised therefore, at the same period, throughout all Europe. (CE 36)

Wilberforce writes: "the Northern nations, who, seeking for a more genial climate and a more fertile Soil, in the finest provinces of both the eastern and western empire, overran the civilized world in the fifth century after Christ" (WL 78).

The use of the words "inundation", "rude shock" and "overran" makes it clear that the fall of the Roman Empire is seen as something negative. While the Romans are portrayed as imperial lords ruling over vast portions of the then known world, the northern nations are portrayed in a more embodied way; they inundate with their sheer mass. The passage also shows that medieval serfdom is constructed as conceptually different from ancient slavery.

Ramsay perhaps voices the final victory of the 'northern nations' over the Roman Empire in the most striking way. He asks:

> ... how would it have hurt the pride of an overweening Hume [i.e. David Hume] among the Romans, to have been told, that the time would come when his sons should be emasculated to fit them for entertaining on a stage the barbarous Britons with effeminate music? (RE 204 fn).

One detects a measure of national triumphalism of the "barbarous Briton" over the rulers of the ancient world.

3.5 Middle Ages and Feudalism

Another theme of historical narrative that received attention in the discussion of slavery was the emergence of feudal states during and after the period of migration. European feudalism is described as conceptually different from the slavery of the ancients. Clarkson, for example, evaluates different explanations for the origin of "that general liberty, which at the close of the twelfth century, was conspicuous in the west of Europe" (CE 40) and asks why "this slavery and commerce which had continued for so long a time . . . began as the northern nations were settled in their conquests to decline and upon their establishment were abolished" (CE 36f). He first discusses whether this was "the necessary consequence of the feudal system" and then concludes that it was "the natural consequence of Christianity" (CE 37).

As mentioned above, the Fall of the Roman Empire was very much seen by authors as a watershed moment in history. Interestingly, however, the term 'Middle Ages' as such is hardly used in the texts. Only Wilberforce explicitly refers to the Middle Ages in his 1807 *Letter* (cf. WL 210), noting the term twice. Nonetheless, the underlying concept of a transitional period between 'the ancients' and 'the moderns' can be found in almost all the texts' historical analyses. In his essay on Gibbon's *Decline and Fall*, Pocock writes that:

> in the years of the late Enlightenment ... it was widely held that virtue had subsequently [i.e. after the fall of the Roman empire] been restored in a barbaric form by the Gothic and Germanic invaders, who had set up primitive but effective communities of armed freeholders ...: (Pocock, *Gibbon* 288, 291).

Gibbon himself describes the northern invaders of the late Empire as "the barbarians of Germany and Scythia, the rude ancestors of the most polished nations of modern Europe" (Gibbon, *Decline* xiii). Furthermore, he writes that "... when the fierce giants of the north broke in ... They restored a manly spirit of freedom; and after the revolution of ten centuries, freedom became the happy parent of taste and science" (Gibbon, *Decline* 36).

There seems to be a general narrative of the progress of European freedom and individuality in which the Middle Ages function as a period of transition. In this context, the period of Humanism and the Renaissance becomes the time when the individual was reinvented. In his *Slavery and Human Progress*, Davis asserts that in most traditional societies, the antithesis to slavery is not free autonomous individuality, as the abolitionists would have it, but rather the state of belonging to the dominant group. In other words, those who do not belong to the in-group are automatically termed 'slave' and even their assimilated offspring often retain a different status from those who are considered kinspeople (cf. Davis, *Human Progress* 15). It is very interesting that within this context, Davis remarks that:

> in a sense, slaves were the world's first 'modern' people. The archetypical slave was a foreigner, and outsider torn from her or his protective family matrix ... the modernity of the slave lay in his continuing marginality and vulnerability, in his incomplete and ambiguous bonding to a social group (Davis, *Human Progress* 14f).

This point of view resonates with what Agamben writes about the emergence of the modern subject in *Homo Sacer*, namely that "the original political relation is the ban" and that "the [modern] juridico-political order has the structure of an inclusion of what is simultaneously pushed outside" (Agamben, *Homo Sacer* 181 and 18). The European Middle Ages and their romanticised residues, for example, in the image of the happy peasant (cf. WL 5), are represented in the discourse on slavery as a period of time when the alienation which characterises the modern subject/labourer was not yet in place. Such a period of non-alienation had an important function in the European paradigm of human progress. Drescher writes in his *Mighty Experiment* that "the classic Enlightenment paradigm, derived from its concept of human progress, was based on the decline of slavery and serfdom in Western Europe. Its master narrative entailed a shift from medieval servitude to modern, free, contractual bargaining" (Drescher, *Experiment* 5). Thomas Clarkson posits the universal necessity of a period of transition when he compares the ancient Greeks with the moderns:

> The political state of Greece in its early history, was the same as that of Europe, when divided, by the feudal system, into an infinite number of small and independent kingdoms ... the Grecians in short, in heroic, were in the same situation in these respects as the feudal barons in the Gothic times. (CE 38)

Clarkson also hints at the emergence of modern freedom being a result of the renewal of virtue by the northern invaders when he quotes Tacitus on the original situation of the Germanic peoples:

> They [i.e. the Germans] had their national councils, like the Gauls, in which the regal and ducal offices were confirmed according to the majority of voices. They elected also, on these occasions, those only, whom their virtue, by repeated trial, had unequivocally distinguished from the rest ... We might appeal for a testimony of this, to the history of the Goths; to the history of the Franks and Saxons; to the history, in short, of all those nations, from which the different governments, now conspicuous in Europe, have undeniably sprung. (CE 64f)

The existence of a transitional period was an integral part of the idea of making slaves "fit for the enjoyment of British freedom" (WA 73), which goes hand in hand with the concept of individual improvement, progress and learning as a means of "man's emergence from his self-imposed immaturity", to quote Kant's famous dictum. Wilberforce describes the "real state" of slaves in African societies "in truth to be a species of feudal or rather of patriarchal vassalage" (WL 91). Accordingly, he also suggests the introduction of feudal structures on West India estates (cf. WL 191) as was actually the case in Joshua Steele's famous experiment.

Clarkson writes about what Drescher refers to as a "modest experiment in quasi emancipation" (Drescher, *Mighty Experiment* 111) that:

> Mr. Steele took the hint for the particular mode of improving the condition of his slaves .. from the practice of our Anglo Saxon ancestors in the days of villainage, which ... was 'the most wise and excellent mode of civilizing savage slaves' (CT 37).

Juxtaposing the Africans' situation with a universalised European narrative of progress from medieval servitude to modern freedom encapsulated free Africans and slaves alike in a Eurocentric discourse of betterment, portraying a feudal organisation of society as a necessary precursor of the modern state.

Pro-slavery authors, perhaps merely for the sake of disagreeing, tend to paint a less positive picture of feudalism. "William the Concqueror, who introduced the Normal feudal system, which was of a milder nature, but still there was not interposition of the legislature to prohibit personal servitude: The act of Car. 2d [i.e. the 1660 Tenures Abolition Act] abolished feudal tenures among free British subjects, but did not mention foreign slaves" (AA 30). In his answer to Clarkson, Gilbert Francklyn is anxious to maintain the conceptual overlap between vassalage and slavery while at the same time emphasising British liberty,

> by degrees vassalage and slavery have disappeared in most of the polished parts of Europe ... Enfranchisement of villains seems to have been complete in England about the middle of Queen Elisabeth's reign ... Vassalage still subsists in many parts of France and Germany, and in Russia, Poland, Hungary, and Dalmatia. ... In several of these place the common people are as strictly slaves, as they were formerly in those countries where the severity of the feudal system has been since softened and relaxed. (FA 81)

At the end of the day, anti-slavery authors were more successful in contrasting the horrors of slavery to the feudal blessings of the European past. Davis writes that:

> British antislavery provided a bridge between preindustrial and industrial values. ... The slave owner's claims contrasted sharply with those of the idealised British squire, whose authority was constrained by law and custom, and with the rights of the rising capitalist, who was content to purchase labour on the market like any other commodity (Davis, *Hegemony* 170f).

3.6 Orient versus Occident

3.6.1 Islam as the Ultimate Other

Despite the unquestionable authority of and interest in classical antiquity, there is one main difference between the 'ancients' and the 'moderns': the former's lack of Christianity. This is evidenced by Ramsay summarily referring to the ancients as "those nations that had not the light of revelation to direct their conduct" (RE 21) and also by the dispute between Thomas Clarkson and Gilbert Francklyn as to whether the reason for the "general liberty" which came to prevail during the Middle Ages was a result of feudalism, Christianity or the contact with the Orient, as Francklyn boldly argues when he attributes European freedom rather to:

> the influence of the Mahomendan than to the Christian religion . . . The voyages and travels of so many Princes and Nobles to Greece and Asia, where still remained such traces of ancient arts, sciences, and magnificence, could not fail to have considerable influence on the manners of the barbarous people of the northern parts of Europe, and contribute to their civilization. (FA 83)

Although there are minor differences in the image of the Orient which is created in the texts, the concept seems very much to function as a projection screen onto which everything that was meant to be 'Other' could be cast. Clarkson summarily styles oriental societies as slave societies when he writes, "we find all Eastern nations unanimous in the practise [i.e. slavery]" (CE 7).

There is an interesting contrast between the images of the Orient and the one of sub-Saharan Africa. At the risk of oversimplifying the case, one can say that Africa is more or less constructed as a blank spot on the map with (noble ?) savages living in a relative state of nature. The Orient, however, is constructed as a space with a very distinct cultural history of its own. The existence of such a potential counter-empire was certainly a threat to, but also fulfilled an important function in, the internal logic of an emerging British Empire. Edward Said writes of this: "Each great metropolitan centre that aspired to global dominance has said, and alas done, many of the same thing. . . . there is the horrifically predictable disclaimer that 'we' are exceptional, not imperial, not about the repeat the mistake of earlier powers . . ." (Said, *Imperialism* xxvi). The discursive struggle of integrating this Other empire within the universal Eurocentric narrative of one source of civilisation in the form of classical antiquity becomes evident when Wilberforce writes that ". . . it should be remembered, that while the Mahometans, who overran the various provinces of both the eastern and the western empires, became civilised by the nations they subdued, as Rome had been before by her conquest of Greece . . ." (WL 78). The text attempts to create a sort of sanitised, mimetic Other.

Pro-slavery authors employ the image of the Orient rather more bluntly. The anonymous authors of St. Christopher call "Mahomet the false Prophet and establisher of a false religion" (AA 29), referring to Islam in their personal rant against James Ramsay, in which they mention an "honourable gentleman of St. Christopher", and remark of Ramsay's attitude that, "such a doctrine was fitter for a Disciple of Mahomet, than a Christian Minister" (AA 19). James Tobin propagates his own image of Arabic culture in a quite straightforward way when he writes, "The lower ranks in Spain are avowedly debased, by their long intercourse with the Moors" (TC 118 fn).

3.6.2 Arabic Slave Trade

What all authors seem to concur on is an image of the Orient as a cultural space featuring slavery. Quoting the ancient Greek historian Ctesias on the legendary Assyrian queen Semiramis, Gilbert Francklyn writes "that this queen and her more infamous successors, were attended by eunuchs, in the same manner as all the other princes of the east are at present" (FA 48).

It is a bit ironic that the existence of Arabic slavery could both be used in the pro- and anti-slavery argument. The pro-slavery argument rests on two tenets: Firstly, the claim that it was not the Europeans who actually started the slave trade was used to show "The Antiquity, Universality, and Lawfulness of Slavery" (FA title). James Tobin writes that:

> the Moors of the north of Africa traded for slaves with the inhabitants of the different branches of the river Niger, by an inland communication, as far back as history furnishes us with any account of those countries, and long before the seacoasts of Guinea were discovered by the early Portuguese adventurers who found this trade firmly established on their first visiting those countries (TC 16f).

The second assumption was that the Christian Europeans were saving the Africans from being enslaved by the 'Moors'. Francklyn writes of the Portuguese that they:

> ... did not revive that commerce, nor were the first who carried Africans into slavery.... they only diverted a part of that commerce from the east to the west part of that continent, by doing which, they have enabled the Christians to purchase some of those slaves which would otherwise have been sold to the Mahomedans.... Perhaps a Christian divine, zealous for the conversion of the negroes, Mr. Clarkson may be alarmed at so many of them being made Mahomedans, (if the European trade with Africa should cease,) who have now some chance of being made Christians. (FA 153f)

Two pages later, Francklyn puts his argument that the Europeans are actually doing the Africans a favour even more clearly, when he emphasises that otherwise the slaves "would be returned to the 'antient' channel, which has never been entirely shut, and obliging the natives, who possess slaves, to dispose of them to the Moors and Arabs" (FA 155).

3.6.3 Islamic Influence in Africa as "Some Feeble Light"

The role of Islam in the anti-slave trade argument is slightly more complex. While the topic of Islam receives quite some treatment in texts up to 1807, it seems to be largely absent in the emancipation debate. The reason for this might well be a geographical one since the latter discourse was spatially located primarily in the West Indies, while part of the negotiation of the slave trade pertained to the African continent and the circumstances there. In particular, Thomas Clarkson's *Letters on the Slave Trade* and William Wilberforce's *Letter on the Abolition* contain a more extensive discussion of the influence of Islam in Africa.

Clarkson describes the influence of the Moors in Africa as a very damaging one. He writes of the country of Oualo (Walo?) that "The Moors made incursions onto this country about five years ago, and killed the king. Deeming themselves from this moment the lords and disposers of the soil, they took the liberty of appointing to the throne" (CL 19). Clarkson writes that they appoint a weak king who was to remain tributary to them and "who considering him a creature of their own, rob and plunder in his territories as often as they think proper" (CL 19). This sort of empire based on crude force instead of a civilising mission serves exactly the function which Said refers to above. In this context, it is also worth considering the Islamic expansion in the whole Maghreb region. It has been stated above that Wilberforce and other authors write that the Arabs were civilised by the peoples they conquered. Clarkson writes that, "there was another eruption of Cushites into these parts, under the name of Saracens and Moors, who over-ran Africa to the very extremity of Mount Atlas!" (CE 182). The difference with the Roman empire is palpable: while the Romans are seen as the ones who first sowed "the seeds of civilization" in the northern regions of Europe (cf. WL 76), the Arabs merely overrun in their conquest. This constitutes an example of an 'Other' empire which failed to last.

Clarkson's description of the Moors in Africa is an extremely negative one. He explains that they "have no houses or fixed habitations, but live in tents ... These people live almost entirely by plunder, ... all that comes out of their hands may be set down as the produce of treachery and force" (CL 20). Clarkson solidarises with the African natives against the Moorish invaders and explains the Africans' view of the Moors, "The name, by which the Moors have always been known to them is Nars, ... this word ... has become a word in the language of the Negroes to convey to the hearer the united characters of a liar and of a thief" (CL 23). Clarkson's invective against the Moors continues:

> Mr. de Villeneuve informs me that the Moors are so habituated to robbery, that scarcely any person of any complexion can escape without losing something if long among them. They are even expert at thieving with their feet ... Their whole life, in short, is a scene of robbery and the negroes have well applied their national name to denote the character described. (CL 23 fn)

The argumentative aim of all this seems to be to strengthen the image of Africans as noble, uncorrupted and largely unspoilt savages against the other of the Moors. Seen from the internal logic of a Eurocentric civilising mission, the *tabulae rasae* of the Africans are certainly more receptive for receiving 'the seeds of civilization' than the Moors who are already strategically located within the concurring sociocultural discourse of the Orient. The contrast between Africans and Moors is further exemplified by Clarkson's description of King Almammy of the dependent Poules, who valiantly defies the incursions of the Moors and even abolishes the slave trade in his African dominion (cf. CL 30ff). Against this background, it is hardly surprising that Clarkson seems to be anxious to point out that although the countries he is writing about in his *Letters* seem to be under a strong Islamic influence, "the bulk of the people, they seldom or ever assemble except for circumcision. They know little about the religion of the country, and, a few external rites excepted, are little of Mahometans but by name!" (CL 47). It appears as if Clarkson feared that presenting Africans as Muslims would somehow damage their reputation.

Quoting the explorer Mungo Park, Wilberforce portrays Islamic influence in Africa in the form of Islamic schools as s sort of counter model to the European Enlightenment.

> By establishing small schools in the different towns, where many of the Pagan as well as Mahometan children are taught to read the Koran, and instructed in the tenets of the prophet, the Mahometan priests fix a bias on the mind and form the character of their young disciples, which no accidents of life can ever afterwards remove or alter. I . . . heartily wished they had had better instructors and a purer religion. (WL 44f)

The author clearly sees the influence of Islam as an impediment and a competitor to the spread of European influence in the form of Christianity on the African continent. Wilberforce again quotes Mungo Park, who writes that while "the Negroes in general have a very great idea of the wealth and power of the Europeans, I am afraid that the Mahometan converts among them think but very lightly of our superior attainments in religious knowledge" (WL 45f). The author goes on to quote Park, who recommends "from motives of Christian zeal as well as of humanity, . . . to introduce the light of true religion into that benighted land" since it was "a matter of regret, to observe, that while the superstition of Mahomet has in this manner scattered a few faint beams of learning among these poor people the precious light of Christianity is altogether excluded" (WL 45f).

Wilberforce uses these observations to back up his case against the slave trade. It sheds some light on his view on Islam as well as on his wish for European intervention on the African continent when he portrays it as a paradoxical situation that:

> native superstitions . . . have continued in full force in those very districts, where the intercourse with the Europeans has been the longest, and the most intimate; while in the interior, the same barbarous practises have either gone into decay of themselves, or seen to have faded away before the feeble light of Mahometanism (WL 31).

He portrays the effects of the slave trade as "disgraceful to us as a Christian nation as when we contemplate them in connection with the benefits which the Africans derive from their intercourse with the Mahometans" (WL 43) and regrets "with what shame must we acknowledge that in Africa, Christianity and Mahometanism appear to have mutually interchanged characters" (WL 43f).

The Otherness of Islam is also reflected in the metaphors Wilberforce uses: while Africa is "benighted" (WL 45f) and full of "darkness" (WL 78f), both Christianity and Islam are referred to in terms of light. However, Islam comes in the form of "a feeble light" (WL 31) and "faint beams of knowledge and civilization" (WL 78f) while Christianity is the "purer religion" (WL 44f) and a "precious light" (WL 45f). This shows that the portrayal of the relationship between Islam and Christianity is a mimetic one of "almost the same but not quite" (Bhabha, *Culture* 122).

3.7 Modernity and the Atlantic System

The European historical master narrative posits a transition from the Middle Ages to Modernity around 1500. The transition coincides with the European 'discovery' of previously unknown parts of the globe. It is the aim of this chapter to trace the historical narrative(s), which the texts in my corpus construct about the period from roughly 1500 up to the 1820s. The historical discourse comprises several discursive strands.

3.7.1 African History

Georg Hegel famously declared Africa to have no history (cf. Hegel, *History of Philosophy* 103); however, the discourse on slavery does not completely support this conviction. The texts, at least the ones from the abolition phase, do discuss events of African history in quite some detail. Also, Philip Curtin points to the fact that "two out of the sixteen folio volumes of the Modern History section [of the *Universal History* published between 1736 and 1765] were devoted to Africa—one eighth of the total" (Curtin, *Image* 12f), which shows the interest in the history of the African continent. Producing scientific knowledge about Other peoples and countries is of course always part of establishing certain power relations. Edward Said famously wrote about a similar process of systematic production of knowledge about the Orient in his seminal work. He states that "to have such knowledge of a thing is to dominate it, to have authority over it" (Said, *Orientalism* 32).

The references to African history start with Trans-Saharan contacts of various Arabic and Berber states of the Maghreb region, which have already been dealt with in the previous chapter. James Tobin, for example, refers to Al Idrisi's *Geographia Nubiensis* to establish the long existence of an 'inland communication' of the Moors across the Sahara. He also refers his readers to the Moroccan Hassan ibn Muhammad al Fasi, who wrote a detailed description of the African kingdom of Songhay under his Christian name, Leo

Africanus (cf. TC 16fn and Shillington, *Africa* 111f). Gilbert Francklyn quotes the "Universal Mod. History Vol. 16 p.157", which mentions "a famine on the Gold Coast in the 15th century, occasioned by locusts", which reduced the population

> to such extremity, that the parents were forced to decimate their children, and sell one to help support the rest; insomuch, that the markets for slaves were so overstocked, that the Portuguese merchants had not ships to transport them to the Brazils; insomuch that the kingdom must have been depopulated by the famine, and the pestilence which followed, had not the Portuguese come to their assistance, and furnished them with proper physic, and wholesome food. So dreadful was the miserable condition of the people, that many persons of quality, and even princes of blood, voluntarily sold themselves for slaves, and submitted to be sent chained, to the Portuguese plantations, with the common herd, in hopes to meet with some relief, even in this sad exchange of misery. (FA 150f)

I have already mentioned that, of course, it helped the pro-slavery argument to emphasise that the Moors had long carried on a slave trade across the Saharan desert; in a similar argumentative ploy, James Tobin is anxious to point out that it was actually the Portuguese who started the trade in African slaves:

> At first the Portuguese carried off the natives by force, but about the year 1444, Gonzales, one of their leaders, returned from the coast of Guinea with a cargo of negro slaves regularly purchased; and they soon after settled proper markets, on different parts of the coast, for that purpose. This traffick soon increased, so that in 1445 not less than seven or eight hundred Negroes were annually brought as slaves to Lisbon. It was not, however, till the beginning of the sixteenth century that the Spaniards and Portuguese thought of exporting negroes to their settlements in the western world, which began to be most dreadfully depopulated by the unusual labour the natives were [18] forced to undergo, and the despair occasioned by such a heart breaking change of circumstances; and it was many years afterwards that the English endeavoured to follow so promising an example. (TC 17f)

Gilbert Francklyn extensively quotes from Astley's *Collection of Travels*, which was published between 1745 and 1747. He cites Astley's account of Villault, who was at the Gold Coast in 1663 and reported on a war in Akim "in which 60,000 men were destroyed"

(FA 118f). Drawing on the same source, Francklyn refers to the conquest of the coastal kingdoms of Allada and Whydah by King Agaja of Dahomey (cf. Shillingon, *Africa*, 199 and FA 121f). Among the European explorers whom Francklyn refers to from Astley are the Chevalier des Marchias, William Smith and Francis Moore (cf. FA 119,111,111 respectively). Later in his work, Francklyn points his readers to the rise of the Ashanti Empire (FA 126). Further events of distinctly African history include the British capture of the French settlements of St. Louis and Goree in Senegal and Gambia, which had to be given back to France after the Treaty of Paris in 1783.

The travels of the Swedish explorers Sparrman, Wadström and Arrhennius entered the discourse mainly because of their examination as witnesses before the Privy Council (cf. CL 32). Of course, the foundation of the British settlement at Sierra Leone with former American slaves who had defected to the British army in the American War of Independence is also frequently referred to (cf. FA 207f, 226f, 188. AF 49. WA 64. CT 16ff).

Perhaps the most influential African explorer who entered the discourse was Mungo Park, in relation to his travels on the river Niger. Wilberforce quotes Park extensively (11 direct quotes), and the anonymous pro-slavery writer Mercator refers to Park five times. While Mercator mainly refers to Park as proof of the existence of slavery in Africa, Wilberforce uses similar facts in his argument to underline the pernicious effects of the slave trade on African society, engulfing it in a Hobbesian war of all against all (WL 22). Apart from this, Wilberforce uses Park's account to report on the spread of Islam and the resulting need of "endeavouring to introduce the light of true religion in that benighted land" (WL 45).

Apart from these, the references to Africa, although frequent, are so general in nature that they do not yield any historical facts.

3.7.2 Slave Trade and Abolition

Both pro- and anti-slavery writers point out that Portuguese explorers started the slave trade. Tobin probably refers to Nuno Tristão when he remarks that the Portuguese trade "had its beginning so soon as 1443, many years preceding the discovery of America." (TC 17). The same person writes about the practice of the slave trade that:

> At first the Portuguese carried off the natives by force, but about the year 1444, Gonzales, one of their leaders, returned from the coast of Guinea with a cargo of negro slaves regularly purchased; and they soon after settled proper markets, on different parts of the coast, for that purpose. (TC 17)

In pursuit of his defence of slavery, Tobin does not fail to mention Pope Nicholas V's bull *Romanus Pontifex* (Harmer, *Companion* 3). Tobin describes the papal document as "the celebrated bull by which he [i.e. Pope Nicholas V] presented the new and unknown world to the Spaniards and Portuguese, not only permitted, but expressly ordered, the Christians to reduce all the infidel inhabitants into slavery" (TC 13f). Clarkson writes of the beginnings of the trade that, "The Portuguese erected their first fort at D'Elmina, in the year 1481, about forty years after Alonzo Gonzales had pointed the Southern Africans out to his countrymen as articles of commerce." (CE 44 fn).

After Columbus's 'discovery' of the Americas, the next discursive event is the establishing of the First Atlantic System primarily by the Spanish and Portuguese. Tobin writes:

> It was not, however, till the beginning of the sixteenth century that the Spaniards and Portuguese thought of exporting negroes to their settlements in the western world, which began to be most dreadfully depopulated by the unusual labour the natives were forced to undergo, and the despair occasioned by such a heart-breaking change of circumstances; and it was many years afterwards that the English endeavoured to follow so promising an example. (TC 17f)

The harsh treatment and the introduction of new diseases had a devastating influence on the indigenous peoples of the Americas and the Caribbean islands (cf. Shillington, *Africa* 180), which had forced the colonial empires to satisfy their need for labour on the African continent. The Bishop of Chiapa, Bartholomew de las Casas, protested to Spain's King Charles V about the inhuman treatment of the native population in the new settlements. Thomas Clarkson naturally styles de las Casas' intervention as a precursor of the abolition movement:

> Among the well disposed individuals, of different nations and ages, who have humanely exerted themselves to suppress the abject personal slavery, introduced in the original cultivation of the European colonies in the western world, Bartholomew de las Casas, the pious bishop of Chiapa, in the fifteenth century, seems to have been the first. This amiable man, during his residence in Spanish America, was so sensibly affected at the treatment which the miserable Indians underwent that he returned to Spain, to make a publick remonstrance before the celebrated emperor Charles the fifth, declaring, that heaven would one day call him to an account for those cruelties, which he then had it in his power to prevent. The speech which he made on the occasion, is now extant, and is a most perfect picture of benevolence and piety. (CE v)

The argument that de las Casas might be held responsible for the introduction of African slaves instead of native ones (cf. Harmer, *Companion* 5 and Ashcroft, *Studies* 195) seems to have served the pro-slavery writers better. Francklyn relativises de las Casas' virtue when he asks: "What opinion will the public entertain of Mr. Clarkson's integrity, when they are told, as the fact is, that the introduction of the African slaves into the colonies was first conceived and recommended by this very 'amiable man?'" (FA 162).

The year 1562 saw the British enter the transatlantic trade with John Hawkins, whose second voyage in 1564 is considered to have been the first 'successful' triangle run by a British crew (cf. Harmer, *Companion* 1564). Both Ramsay and Clarkson see this as an hour of British national embarrassment. Ramsay writes that, a nation most highly favoured of liberty, is viewed as taking the lead in this odious traffic, and as bending down the soul in utter darkness, the more effectually to enslave the body; freedom must blush indignantly, while humanity mourns over the reproachful tale. (RE 34).

Clarkson, however, rushes to the defence of Queen Elizabeth I, writing that she "expressed her concern lest any of the Africans should be carried off without their free consent, declaring, 'that it would be detestable and call down the vengeance of Heaven upon the undertakers'" (CT 12; cf. also Harmer, *Companion* 6). Despite the fact that Elizabeth herself invested in Hawkins' second voyage (cf. Harmer, *Companion* 6), Clarkson obviously wants to protect the reputation of the maiden Queen when he tells the readers of Hawkins' betrayal,

> Capt. Hawkins promised to comply with the injunctions of Elizabeth in this respect. But he did not keep his word; for when he went to Africa again, he seized many of the inhabitants and carried them off as slaves . . . (CT 12)

Thus the transatlantic triangle trade had been established, the Middle Passage of which saw the shipping of at least ten million Africans to the Americas and the Caribbean over a period of 300 years (cf. Shillington, *Africa* 180). With the 1713 Treaty of Utrecht, the Spanish ceded their monopoly of supplying slaves to Spanish America, paving the way for Britain to become the leading slave trading nation (cf. Harmer, *Companion* 9).

The narrative trope used to describe the Middle Passage has remained relatively unchanged since the days of the abolition debate. Recent works, such as Shillington's *History of Africa*, feature surprisingly similar elements as the 18th-century texts by authors such as Thomas Clarkson. The slaves are captured in the interior and then marched to the coast, and then have to undergo humiliating treatment, including being inspected naked by the slave traders. The trip across the Atlantic has perhaps been most famously illustrated in Thomas Clarkson's 1786 *Essay*, in which he had an African bystander explain the process of marching Africans from the interior to the coast,

> the cloud that you see approaching, is a train of wretched slaves. They are going to the ships behind you. . . . They were last night drawn up upon the plain which you see before you, where they were branded upon the breast with an hot iron; and when they had undergone the whole of the treatment which is customary on these occasions, and which I am informed that you Englishmen at home use to the cattle which you buy, they were returned to their prison. . . . Scarcely were these words spoken, when they came distinctly into sight. They appeared to advance in a long column, but in a very irregular manner. There were three only in the front, and these were chained together. (CE 188f)

On board the slave ships, the appalling conditions due to the confined space dominate the descriptions. Thomas Clarkson visualised this through his cross-sectional diagrams and models of a slave ship:

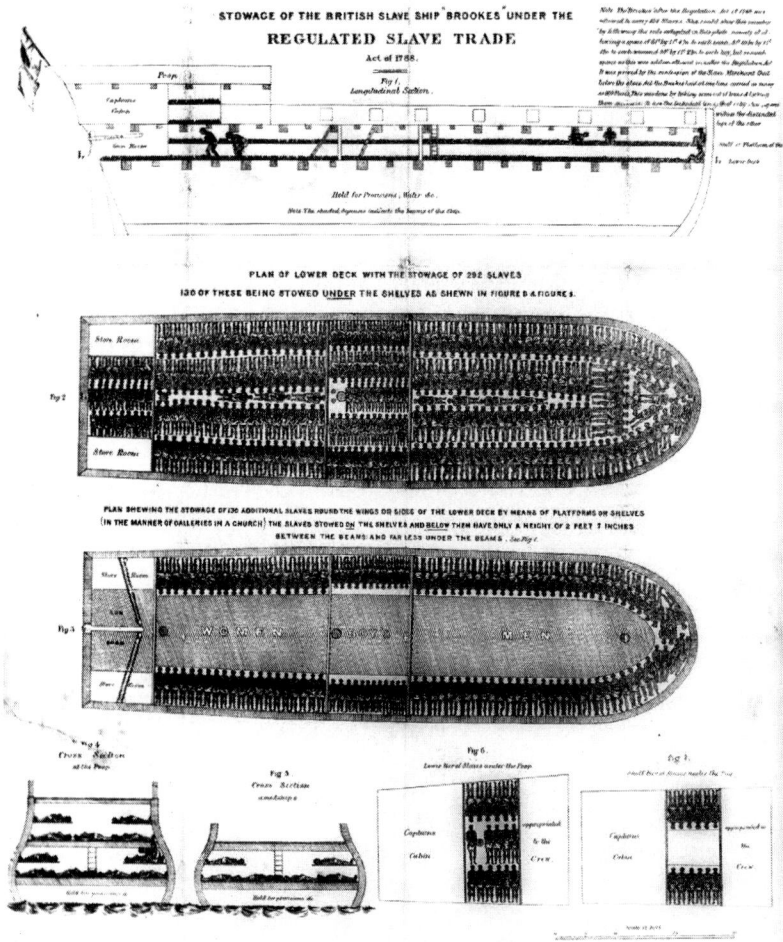

Fig. 7: Slave Ship (Wikimedia Commons. Public Domain)

The same author writes of the conditions during the Middle Passage:

> As much has been said by the advocates for this trade, of the accommodation which slaves experience during the Middle Passage, I shall say a few words on that head. The height of their apartments varies of course according to the size of the vessel, but may be stated to be from six feet to less than three; so that it is impossible for them to stand erect ... I cannot compare the scene on board this vessel, to any other than that of a pen of sheep; with this difference only, that the one have the advantages of a wholesome air, while that, which the

others breathe, is putrid. . . . Being stowed then in the manner thus described, they soon begin to experience the effects, which might naturally be presumed to arise from their situation. In consequence of the pestilential breath of so many confined in so small a space, they become sickly, and from the vicissitude of heat and cold, of heat when confined below, and of cold when suddenly brought up for air, a flux is generated. Whenever this disorder attacks the, no pen can be adequate to the task of describing their situation. Imagine only for a moment the gratings to be opened, but particularly after a rain, which has occasioned them to be covered for some time. The first scene that presents itself, is a cluster of unhappy people, who, overcome by excessive heat and stench, have fainted away . . . and who are wallowing in the blood and mucus of the intestines, with which the floor is covered. (CE*88* 91ff)

After undergoing this terrible ordeal, the human cargo of the slave ships arrived in the New World and were again subjected to a variety of degradations when being sold. In connection with this, nakedness in front of potential customers is always part of the narrative trope. Wilberforce quotes "Dr. Pinkard's Notes on the West Indies" (WL 134 fn) to provide a description of a "Negro Sale":

> The poor Africans, says he, who were to be sold, were exposed naked, in a large empty building like an open barn. Those who came with intention to purchase, minutely inspected them; handled them, made them jump, and stamp with their feet, and throw out their arms and their legs; turned them about; looked into their mouths; and, according to the usual rules of traffic with respect to cattle, examined them, and made them shew themselves in a variety of ways, to try if they were sound and healthy. All this was distressful and humiliating; but a wound still more severe was inflicted on the feelings, by some of the purchasers selecting only such as their judgment led them to prefer, regardless of the bonds of nature and affection. (WL 134f)

Francklyn mentions unsuccessful rebellions on slave ships in 1718 and 1721 (FA 180f). The middle of the 18th century also saw the beginning of popular resistance against the slave trade. In 1754, the American Quaker, John Woolman, published *Some Considerations on the Keeping of Negroes*. Clarkson writes:

> Till this time it does not appear, that any bodies of men, had collectively interested themselves in endeavouring to remedy the evil. But in the year 1754, the religious society, called Quakers, publickly testified their sentiments upon the subject, declaring, that 'to live in ease and plenty by the toil of those, whom

fraud and violence had put into their power, was neither consistent with Christianity nor common justice. (CE vii)

Another early opponent of the slave trade mentioned by Clarkson and Francklyn (CE 230 and FA 225f) was William Warburton, the Bishop of Gloucester, who condemned slavery in sermons before the Society for the Propagation of the Gospel in Foreign Parts and the House of Lords (cf. Young, *Warburton*).

A first important legal success of the anti-slavery cause was the famous 1772 Somerset Case, in which Lord Chief Justice Mansfield ruled that under British law the former Virginia slave James Somerset was not to be returned to bondage. Thomas Clarkson's triumphant reference to this as "the famous decree in the case of Somersett, that as soon as any person whatever set his foot in this country, he came under the protection of the British laws, and was consequently free" (CE xiiif) characterises the popular interpretation of this event to the present day. The same author alludes to Mansfield's ruling, when he describes Britain as "that illustrious island, the very air of which has been determined, upon a late investigation of its laws, to be an antidote against slavery" (CE ii). The pro-slavery argument primarily used this event to point to the 'problem' of what Tobin refers to as "the great number of negroes at present in England, the strange partiality shewn for them by the lower orders of women, and the rapid increase of a dark and contaminated breed" (TC 118 fn). The anonymous author of the 1792 pamphlet, *Fugitive Thoughts*, clearly held the Somerset decision responsible for this 'evil':

> When by a decree in Westminster Hall, negroes were released from slavery, the moment of landing on British ground, the gentlemen were obliged to put their black servants on wages; not knowing the use of money, and being incontinently fond of liquor, they became so insolent and licentious, that their masters turned them out of doors, and the streets were infested with black mendicants (AF 29)

The next key event in the history of British anti-slavery was certainly the infamous *Zong* Massacre, which was later to be commemorated by Turner's famous painting, *The Slave Ship*. In an attempt at insurance fraud, Captain Luke Collingwood 'jettisoned' 132 Africans from the vessel *Zong*. Thomas Clarkson describes the horrible events in his *Essay*:

> in the summer of the year 1781, when an hundred and thirty two negroes, in their passage to the colonies, were thrown into the sea alive, to defraud the underwriters ... This instance happened in a ship, commanded by one Collingwood. On the 19th of November, 1781, fifty four of them were thrown into the sea alive; on the 30th forty two more; and in about three days afterwards, twenty-six. Ten others, who were brought upon the deck for the same purpose, did not wait to be hand-cuffed, but bravely leaped into the sea, and shared the fate of their companions. It is a fact, that the people on board this ship had not been put upon short allowance. The excuse which this execrable wretch made on board for his conduct, was the following, 'that if the slaves, who were then sickly, had died a natural death, the loss would have been the owner's, but as they were thrown alive into the sea, it would fall upon the underwriters.' (CE 131)

When the insurance company refused to pay, the case came to trial before Lord Mansfield, who found in favour of the insurers. What outraged early anti-slavery activists such Granville Sharpe and Olaudah Equiano, apart from the horrific event itself, was that the case was tried strictly as a civil insurance dispute and not as a case of homicide. Although the case received little press coverage itself (cf. Hochschild, *Chains* 81f) "a passionate salvo of letters [Granville] Sharp wrote spread the word of what had happened on board the ship, and several prominent clergymen later mentioned the case in sermons, essay, and letters" (Hochschild, *Chains* 82). In 1784, James Ramsay, published one of the first British mainstream texts against the slave trade. The text seems to have hit home to such a degree that Clarkson refers to it in his own *Essay*:

> This *Essay on the Treatment and Conversion of African Slaves*, contains so many important truths on the colonial slavery, and has come so home to the planters, (being written by a person who has a thorough knowledge of the subject) as to

have occasioned a considerable alarm. Within the last eight months, two publications have expressly appeared against it. . . . (CE xvf).

Ramsay's text was certainly the beginning of a period of intensive publishing on the topic of slavery. Peter Hogg's bibliography on the topic cites no less than 460 titles, which were published between 1784 and 1812 (cf. Hogg, *Slave Trade* 149–185). The increased public interest in the topics of slavery and the slave trade is also reflected in the fact that the University of Cambridge chose *Anne liceat invites in servitutum dare*[4] as the topic for its annual Latin dissertation competition for 1785, which Thomas Clarkson won and which marked a life-long involvement in the anti-slavery cause for a man who was famously described by Coleridge as "a moral steam engine" (qtd. in Hochschild, *Chains* 89f). After an often-cited moment of epiphany in the summer of 1785 "in sight of Wades Mill" (Clarkson, *History I* 210). Thomas Clarkson decided that:

> I could translate my Latin dissertation. I could enlarge it usefully. I could see how the public received it, or how far they were likely any serious measures, which should have a tendency to produce the abolition of the Slave-trade. (Clarkson, History I 211)

In 1787, Thomas Clarkson, Granville Sharp, Josiah Wedgwood, William Dillwyn and others founded the Society for Effecting the Abolition of the Slave Trade (cf. Clarkson, *History* I 288). They famously argued their decision not to tackle slavery itself, but rather the trade as:

> . . . laying the axe at the very root. By doing this, and this only, they would not incur the objection, that they were meddling with the property of the planters, and letting loose an irritated race of beings, who in consequence of all the vices and infirmities, which a state of slavery entails upon those who undergo it, were unfit for freedom. (Clarkson, History I 286f)

In the wake of Clarkson's subsequent fact-finding mission, which took him 35,000 miles across Britain over the next seven years, anti-

---

[4] Trans: Is it right to make slaves out of the unwilling?

slave-trade societies sprang up all across the country and began petitioning parliament (cf. Brogan, *Clarkson*). Among the evidence which Clarkson collected in the country's main slave ports were the muster rolls of various slave vessels. These were to be used in his 1788 *An Essay on the Impolicy of the African Slave Trade* to prove, among other things, that the slave trade "is the grave of our seamen, destroying more of them in one year, than all the other trades of Great Britain, when put together destroy in two" (Clarkson, *Impolicy* 132).

The evidence that Clarkson supplied was used for the abolitionist cause before the British parliament. In 1788 and 1789, a Committee on Trade and Plantations of the Privy Council held hearings on the slave trade (cf. Hochschild, *Chains* 153f) and published an 850-page report on the subject in 1789 (cf. Hochschild, *Chains* 158). The issue of the slave trade was first discussed before the House of Commons on 9 May 1788 (cf. Clarkson, *History I* 503f) and in the same year, the British parliament passed the first legislation on the slave trade. The Dolben Act of 1788 limited the number of people on slave ships.

William Wilberforce, whose health had not permitted him to partake in the parliamentary debate on the slave trade up to then, made his first great abolitionist speech before the Commons on 12 May 1789 (cf. Clarkson, *History II* 40). It would, however, not be until January 1807, after several unsuccessful attempts, that Wilberforce would eventually get the Slave Trade Bill passed in both houses of the British Parliament.

In the 1820s, both Clarkson and Wilberforce renewed their efforts for the cause of African slaves when they supported the organisation with the rather timid title The Society for the Mitigation and Gradual Abolition of Slavery Throughout the British Dominions, which was formed in 1823. The British Parliament finally passed the Abolition of Slavery Bill in 1833 after compensation of £15 million was paid to the former slave owners and a five-year period of 'apprenticeship', during which the freed slaves had to continue working for their former masters. British slaves were finally freed in 1838.

3.7.3 British History

It has been noted that the British historiography of abolition and emancipation was for a long time characterised by a "national triumphalism" (Drescher, *Experiment* 4). The same statement holds true for the representation of British history in texts on slavery. Anti-slavery authors, in particular, strove to define Britain as "free soil" (Davis, *Hegemony* 168) by contrasting it with the slave colonies. Ramsay refers to Britain as "a nation most highly favoured of liberty" (RE 34), Wilberforce is perhaps the most vociferous advocate of British liberty and describes Britain as "[f]avoured in an unequalled degree with Christian light, with civil freedom, and with a greater measure of national blessings than perhaps any other country upon earth ever before enjoyed" (WA 74f), emphasising that "[w]e enjoy a political constitution of government, eminent above all others for securing, to the very meanest and weakest the blessings of civil liberty, of personal security, and equal laws" (WL 42). In the colonies, Wilberforce explicitly wanted to make the African slaves fit for "the enjoyment of *British*[5] freedom" (WA 73). Also, Thomas Clarkson writes of Britain as "a country, the basis of whose government is *liberty*" (CE xi). The list could be continued. Accordingly, the authors present British history as a series of events leading up to a "land of liberty and humanity" (WA 60).

One of the earliest events of British history is the law code of Alfred the Great, whom Clarkson invocates as, "Immortal Alfred! father of our invaluable constitution! parent of the civil blessings we enjoy!" (CE 154). In his *Commentary* on Clarkson's *Thoughts*, pro-

---

[5] My emphasis.

slavery author John Hampden cites Henry's History of Great Britain about "a great council held at St. Peter's, Westminster, A.D. 1102", "Let no man for the future presume to carry on the wicked trade of selling men in markets like brute beasts, which has been the common custom of England" (HC 198 fn), to point out that legislation like this never had an influence on colonial slavery. Later on, the same author points to an unsuccessful bill for the greater freedom of bondsmen, in 1526. The aim of this argument was to prevent metropolitan interference with colonial legislation since "what could not be effected at once by law, was gradually accomplished by humanity" (HC 198 fn). His fellow pro-slavery writer, Gilbert Francklyn, states that "enfranchisement of villains seems to have been complete in England about the middle of Queen Elizabeth's reign—the last charters of that kind, which I have heard of, bear date in 1754" (FA 82). However, as can be seen in many a pro-slavery text, Francklyn also points to the fact that not everything is as libertarian as the abolitionist side would have it, when he writes that "the abolition of hereditary jurisdictions in Scotland took place but very lately; and the emancipation of those people who were bound to work in the mines and saltworks of that country, only a few years since" (FA 82).

Despite all the commitment to British liberty, the English Civil War and the Glorious Revolution are only explicitly referred to in passing by some of the pro-slavery authors (cf. FA 235). The only reference to the Glorious Revolution in Ramsay's *Essay* is his mentioning that:

> Soon after the revolution, Scotland was afflicted with four or five successive unfruitful years ... which is still remembered under the name of the Dear Years. Many died of want, and thousands, all over the country, were reduced to beggary; the Highlanders, especially, suffered greatly, and came down and overspread the low-lands; and, where did not succeed by begging, made no scruple to steal and rob, to supply their wants. (RE 37f)

Ramsay dedicates a whole 15-page section of his essay to a discussion of the 1698 plan of Fletcher of Saltoun:

> In this situation of things, when the poor were numerous, few manufactures established, and the fisheries lay neglected, did Fletcher propose his plan of slavery, founding it on a statute enacted Anno 1579, which empowered any subject of sufficient estate to take the child of any beggar, and educate him for his own service, for a certain term of years, which term was extended Anno 1597 for life. (RE 38)

Ramsay seems to have principally approved of this scheme since he calls "vagabond beggars ... a nuisance which call loudly for redress" and suggests that "a day be fixed by proclamation for apprehending them throughout the kingdom" and "their service be sold for seven years to such as have employment for them" (RE 41 fn). Ramsay's whole attitude suggests that the abolitionist notion of freedom was, perhaps with the exception of Thomas Clarkson, largely quite a middle-class one. An often-cited fact in this respect is that Jeremy Bentham proposed his model prison in the same year as Ramsay published his *Essay*. He also argued for the buildings of houses of industry based on his panoptical principles in the 1790s, while at the same time condemning the "dehumanization of West Indian slavery" (Davis, *Revolution* 456). Davis, furthermore, refers to the striking parallels "between the rise of anti-slavery and a profound transformation in attitudes towards the English poor" (Davis, *Revolution* 356),

> In 1834, the same year that witnessed the nominal emancipation of West Indian slaves the Poor Law Amendment liberated the English workers from public welfare and offered the unemployed a choice between starvation and the humiliating workhouse. (Davis, *Revolution* 357)

William Wilberforce cites the opposition's claim against the 1775 Colliers and Salters Act that "without the admission of slavery in this particular instance, the collieries could not be worked" (WL 276). When "the whole idea of the collieries being in the least hurt by the abolition of this sort of slavery vanished into smoke" (WL 276), Wilberforce saw this as proof of the superiority of the free labour ideology.

The Gordon Riots of 1780 in London are referred to in particular by the pro-slavery side. They blame the abolitionists for "endeavouring to halloo the mob against a commerce of the greatest utility to Britain" and warn that "the same conflagrations may take place in Liverpool and Bristol, as were experienced in London, under a pretended zeal for the Protestant religion in 1780" (FA 4).

3.7.4 The American Revolution

It has already been pointed out above that the period of abolition was certainly characterised by an interest in the 'decline and fall' of empires, which is reflected both by the frequent historical references in my primary sources as well as by the publication of Gibbons' famous work between 1776 and 1789. This interest ought to also be understood in the context of the American Revolution in which the British Empire lost its 14 North American colonies. As "the old empire crumbles" (Curtin, *Image* 88), it was necessary to make certain ideological adjustments. The discourse of slavery certainly provided a channel for demonstrating the British Empire's investment in humanitarian values. The anti-slavery side of the debate, in general, used this massive colonial setback as proof for the necessity of the restoration of national virtue through the abolition of the slave trade in order to prevent the British Empire from suffering a similar fate as the Roman one. Pro-slavery authors, on the other hand, especially those of West Indian origin, often used the revolution against the mother country of the American colonies to create a more or less subtle threat against the interference of metropolitan Britain with what they considered colonial affairs. They tried to achieve this, on the one hand, by underlining the patriotism and Britishness of the white West Indians and, on the other hand, by hinting at the possibility of revolutionary ideas spreading among the West Indians. The anonymous authors of *Observations on the Project for abolishing the Slave Trade*, for example, draw a parallel between their situation and the American one when they assert that "Surely we have had enough of interfering with property and of shutting ports in America" (AO 10).

The authors reflect the ideological basis of the American Revolution in different ways. Ramsay writes that the "friends of America":

> contended not for the equality of men, considered as individuals unconnected in society, till mutual benefit brought them together, and formed the distinction of ranks; . . . But they contended for the present actual equality of all men, with an exception to their own slaves. And again, to support the argument, they were obliged to suppose society dissolved, and men reduced to that solitary, savage state, where such equality only can take place. For society cannot be maintained, even in idea, but by the inequality of condition, and various ranks necessarily arising from the social compact —So easy is it for men to take such parts of reasoning as best suit their present purpose. (RE 17 fn)

The anonymous authors of *Fugitive Thoughts* present the Americans as "descended from a race of men, who thinking their liberties infringed upon, left their native homes and crossed the Atlantic, dreading less the unlettered savages of America, than the control of learned sages in their own country" (AF 42). The anonymous "Gentlemen of St. Christopher" similarly brand the American revolutionaries as religious fanatics when they quote the equally anonymous "African Merchant":

> Mr. Benezet of North America who wishes the West-India islands sunk in the sea rather than we should carry on the slave trade for their service, may possibly have the same kindness and good will to Great Britain, and may sincerely long to see the seat of empire travel Westward and the dominion of the Saints established in Boston. This last conjecture has been since verified to our great national loss. (AA 31)

It is remarkable that even pro-slavery writers are invested in the construction of a distinctly British concept of liberty which stands in contrast to French and American ones.

Apart from its influence on the concept of empire, the American Revolution was quite simply seen as a watershed moment in

British history and often used quite pragmatically to signify the beginning of a new era. The Treaty of Paris, which concluded the war between Britain and the US, brought about substantial changes in colonial boundaries. In Africa, Great Britain had to hand over the island of Goree and the Gambia to the French. The author of *Fugitive Thoughts* cites this fact not without some regret:

> At the last peace, when the island of Goree, the Montpellier of Africa, was restored to the French, and the rest of the province of Senegambia given to the African company without any stipulated compensation even to the officers on this staff, (AF 51)

That the War of Independence was certainly seen as a caesura can also be seen in the more trivial fact that James Ramsay, for example, points out that his calculations about colonial production were made "before America was made independent" (RE 85, 110).

An early reference to American history is General Braddock's failed expedition against the French settlements in the American theatre of the Seven Years' War, which saw the establishment of a British dominance over the French in present day USA and Canada (cf. AF 27). The stricter colonial policy of the British Empire in the wake of this conflict eventually led to the protests of the 14 colonies, which was most famously expressed in the 1773 Boston Tea Party. Although Ramsay acknowledges that "the law that shut up Boston Port was hard" (RE 7) he clearly takes the side of a strict colonial policy when he writes:

> A law to shut up every port, where the revenue laws are resisted, would be just and equitable. Thus might a dictatorial authority, (I mean a latent power to be occasionally called forth) which is necessary in every state, be established on a legal foundation, and be kept from transgressing its due bounds. (RE 7f)

Another episode from the American War of Independence which obviously lent itself to being used in the discussion of slavery was the promise of freedom to any American slave who "deserted a rebel master and joined the British army" (Hochschild, *Chains* 98).

These former slaves were eventually brought to the British settlement at Sierra Leone after a temporary stopover in Nova Scotia (cf. AF 50, 29 and CT 17ff). The anonymous "Gentlemen of St. Christopher" juxtapose an emancipation of West Indian slaves with the British tactic in the American War and predict that this would "deprive us of these colonies also and rob England of her sugar, the only stable commodity now left for importation" (AA 31).

The final reference to the by then United States can be found in Wilberforce and Clarkson, when they refer to the war of 1812 in which deserted slaves were again enfranchised by the British army and settled in Trinidad after the conflict. Thomas Clarkson cites the march of the British to Washington in 1814, where they "burnt most of its public buildings" (CT 17). Both authors use this episode to show that the former slaves were emancipated without danger and were even seen "as a valuable acquisition to the colony" (WA 68).

3.7.5 History of the Caribbean Islands

Concerning the Caribbean islands, two topics seem to be of foremost importance in the texts under investigation: the history of the slave revolts and the history of the Caribbean in terms of the changing influence of the European powers.

James Tobin mentions a plot for a revolt on the island of Barbados as early as 1640 (cf. TC 124 fn). An important piece of legislation for early French master-slave relations was the 1685 *Code Noir*, which King Louis XIV of France decreed as a reaction to the "fear that ill-treatment of slaves by their owners would provoke revolt" (Harmer, *Companion* 193). While the *Code Noir* introduced minimum standards to ensure slaves' survival and gave the slaves the possibility of complaining about violations to an agent of the King, it also enshrined segregation by prohibiting sexual relations and intermarriage between whites and blacks and introduced Roman Catholicism (cf. Harmer, *Companion* 193). Both abolitionists and pro-slavery writers saw this piece of French legislation as something fundamentally positive. Tobin describes it as "a check upon the natural abuse of unlimited authority" (TC 24) and Ramsay refers to the *Code Noir* as "an instance of attention and benevolence in the French government, that may well put British negligence to shame" (RE 53f). Despite its liberal intentions, the French slave code and other similar pieces of legislation began to be eroded and largely ignored in the course of the 18th century. William Wilberforce wrote in 1807 that "the *Code Noir,* and various other edicts, which from time to time had been issued, concerning the treatment of Slaves, were become a mere dead letter" (WL 233). Other West Indian legislations referred to in the texts under investigation include the 1784 Consolidated Slave Act of Jamaica (Harmer, *Companion* 22) and the 1798 Amelioration Act of the Leeward Islands (WA 19).

The pro-slavery author Gilbert Francklyn refers to several mutinies on board slave vessels in 1718 and 1721 (cf. FA 180 fn). Also, Thomas Clarkson mentions a thwarted attempt at mutiny on "[a] certain vessel" which "had procured a hundred and ninety slaves from the Windward Coast, and had put to sea." (CE*88* 94). It was, however, the Haitian Revolution which was soon to become a lasting symbol of slave rebellion. Most British authors were afraid that something like this, or like the Revolution in Metropolitan France, might also happen in Britain or its colonies. The stock phrases to refer to the revolution in what was then called St. Domingo were either "the horrors of St. Domingo" (ML 16) or "the lessons of ... St. Domingo" (WL 321). At the risk of oversimplifying, one can say that pro-slavery authors tended to emphasise the massacres and dangers of uprisings, while anti-slavery authors like Wilberforce took a more understanding stance. He emphatically warned of the danger of insurrections spreading to the British colonies and even compares the West Indians to "the short sighted inhabitants of Puzzoli or Terra del Greco [who] are insensible to the approaching lava, which is about to desolate their dwellings" (WL 325). However, Wilberforce's argument was, of course, that the "approaching lava" of a slave rebellion could easily be averted through better treatment of the slaves.

Thomas Clarkson's attitude to both the French and the Haitian revolutions seems to have been a more radical one than that of the MP Wilberforce. Not only did Clarkson spend some time in revolutionary France attempting to persuade the national assembly to abolish the slave trade (cf. Brogan, *Clarkson*), in his 1823 *Thoughts* he also explicitly cites the Haitian revolution as an example of how an emancipation of slaves could be undertaken without danger (CT 22ff). Wilberforce, on the other hand, in his *Appeal* of the same year, is careful to avoid the topic of St. Domingo altogether and only theoretically proposes emancipation as the means to prevent "the dreadful explosion that may otherwise be expected" (WA 72).

Other references to slave rebellions on a smaller scale include Thomas Clarkson's mentioning of "an insurrection . . . among some slaves in Barbadoes" in 1816 (CT 4), which probably refers to the revolt under Bussa which saw one white person killed and over 200 slaves executed and others deported to Sierra Leone (Harmer, *Companion* 59f). Elizabeth Heyrick writes about the "the insurgents of Demerara and Kingston" (Heyrick, *Abolition* 21), which probably refers to the 1823 rebellion of thousands of slaves in the Demerara Plantations of Guiana and the uprisings in Jamaica following a rumour that an emancipation granted by the British Parliament was being withheld from slaves (cf. Harmer, *Companion* 60).

Altogether, while the theme of slave rebellion is certainly present in most of the texts, the authors deal with it in surprisingly little depth in comparison to what I would have expected. Interestingly, historical factuality does not seem to be the most important thing in this respect. While general references to rebellions, insurrections and massacres are relatively frequent, authors refer to actual historical events much less often. The reason for this could well have been that the narrative trope of the slave rebellion was so widespread that authors did not feel the need to back it up with historical evidence.

The second historical narrative about the Caribbean islands is about the influence of the European concert of powers on the various islands. In the treaty of Paris of 1763 France had to cede several islands, which "represented the British Empire's first major Caribbean acquisition in a century" (Quintanilla 14). When the American Revolution broke out, a first direct effect on West Indian islands was that the British banned all trade from the North American colonies in 1774 as a reaction to the boycott of British products by the Americans. Ramsay writes of this:

> When our late North American brethren were pleased to threaten our sugar islands with famine, this custom [i.e. growing foodstuff directly on sugar plantations instead of importing] began again to be renewed, and with such success as might have encouraged them, never, in time to come, to have made themselves as dependent on North America as formerly for their daily bread. (RE 79)

The Caribbean theatre of the American War of Independence saw various naval encounters between French and the British forces. The anonymous "Gentlemen of St. Christopher" refer to some of these events in particular. In 1779, the French captured the island of Saint Vincent and in 1781, Tobago. The year 1782 saw a naval encounter off the island of St. Kitts (then St. Christopher). The "Gentlemen of St. Christopher" exploit the gallantry of the native militia in the battle of Brimstone Hill, which was part of the same action both to underline the patriotism of the inhabitants and to expose James Ramsay, who resided on the island of St. Christopher at the time, as having allegedly conspired with the French invaders.

Reading the Gentlemen's account of the role of their native island in the American War of revolution is quite fascinating. Although they portray themselves as patriotic British subjects, there seems to be a lingering threat between the lines. Referring at such length to this kind of instance of colonial patriotism in a war in which 14 colonies were to assert their independence from their mother country, and in a text which discusses the limits of metropolitan influence on the colonies, certainly contains a more or less subtle threat. I think most contemporary readers would have understood the implication that the inhabitants could have also reacted differently in this situation.

The third type of historical event which some of the authors refer to is natural disasters on the various West Indian Islands. Clarkson writes of the 1692 earthquake in Jamaica in his *Essay*:

> The first noted earthquake at Jamaica, happened June the 7th 1692, when Port Royal was totally sunk. This was succeeded by one in the year 1697, and by another in the year 1722, from which time to the present these regions of the globe seem to have been severely visited, but particularly during the last six or seven years. (CE 254 fn)

Clarkson leaves no doubt that these

> ... violent and supernatural agitations of all the elements, which, for a series of years, have prevailed in those European settlements, where the unfortunate Africans are retained in a state of slavery, and which have brought unspeakable calamities on the inhabitants, and publick losses on the states to which they severally belong, are so many awful visitations of God for this inhuman violation of his laws. (CE 254f)

3.7.6 Larger Historical Context — British and European History

Among the more general historical events that are referred to in the text, the antagonism between France and Britain is most characteristic of the discourse. James Tobin calls the French "our inveterate and natural enemies" (TC 23) and some of the main lines of argument in the discourse on slavery are drawn from the Anglo-French rivalry. A frequent argument was that if the British were to stop the slave trade, other nations would simply take over. This kind of reasoning was all the more effective since the pro-slavery side argued that the slave trade was a "nursery for our seamen" (Clarkson, *Impolicy* 30) and thus vital for British naval superiority over the French. Mercator argues that the slave trade "furnishes employment for 200,000 tons of British shipping and 16,000 British seamen; and thus is one of the great supports of that naval power to which she owes her independence and even existence as a nation" (ML 6).

The most significant historical event of European history within the period of the British abolition and emancipation debate was certainly the French Revolution. The earliest reference can be found in Francklyn's 1789 *Answer*, when he mentions "the present disoriented situation of France's finances" (FA 4). The authors, with the notable exception of Thomas Clarkson, who even spent some time in revolutionary France during the early stages, seem to have a profound fear of the revolutionary changes in the France. Clarkson's relatively radical stance was underlined by the fact that his 1791 *Letters on the Slave Trade* are literally written from within revolutionary France. The anonymous author of *Fugitive Thoughts* writes:

> Every day's experience shews us how dangerous it is to attempt a reform, the French troops delighted with the American spirit of independence, on that continent, inhaled it, and on their return breathed it throughout the land, and the flame of liberty was kindled, but they did not foresee the consequences, it was like putting a sword into the hands of a man who only appeared tame whilst under the care of his keeper. (AF 51)

The idea of the rule of the mob seems to be what primarily troubled the author, who emphasises the importance of aristocratic control when he compares the popular support for abolition in Britain with the situation in France:

> Had such a ferment been in France against the slave trade, the National Assembly must have acquiesced with the request of the people, no upper chamber of control is there, and majesty must have ratified an abolition, though in his own judgment, signing a decree that must materially injure the commercial interest of his kingdom, and diminish the naval strength; happy for this nation that we have a prince who has personally examined into the nature of the slave trade abroad, and other peers who have fortitude and abilities to silence wish to suppress so benevolent and advantageous a commerce. (AF 61)

In this context, the same author is probably being sarcastic when he writes that "the French revolution [has] nothing to alarm us, the minds of the people are divided between a parliamentary reform and an abolition of the African slave trade" (AF 66). The intended meaning in this case is probably to point out that there would have been more serious matters to be considered at that moment than the slave trade.

Mercator explicitly compares the potential consequences of abolition with the horrors of the French Revolution when he claims that "the abolitionists are not aware of the dreadful events to which their favourite measure leads, nor did the first leaders of the French revolution foresee the horrors that would mark its progress" (ML 16). In another place, the same author warns of legislation that is governed by feelings rather than judgement, since "a false philosophy lately deluged France with blood and revolutionary horrors, so a false philanthropy is preparing similar evils for Great Britain" (ML 19f).

In the other texts, the French Revolution is indirectly present in the form of the Haitian Revolution, which is, of course, intensively discussed. Wilberforce even makes abolition a matter of national security to prevent Napoleon from instigating "the Negroes of St. Domingo . . . to invade Jamaica, and stir up in all our islands insurrection and revolt" (WL 329). Thomas Clarkson's *Thoughts* is the text which deals with the Haitian Revolution in most detail, dedicating a whole section to the "slaves of St. Domingo as they were made free at different intervals in the course of the French Revolution" (CT 22ff). As it is Clarkson's aim to show that emancipation is possible without causing danger, he states that the animosities in Haiti were not simply a matter of slaves against masters, but part of the larger French revolution and "augmented by political party-spirit, according as they were royalists or partisans of the French Revolution" (CT 22). The author then refers to "the abolition of slavery throughout the whole of the French colonies . . . by the Conventional Assembly of France" (CT 24). Furthermore, Clarkson cites the failed attempt of General St. Vincent to dissuade Napoleon from the invasion of St. Domingo under Leclerc (28), concluding that:

> The hellish expedition at length arrived upon the shores of St. Domingo:-a scene of blood and torture followed, such as history had never before disclosed, and compared with which, though planned and executed by Whites, all the barbarities said to have been perpetrated by the insurgent Blacks of the North, amount comparatively to nothing. (CT 29)

The pro-slavery author John Hampden (a pseudonym) is naturally less positive about the goings on in St. Domingo when he calls the revolution there:

> a revolution in its principles, its progress, and its consequences, worthy of its parent and prototype—the French Revolution; and certainly exhibiting the most awful warning that could be recommended to our notice in the midst of such speculations. It must be admitted by the most infatuated admirers of the name of liberty, that it is purchased too dearly at the price of so much blood, by the dreadful excesses of human wickedness and misery, which, in the Kingdom of Hayti, have erected a monument to the disgrace of human nature. (HC 164)

3.8 Conclusion

The discourse of slavery has a strong historical dimension, going back to a discussion of the original state of mankind. While anti-slavery authors have a more romantic view of the state of nature, pro-slavery ones tend to conceptualise man's original state in a more Hobbesian way. Anti-slavery authors propose a concept of human societies going through distinct stages of progress. The Bible is used by both pro- and anti-slavery authors as a historical source in a quite literal sense. The passages that most frequently appear in discussions of the Africans' blackness are the curse of Ham (Genesis 9:25) and the mark of Cain (Genesis 4:15). Greco-Roman antiquity is a period of profound influence on European humanism and, thus, on the discourse of slavery. The "light from antiquity" (CT 16) was a powerful source of authority for thinkers of the Enlightenment. Authors saw a single source of civilisation which was handed down to the moderns via the Greeks and the

Romans. This supported the Eurocentrism of later imperial projects. The decline of the Roman Empire was a topic that frequently served as a warning example of a similar fate of the British Empire, which had just lost 14 colonies in the American Revolution. The European Middle Ages and the feudal system also received some attention in the discourse on slavery in providing the Romantic *topos* of the happy peasant. The existence of a transitional period between antiquity and modernity in the historical narrative suggested the necessity of a similar period of transition in the case of emancipation. The long-existing contact of Arabic societies with sub-Saharan Africa is received as a potentially threatening one in the discourse of slavery. As a potential counter-empire from which Africa has already received "some feeble light" (WL 31), the representation of Islamic influence is a predominantly negative one. Many of the texts deal with events of African history, especially in the form of European travel narratives such as found in Astley's collection of travels. Later, Mungo Park became a prominent source. Another topic of profound influence on the whole discourse was the history of the transatlantic slave trade. The discussion of colonial slavery was, of course, charged in terms of power relations between the colonial centre and the periphery. In this respect, the American Revolution was frequently used as a threatening example against too much metropolitan influence. The history of the West Indian islands themselves is mainly present in the discussions of various slave revolts, among which the Haitian revolution perhaps features most prominently. The French Revolution is also discussed. The authors, except for Clarkson, seemed to be quite critical of what they saw as the rule of the mob.

4 The Discourse on Slavery

As already mentioned in the Introduction, fifteen texts form the basis of the present thesis. I have attempted to select texts which were written at different stages of the discussion of slavery in Britain. The three anti-slavery authors, Ramsay, Clarkson and Wilberforce, feature most prominently. Where possible, an attempt has been made to select such pro-slavery texts as directly respond to texts by these authors. The most recent text in the corpus is one by Elizabeth Heyrick, the only woman who wrote an argumentative prose-text on the topic. In terms of genre, the texts are all either argumentative essays or letters.

4.1 Corpus-based Appreciation of the Discourse as a Whole

When dealing with a substantial collection of 'discourse fragments', one is faced with the problem of finding a starting point. The present work begins by seeking to establish some general features of the discourse as a whole before analysing single discourse fragments. The aim of this chapter is, therefore, to try to identify key themes and topics of the primary texts that form the basis of this thesis. An appraisal of the text corpus' most frequent nouns will be used to gain some insights into the most important semantic fields.

The tables below show the ten most frequent nouns of the corpus and a thematically arranged selection chosen from the corpus' 150 most frequent nouns, which will be used in order to arrive at an assessment of the important themes founded on a substantial amount of textual data.

4.1.1 The Ten Most Frequent Nouns

TOP 10 Nouns – Corpus	
1846	slaves
1013	slave
786	mr
683	negroes
653	time
631	slavery
630	trade
622	men
602	man
557	people
8023	**TOTAL**

Fig. 8:   Ten most frequent Nouns

A brief appreciation of the ten most frequent nouns of the text corpus allows for the following hypotheses. In terms of the image of Africans, it is evident, that—unsurprisingly—Africans are primarily represented as slaves, but also in terms of their complexion when considering the high frequency of the word "negroes". It has to be noted that both negroes and slaves and, consequently, the Africans who are thus denoted appear frequently in their plural forms. The most frequent representation of Africans is, therefore, as a multiplicity rather than individuals. That the word "Mr." is the third most frequent noun is due to the frequent referrals of one author to the other, which is partly a result of my mode of selecting texts, which favours responses over stand-alone texts. However, it also suggests that the whole discussion on slavery was at heart led by white male British middle-class authors, with the notable exception of Ottabah Cugoano, whose essays have not been included in the present thesis for reasons of thematic uniformity.

Finally, the fact that "men", "man" and "people" are included in the list of the ten most frequent nouns shows that the discourse of slavery was more than a mere negotiation of colonial procedures. The question of whether slavery was a legitimate form of extracting labour from a workforce was strongly linked to bigger discourses on the conception of the human as such. This probably holds especially true in what Hobsbawm called "the Age of Revolution", in which many fundamental assumptions about humans and society were re-negotiated.

4.1.2 Thematic Selection from the 150 Most Frequent Nouns

This is also shown in the second table (cf. below), since by far the largest thematic group of nouns, with total frequencies of 8,240, are those that in some way refer to humans. A discussion of slavery is of course fundamentally a discussion of the basic rules governing the relationship between society and individual. This is also shown by the fact that the greater part of these nouns explicitly refers to humans in the plural (underlined) and that quite a few imply some sort of power relation (*italicised*). An analysis of how authors constructed concurring conceptions of the subject and society in the discussion of slavery can deepen an understanding of the changes that these concepts underwent at the threshold of late modernity. This will be done below in the discussion of primary sources.

It is of course not very surprising, given the common topic all these texts, that the nouns "slaves" and "slave", which, by the way, also refer to humans, are the two most frequent ones. Since the plural form is almost twice as frequent as the singular, one can speculate that the image of Africans conveyed by these texts is one of a multitude rather than one of single individuals. Quite possibly, Africans were not represented in terms of what Stuart Hall describes, as a the "Enlightenment subject", which was defined by the ability to think logically and rationally and based on "a conception of the human person as a fully centred, unified individual, endowed with the capacities of reason, consciousness and action, . . ." (Hall, *Cultural Identity* 275).

The table also shows that the thematic group of nouns referring to slavery and the slave trade is the second largest, with a total frequency of 5,291. In these texts, the fact that Africans are slaves is used to create meaning more often than their ~~race~~ or their geographical provenance. The group of nouns referring to Africans shows that the most frequent way of referring to Africans was as "slaves" and "slave", followed by the ~~race~~-based representation as "negroes" and "negro", while the reference to their geographical provenance as "Africans" comes only in the third place.

Another large thematic group of nouns is the one which denotes place. This is interesting in two respects. On the one hand, it shows that the discussion of slavery was, of course, a global topic, which, for practical reasons, made it necessary to locate things. In doing so, the debate about the abolition of slavery also served as a dividing line to define the differences between the colonial centre, where it was absent, and the colonial periphery, where it existed. The second consideration that comes to my mind when faced with this large group of nouns is that the action of placing things has, of course, more far-reaching implications. All texts very much seem to discuss the human and groups of humans. In *Discipline and Punish*, Foucault brilliantly comments on the importance of placing things for the creation of disciplined modern subjects. He describes "disciplines [as] techniques for assuring the ordering of human multiplicities" and points out that they gained importance during the 18th century due to an "increase in the floating population [and that] one of the primary objects of discipline is to fix; it is an anti-nomadic technique" (Foucault, *Reader* 207). That human multiplicities are a key topic of these texts has been pointed out above.

The enormous concern of the discourse on slavery with discipline and control is further evidenced by the fact that the third biggest group of nouns are those that refer to various forms of control. Any discussion on slavery is fundamentally a discussion of the power of employers over the employed and of the means which are acceptable for one group of humans to make others work for them, which also explains the relatively large group of nouns denoting work. It ought to be said here that the group of nouns referring to forms of freedom is much smaller than the one about control. David Brion Davis once wrote that "the Enlightenment was torn between the ideal of the autonomous individual and the ideal of a rational and efficient social order" (Davis, *Revolution* 263). The abolitionists' bold claims for the emancipation of the large colonial slave populations made necessary carefully crafted arguments as to why such a step would not endanger the social order, which is what most antislavery texts largely deal with.

The connection between the abolition of colonial slavery and the rise of capitalist elites in Great Britain has widely been discussed in the scholarly debate (cf. Davis, *Hegemony*). The overall opinion seems to be that there exists an ideological affinity between abolition and the interests of the rising middle classes, who both produced and read texts on slavery. In other words, there was a vested interest that the utopias these texts envisioned for post-slavery societies did not contradict capitalist concepts of man and society. The standards set by these texts' images of Africans can, therefore, be seen as having had further repercussions on the more general view of a global working class. The fact that the slave trade was a global issue gave the norms that these texts constructed a special authority by linking the specific with the general and the local with the global. It has been argued that by defining Britain as free soil (cf. Davis, *Hegemony* 168f), the debate on slavery served as a screening device to hide the domestic exploitation of workers. On the other hand, the colonial centre attempted to put itself in a hegemonic position, by exporting such a conception of the human in general and especially of Africans, to the colonies, which best served metropolitan interests. Thus, the debate on the slave trade possibly helped the self-assigned civilising missions of European powers in the age of imperialism and were an outcome created by the discourse on slavery.

The noun groups labelled "truth", "parts", "cause + effect" and "reference" are symptomatic of the way in which authors presented their arguments. The discourse as a whole was, of course, very much influenced by the philosophy of the Enlightenment (cf. Drescher, *Experiment* 5). James Ramsay, for example, whose *Essay* triggered off the public debate, was taught by Thomas Reid, the proponent of the Scottish Enlightenment and a contemporary of David Hume (cf. Watt). Apart from its commitment to personal freedom, Enlightenment thought is also characterised by a belief in authority based on reason. The high frequency of the form of address "Mr." is both due to the nature of the texts as part of a discussion in which writers responded to each other and also a sign of how the various texts quoted other texts in order to lend authority to their arguments. The OED defines the term Mr. as "a title of courtesy prefixed to the surname or Christian name of a man (not entitled to be addressed as 'Sir' or 'Lord')" (OED 'Mister'); the frequent use of this specific form of address is evidence of the male middle-class nature of the discourse. It also brings back to mind that the discourse on slavery was an almost exclusively male one; all the texts, except for Elisabeth Heyrick's, were written by white male middle-class authors, as has been pointed out above.

The Enlightenment's strong belief in reason is shown by the groups of nouns "truth" and "cause and effect". One of the reasons for the relatively sudden criticism of slavery in British colonies at the end of the 18th century can perhaps be found in the universal claims of the Enlightenment's reasoning and its belief in truth and reason in the form of cause and effect. It seems to have been no longer acceptable to middle-class authors that deviant forms of social reason, such as the acceptance of slavery, should remain in place and should even determine colonial policies. If nothing else, the debate on slavery was the fight for the hegemony of metropolitan and colonial reasoning, in which the former finally proved successful over the latter.

The groups "state" and "time" show another interesting feature of the discourse fragments. The debate on slavery is, of course, a discourse of change, and authors both refer to historical precedents and present their utopias for future situations, both of which make necessary a temporal location. The group "state" shows the typical mode of social analysis which these authors use; they did not so much understand the social realm as being subject to permanent change, as suggested by Norbert Elias (19), but applied static analyses of the state of affairs, conditions, situations and circumstances. This kind of analysis can again be linked to the construction of disciplines and the ordering of human multiplicities. Living human societies are perhaps by definition chaotic and disorderly. The idea of simplifying complex processes by reducing them to ideal-typical phases or still images is a central method of modern scientific method. The social analysis of these authors resembles the anatomist who gains his insights not by studying living human beings but only their dead bodies. I would like to suggest a critical approach to this kind of analysis, since it is driven by the desire to gain power over living beings by reducing them to frozen, dead images.

102 'MALLEABLE AT THE EUROPEAN WILL'

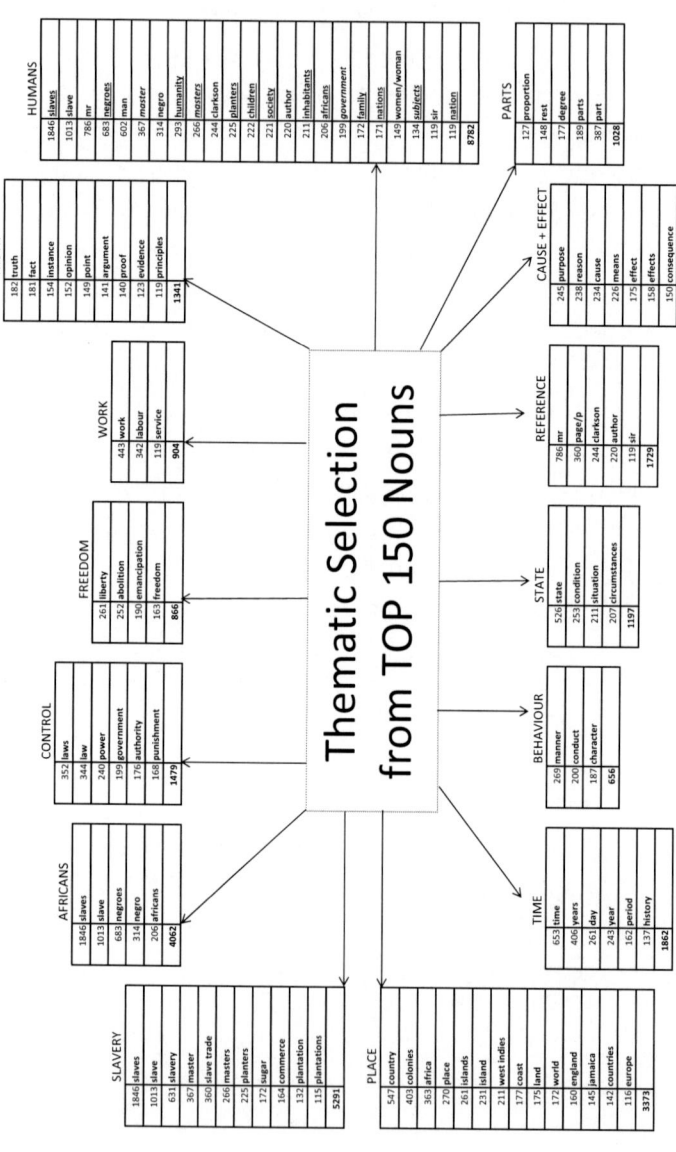

Fig. 9: 150 most frequent nouns – thematically arraganged

4.2 James Ramsay's *Essay* (1784)

4.2.1 *James Ramsay — Biography and self-representation in the text*

James Ramsay was born in 1733 in Fraserburgh, Aberdeenshire, to respectable parents of modest means. In 1749, he entered the University of Aberdeen to be educated in the liberal arts. There he was taught by Thomas Reid, the Scottish philosopher. After graduating with a Masters of Arts in 1753, Ramsay went to London to study surgery and pharmacy. In 1755, he entered the Royal Navy as a surgeon. In 1759, he was on duty aboard the vessel *Arundel* under the command of his later benefactor, Sir Charles Middleton, when their fleet encountered a slave ship in distress due to an epidemic raging both among the slaves and the crew. Ramsay was the only surgeon in the whole fleet who dared to expose himself to the epidemic in answer to the slave ship's request for medical assistance. Ramsay saw and was deeply shocked by the horrible conditions under which the slaves were transported across the Atlantic in the body of a slave ship. Although he escaped contagion, he broke his thighbone when returning to the *Arundel*, leaving him lame for the rest of his life. As his injury left him unfit for naval service, Ramsay took advantage of the opportunity to take charge of several parishes in the West Indian island of Saint Christopher (present day St. Kitts) (cf. Shyllon 6ff).

For the next 19 years, from 1763 to 1781, Ramsay lived on St. Christopher, remaining in charge of several parishes. He extended his religious work not only to the white members of the community but also to African slaves whom he welcomed and instructed in his church. By doing this, he antagonised the island's plantocracy, who blamed him for encouraging their slaves to rebel. An anonymous group of planters would later write in response to Ramsay's *Essay* that his reflections induced the slaves "to look upon [their masters] as their enemies, whom hitherto they have honoured and esteem'd as their only friends" (AA 73). It should be added here that Ramsay himself also owned slaves, whom he writes about in his *Essay* (cf. RE 166ff).

The ongoing conflicts with the planters of St. Christopher seemed to have troubled Ramsay to such a degree that he decided to return to England with his wife and family towards the end of 1781 (cf. Watt). His former captain, Sir Charles Middleton, presented him with the livings of Teston and Nettleton. It was during his time as Vicar of Teston and Rector of Nettlestead in Kent that Ramsay wrote most of his texts, which were later to earn him some fame as an abolitionist, among them the classic *An Essay on the Treatment and Conversion of African Slaves in the British Sugar Colonies*, which was published in 1784.

The image that Ramsay constructs of himself is one of extreme modesty, taking pains to assure that "neither vanity, nor self-sufficiency, led the author to the attempt" (RE vi) to criticise the situation in the West Indies. He even writes that "[h]e has suffered more from the necessity of doing it [i.e. criticising], than the persons affected will probably do from the application" (RE vii). Ramsay presents the reader with a picture of himself as conforming to very high moral standards and of his text as having been "approved of by many persons of worth and judgement" (RE vi).

Ramsay's text triggered quite a response and he spent the five remaining years of his life answering criticisms and personal attacks from the pro-slavery writers in an acrimonious pamphlet war. The first reply to the *Essay* was the anonymously published *An Answer to the Reverend James Ramsay's Essay* by a group of planters from St. Kitts (1784), which was followed by James Tobin's anonymously published *Cursory Remarks Upon the Reverend Mr. Ramsay's Essay* (1785). Ramsay replied to the personal attacks of these two works in *A reply to the personal invectives and objections contained in two answers, published by certain anonymous persons* (1785). Tobin answered with *A short rejoinder to the Reverend Mr. Ramsay's Reply* (1787) and Ramsay responded in the same year with *A letter to James Tobin, Esq.*

late member of His Majesty's council in the island of Nevis. Tobin seems to have had the last word, concluding the exchange with the claim of having been hit below the belt by Ramsay (cf. Shyllon 69) in his *A Farewel Address to the Rev. Mr. James Ramsay from James Tobin, Esq.* Ramsay died in 1789 after another paper war, mainly in the British periodical, *The Diary*, in which Ramsay meticulously answered the attacks of two anonymous writers under the pseudonyms of Civis and Scipio (Shyllon 97f). He was buried in Teston, Kent, and his fellow abolitionist, Thomas Clarkson, gave the eulogy, in which he called him "the first controversial writer, and one of the most able and indefatigable labourers in [the] cause" (qtd. in Shyllon 112).

4.2.2 Synopsis and Argumentative Aims of the Essay

The present text's position is an interesting one, since it was not the expressed aim of the author to oppose the slave trade or slavery. At least on a superficial level, Ramsay only wanted to make the miserable situation of Africans in the colonies known to his readership. However, he seems to have expected his readers to draw the correct conclusion. Anyway, his arguments seem to have hit home, considering the vehement reaction of several West Indian writers.

Ramsay's text clearly avoids appearing subversive or revolutionary in any form and seeks to align itself with thoughts that the author perceives to be hegemonic. Right at the start, he points out that his work found the approbation of "many persons of worth and judgment" (RE vi) before he dared to publish it. The narrative of his self-image is that he was "a rebel convict against the interest and majesty of plantership" (RE 179) within the West Indian planter society, who returned home to metropolitan England and found that his convictions were not rebellious after all but, on the contrary, conformed to the ideas of "those, who were much better judges than the author could pretend to be, of the present prevailing taste (and many persons of rank and learning have honoured it with a perusal)" (RE iii). Ramsay used his position at the colonial centre to add weight to his ideas and claimed the authority to reform West Indian societies. That a West Indian readership naturally felt marginalised by this is certainly one of the main reasons for the negative reception of Ramsay's ideas in the colonies.

Ramsay's frequent references to various authorities also have to be seen in this context. At several points in his *Essay*, he states that his opinions are shared by "the friends of virtue" (RE 205); "a well-disposed mind" (RE 203) "the more moderate and sensible people" (RE 181), "a virtuous citizen" (RE 8), and "all sober people" (RE 107). The *Essay* starts with a letter by an anonymous writer who addresses Ramsay as "a mind, turned like yours to all the tender feelings" (RE xv). Such epithets are used to underline the hegemony of the opinions he voices.

On the other hand, the text also contrasts the (hegemonic) notions of the author to the ones of those who do not share his ideas. The expressions Ramsay uses to refer to such persons shed some light on this argumentative technique: "the politician, the selfish" (RE v), "masters, who look no farther than present profit" (RE ix), "a selfish tyrant" (RE 3), "a sick monster" (RE 35), "some pretendedly industrious planters, men of much bustle, and no method" (RE 75), "an ignorant, unprincipled master, or a morose, unfeeling overseer" (RE 63), "the illiberal turn of the colonists, accustomed from their infancy to trifle with the feelings, and smile at the miseries, of wretches born to be the drudges of their avarice, and slaves of their caprice" (RE 67) or "an ignorant, low-minded, narrow-hearted wretch" (RE 92). It is quite understandable that people who did not agree with Ramsay's views felt personally insulted. To cite Antonio Gramsci, Ramsay tries to base his arguments on the kind of consent which "is 'historically' caused by the prestige (and consequent confidence) which the dominant group enjoys because of its position and function in the world of production" (Gramsci 12). Ramsay's positioning himself on the side of the hegemonic and his belief in authority is also reflected in his ideas about political philosophy. He holds quite Hobbesian views on authority:

> The sovereign declares and executes the will of the people at large. He must therefore be supreme, or uncontroulable by any particular number, or part of the people. His authority must extend over all ranks, comprehend all possible cases, and conclude every particular district. (RE 5)

Statements like this, of course, prompted his antagonists such as the anonymous authors of St. Christopher to write that "We totally disapprove of his assuming the dictatorial power" (AA 24). The subsequent chapters on texts by West Indian authors will show that they very much saw themselves as victims of a metropolitan government which, by ignoring the colonies' interests, was not fulfilling its part of the social contract. As far as the enslaving of Africans in the West Indies is concerned, this means that Ramsay attempted to use hegemonic ideas to voice his critique, for example, when he formulates his claim for an improvement of Africans in the following way:

> The public, therefore, has an interest in their advancement in society. And what is here claimed for them? Not bounties, or gifts from parliament, or people; but leave to become more useful to themselves, their masters, *and the state*. (RE v) [my emphasis]

It is important to bear in mind that Ramsay's *Essay* is not an abolitionist text in the strict sense. However, his glaring depiction of the situation of the Africans in the West Indies strongly makes the case for aboltion if not even an emancipation of West Indian slaves. It is my conviction that here lies one of the main reasons for the strong reaction the text received. While later writers took great pains to avoid the appearance of meddling with the slave owners' property, Ramsay's portrayal of the wretched state of the West Indian slaves allowed a reading which would induce the audience to oppose slavery as such. The text shares this sort of radicalism with other early abolitionist texts, such as Thomas Clarkson's *Essay*, which seems to have been written from largely humanitarian motives and possibly owe their radicalism to a certain amount of naivety due to an ignorance of the reality of the political struggle. Neither Ramsay and Clarkson were yet fully involved in the abolitionist struggle. Clarkson wrote his text for a Latin essay competition while still at university in Cambridge, and Ramsay was living as a vicar in Teston. Ramsay emphasises his reluctance to publish his sentiments on the subject of slavery, and maintains that it was only the encouragement of his acquaintances which made him consider publication.

The main aim of the text is to claim a common humanity for the Africans and to advocate their improvement and their instruction in religion in order "to make them good and useful subjects" (RE 263). For Ramsay, it is self-evident that a good and useful subject is, of course, a labouring and disciplined one. Therefore, a further aim of the text is to define wage labour as the fair means of obtaining labour from workers. Explaining that a system of wage labour would work with Africans is the umbrella under which all of his other aims can be placed. He depicts the use of brute force to discipline African labourers as a denial of their humanity. He often compares Africans to animals, for example, by referring to them as "stock" (RE ix) or even as "neglected animal, called a negroe slave" (RE 138). His aim seems to be to highlight the glaring inconsistency with what he wants to establish as a hegemonic notion of Africans' humanity.

Ramsay's text is structured as five chapters. In the first, "Of the various RANKS in SOCIAL LIFE" (RE 1), he outlines his ideas of the social contract and the "Ranks in which the Members of a Community necessarily separate" (RE 5). In a further section, he goes on to analyse the organisations of society in ancient (RE 19) and Gothic (RE 29) times before discussing Fletcher of Saltoun's suggestion of a form of slavery to deal with the impoverished people of Scotland after the Glorious Revolution (RE 37f). In the last three sections, the author turns to the situation of slaves in the European colonies, starting with a comparison of the French and the British colonies, in which Ramsay highlights the damage to British national prestige by what he represents as a contradiction, namely that the slaves under French masters and the "Romish church" (RE 52) seem to be treated better than British ones under the British Church of England.

In his second chapter, Ramsay shows that "The Advancement of SLAVES would augment their Social Importance" (RE 102). In the six sections, he describes slavery as an "unnatural state of mankind, [which has] departed from the dictates of humanity" (RE 103). The main point he makes in this chapter is that everyone—planters and slaves—would greatly benefit from an improvement of the slaves' situation and that "a sugar plantation might be cultivated to more advantage, and at much less experience, by labourers who were free-men than slaves" (RE 119). What sets Ramsay's text apart from later abolitionist work is that he actually claims a sort of emancipation for West Indian slaves. At the same time, he maintains "that full liberty would be no blessing to them" and that "the plan proposed to advance and instruct them, must be gentle [and] slow in its progress" (RE 118) so as not to endanger the property of their masters.

In order to make his proposed change of the situation of slaves safe, Ramsay argues in his third chapter that "The Advancement of Slaves must accompany their religious Instruction". A highly interesting section of this chapter is the one in which Ramsay describes his own attempts as privately (RE 167) and publicly (RE 178) instructing and improving slaves. Ramsay seems not to have been very satisfied with his achievements since he describes his attempts as inefficient. He lays his public failure at the planters' door for boycotting him and heaping censure on him (cf. RE 178).

The fourth chapter of Ramsay's *Essay*, entitled "Natural capacity of African slaves vindicated" (RE 197). contains a discussion of the topic of racial difference. In its four sections. the author sets out to consider "objections to African Capacity" (RE 211) based on form (RE 211ff) and anatomy (RE 219ff). Since this is a central area of interest of the present thesis, it will be discussed in depth below.

In his fifth and last chapter, Ramsay summarises his "Plan for the Improvement and Conversion of African Slaves" (RE 263) by recommending their religious education through the establishment of a "a proper number of sober, pious ministers" (RE 267), among them to ensure their discipline by "imprinting on their minds the obligations of virtue, the claims of society, the difference between right and wrong" (RE 270). In the next section, he writes about the general improvement of slaves, making it once more clear that Africans are, of course, anything but equal to Europeans. Ramsay repeats his notion of a dynamic model of difference making slavery responsible for the degraded state of the Africans because "the yoke of slavery made to sit more easy on their necks . . ." (RE 273). "Then, in respect of intellect, would they be found equal to the people of any country." Again, among the main tools, he suggests religion for their improvement (RE 276–278). In the last section "Privileges granted, and Police extended to Slaves", Ramsay advocates making Africans part of the system of state power. In this context, the word "Police" refers to "The regulation, discipline, and control of a community; civil administration; enforcement of law; public order" (OED). Here he advocates that the slaves should not only be confronted with the negative side of the law in the form of penalties but also be entitled to its security (RE 282), so that they are protected from inhumane and cruel punishments (RE 282f). Ramsay then suggests that "such slaves as shewed merit, and promised to make good use of it" (RE 288) should be given their freedom. By this measure:

> the number of free citizens would insensibly increase in the colonies. A new rank of citizens, placed between the black and white races, would be established. They would naturally attach themselves to the white race, as the more honourable relation, and so become a barrier against the designs of the black. (RE 289)

In the conclusion, Ramsay draws on the national glory and benefit Britain could obtain by liberating her slaves and the strengthening effect which the improvement and conversion of so many "fellow creatures, that are now drowned in ignorance" (292) would have on

Christianity, ending with his hope that God will find the Britons "a people worthy of a blessing, so valuable and extensive as the social improvement and conversion to Christianity of our slaves would indisputably be" (RE 298).

4.2.3 Ideology

The author strongly believes in a well-ordered society, and although he certainly criticises the situation of the slaves in the West Indies. he makes clear that personal freedom is of less importance for the interests of society. The first sentence of the *Essay* makes quite clear what sort of society Ramsay envisions:

> THERE is a natural inequality, or diversity, which prevails among men that fits them for society, enables them to fill up all the different offices of polished life, and forms their varied abilities, nay, even their particular defects and wants, into a firm band of union. (1)

He constructs an image of a society in which everyone has their place, working together smoothly to create what he calls a "polished life" and "each man takes that station for which nature intended him; and his rights are fenced around, and his claims are restrained, by laws prescribed by the Author of nature . . ." (RE 2). That statements like this very much legitimised the existing order becomes all the more apparent when Ramsay compares the British labourer to the West Indian slave:

> . . . the slave cannot hope, as the other [i.e. the labourer] may, to raise himself, or his children above their present condition; or by his industry to put himself or them on a footing with his master; a spur to exertion and emulation that must ever distinguish and ennoble freedom . . . (92)

Ramsay's rigid views of society are especially apparent when he deals with Fletcher of Saltoun's proposal of a sort of corrective slavery for the poor masses of Scotland after the famine of 1698 (RE 38ff). Ramsay makes liberty a cornerstone of Britishness when he replies that any sort of slavery is, of course, inacceptable "in a country where liberty is the established birth right of the lowest member of the community" (RE 43). Still, Ramsay idealises the British situation over the West Indian one when he provides a full five pages for the logical explanation of Fletcher's theories in order for the reader to understand his conclusion that "would heaven, that the slavery in our sugar colonies were only what is here proposed" (RE 43). That the liberty which Ramsay envisions is, of course, only a very limited one shows in his footnote on Fletcher's proposal in which he takes the reader aside and tells him his own opinion on how to deal with the problem of "vagabond beggars" who are "a nuisance which call loudly for redress ... a wretch, that regards neither divine nor humans laws but wallows in every impurity and low vice" (RE 41). He suggests that they "be considered as the property of the public [and] a day be fixed ... for apprehending them throughout the kingdom" (RE 41) and goes on to propose that "their service be sold for seven years to such as have employment for them" (RE 41). Ramsay concludes that this, if "properly pursued for one generation, would annihilate the evil ... and would recover the greatest part of them to labour and society" (Re 42). That this is his utopia for an ideal state is illustrated when he criticises the status quo:

> At present our poor laws are calculated to encourage laziness, by supporting an idle man in as much plenty as him who labours and gets his bread honestly. When sick, the poor should be tenderly cared for; but when only idle they should have a scanty coarse fare, and clothes made up of patches, to make their situation irksome to them. Those that have large families should have every reasonable indulgence, and the burden of their children should be made easy to them. All single strollers should be strictly dealt with. (RE 42 fn)

Reading this, it is no longer surprising that the Poor Law Amendment Act of 1834, which was "designed to incarcerate British paupers in workhouses" (Davis, *Human Progress* 122) and ensure industriousness by making their situation more irksome to them than work in field or factory (cf. Trevelyan, *Social History* 538), was passed the year after the Emancipation Act of 1833. It might be true that "no economist even attempted a comparison of the colonial plantation with the factory or the poor house" (Drescher, *Whip* 6); however, the quote shows that, already 50 years earlier, this text on colonial slavery links the two topics, seeing coerced labour as a completely valid means for reform. Thus, free and coerced labour do not necessarily stand in a binary opposition to each other. While free labour is the utopia which is to be achieved, coercion is the means of reform. Considering the issue of free labour in terms of productivity, Ramsay reaches the following conclusion:

> a free-man, labouring by himself, in the earning of his wages, whose food is portioned out by himself, not by an unfeeling boy overseer, who feels his own vigour, who looks forward to the conveniences of life as connected with his industry, will surely exert more strength, will shew more alacrity, than a starved, depressed, dispirited wretch, who drawl out his tasks with the whip over him. (RE 119f)

The quote echoes Adam Smith's idea that the advantage of free labour is a financial one, since "the wear and tear of a slave, is at the expense of his master; but that of a free servant is at his own expense" (*Wealth* 122f). The ideas which Ramsay expresses here can absolutely be interpreted as what Davis calls the kind of utilitarianism which "would become a 'radical' instrument in the hands of middle-class reformers" (*Revolution* 355) and which would eventually bring about "the Poor Law Amendment [which] liberated the English workers from public welfare and offered the unemployed a choice between starvation and the humiliating workhouse" (*Revolution* 357). The contrast Ramsay draws between the "free-man" and the "starved, depressed, dispirited wretch" makes the significance of free labour for the very possession of basic humanity even more palpable.

Replying to the critique of being too simplistic in his view of British anti-slavery as a "'screening device' designed to distract attention from metropolitan exploitation" (Davis, *Hegemony* 170), Davis argues that "the antislavery movement mirrored the needs and tensions of a society increasingly absorbed with problems of labour discipline" (171). I agree with Davis and also with Stuart Hall, who writes in his definition of 'discourse' that while "discourses are not reducible to class-interests, but always operate in relation to power—they are part of the way power circulates and is contested" (Hall, *West* 295). This becomes quite apparent when Ramsay tells his audience the secret for the improvement of slaves, in a footnote

> Now the police that we recommend above, makes the man contribute to the general prosperity, while he imagines himself wholly taken up in pursuing his own interest, and exerting himself in his own business. (RE 196)

This clearly posits the reader as a member of that social class which profits from the man's contribution to the "wealth of the nation", to use Adam Smith's term, all the time thinking he is working in his own interest.

What is truly remarkable about Ramsay's ideas about societal control is his evaluation of the social function of religion. For him, the priests are the "monitors, or censors of the people, . . . appointed to exhort and instruct" (RE 11f); thus, the discipline of the Africans ought to be ensured by "the hopes and fears of religion, and the approbation and displeasure of [the] priest" (RE 62). Religion "would awaken conscience within them, to be a strict overseer, and a severe monitor, whom they could not evade" (RE ix). What Ramsay actually suggests is a rather utilitarian view of religion as a means of social control, which perfectly fits the declared aim of his contemporary, Jeremy Bentham, in his work describing his invention of the panopticon, "a new mode of obtaining power of mind over mind, in a quantity hitherto without example" (Bentham 31).

Ideas about social order and about individuals as the building blocks of society always mutually inform each other. Ramsay's belief in authority can, therefore, offer interesting insights into his fundamental conception of man, as the following quote illustrates.

> the influence of this lust for acting the master has been so universal, and has obtained so long, as to oblige us also, in principle, to deduce it immediately

from that love of power, which, within the boundaries prescribed by nature, makes a part of our constitution. (RE 3f)

The statement hints at a rather Hobbesian understanding of individuals who are driven by a universal human desire for power. It is this fundamentally negative concept of man which justifies the exercise of power by the state. In the following quote, Ramsay relates his convictions about the necessity for state power to what happens within the single individual.

> The great tyrant has not the opportunity of exercising his lust of oppression over individuals, . . . But the domestic tyrant can seize and torment every wretch submitted to his power, every moment of their lives. They cannot eat or sleep, but when and how he pleaseth. Every feeling, every indulgence, is held at his pleasure; and too often he feels a spiteful amusement, an infernal delight, in unnecessarily imbittering their miserable cup, even at the expense of his own ease and interest. (RE 45f)

Interestingly, the passage describes being a tyrant as something not altogether unpleasant, which is indicated by the frequent use of expressions for delight and enjoyment: "lust", "pleaseth", "pleasure", "spiteful amusement" and "infernal delight". The lust for power is a universally human one for Ramsay. At the beginning of the text, he explains that "among our negro slaves, he who cannot attach to himself a wife, or subdue any other creature, buys some half-starved dog, over whom he may exercise his tyrannical disposition" (RE 4). The tyrant is portrayed as a person who abandons himself completely to an excess of desire and lust, unchecked by rationality and logic. The assumption of such a dualistic nature of the human necessitates analogous control mechanisms at the individual as well as at the political level. This fundamental dualism between good and bad is also evident when Ramsay describes slavery as "an abuse of what is natural to mankind, excited and cherished in them by an enemy to their virtue and happiness" (RE 4).

4.3 Anonymous:
An Answer to James Ramsay's Essay (1784)

4.3.1 "Some Gentlemen of St. Christopher"

The first response to Ramsay's Essay was a text entitled *An Answer to the Reverend James Ramsay's Essay on the Treatment and Conversion of Slaves in the British Sugar Colonies* (hereafter referred to as the *Answer*) by an anonymous group of authors who called themselves "some Gentlemen of St. Christopher". Since the authors remained anonymous, it is not possible to give biographic details. However, an evaluation of the self-representation of the "Gentlemen of St. Christopher" ought to introduce my chapter on this text.

The anonymous authors referred to themselves as the "Gentlemen of St. Christopher" on the title page of the *Answer* just above their Latin motto *"absentem qui rodit amicum QUI non defendit alio cuplante HIC niger est"* (transl. he who attacks an absent friend, or who does not defend him when spoken ill of by another; that man is a dark character). The implied pun of referring to Ramsay by the Latin word *niger* and the overall meaning of the motto make it clear that they want to create a contrast between themselves as honourable, white West Indian gentlemen and James Ramsay, who they, in turn, seek to disparage.

The authors refer to themselves as "We" with a capital 'w' since "there is more than one person employed in this work, that it may be directed by public utility instead of private prejudice" (AA 2). Their claim of being a group of authors, whether true or not, is a vehicle for adding more authority to the text. Just like Ramsay, the authors portray themselves as reluctantly taking on the task of criticising when they write:

> We could wish to omit any mention of even these errors and passions of his, which injure us as a society; but We are bound to establish our own character, though at the expence of his credibility. (AA 5)

The anonymous authors obviously want to be seen as writing 'as a society'. It is interesting that the argument they pursue forces them to adopt an identity as "We West Indians" (AA 85), which formed in opposition to Ramsay's alleged attacks, whom they ironically describe as following "the charitable purpose of degrading the West Indians, who, if the fact were true, must be void of common sense as of humanity; and act against their own interests on important occasions to preserve it in trivial concerns" (AA 63). At the same time, however, the authors express their surprise as "loyal inhabitants of St. Christopher" that Ramsay represents them as "men divest of all just principles and affection to their Mother Country" (AA 63).

What seems to be at stake for the authors is their threatened claim to Britishness. It is because of this that they emphasise the bravery of the inhabitants of St. Christopher in the 1782 Battle of St. Kitts (St. Christopher) during the American War of Independence, when they write that:

> the behaviour of the militia on the hill tho' unnoticed by their countrymen, was applauded by their Enemies. Governor De Fresne said, there never was an instance of a colonial militia, who held out so long in a siege of so much danger and distress. (AA 10)

The aim of their short narrative is to show how loyal the inhabitants of St. Christopher were to Britain in the late war.

A central criticism of Ramsay's text is the absentee state of the plantation owners. The authors also address this issue in the following passage:

> the decrease of the number of whites is owing to another cause, namely to the small lots, into which the country was at first divided, being laid together and purchased up by the rich proprietors, who from their affluence can afford to reside in England. Accumulation of wealth has the effect, till the head grows too big for the limbs, and the property is again divided among a set, who have address or force enough to overset the unwieldy carcass. (AA 73)

The metaphor of the head that grows too big for the body is interesting, since it shows that the authors also distance themselves from the absent owners. They present themselves as the limbs of the body of the plantation economy and the rich absentee planters as the head, which grows too big in London until it will be overturned. What is implicit in the passage is a self-image as hardy and virtuous men who are the ones who should really be running the colonies and a feeling of unjust distribution of influence, not based on merit but on wealth. Consciously or unconsciously, the passage draws a strong parallel to the image of Roman citizens during the Principate, who paid mercenaries to protect them and were governed by absolute monarchs and to the image of the Germanic tribes which Gibbon invokes when he tells his readers that "the fierce giants of the north broke in and ... restored a manly spirit of freedom; and after the revolution of ten centuries, freedom again became the happy parent of taste and science" (Gibbon 36). While the absentee landowners in England have a certain parallel with the decadent Roman citizen, the West Indian authors clearly identify with a "many spirit of freedom", a central element of which is their being present rather than absent in the colonies.

However, the passage also contains an implicit threat since the battle was part of the American Revolutionary War, in which 14 other colonies declared their independence and were lost to the Empire. They also use this against anti-slavery writers such as Benezet, blaming him for injuring the British Empire by wishing "the West-India islands sunk in the sea ... and may sincerely long to see the seat of empire travel Westward [which] has been since verified to our great national loss" (AA 31).

4.3.2 Synopsis and Arguments

After some introductory thoughts, which mainly consist of a quite personal attack against James Ramsay's character, the authors set out to deal with Ramsay's text chapter by chapter. To do this, they take over Ramsay's chapter titles to present their own ideas on the various topics. They sometimes use quotes from his *Essay* as a starting point; often, however, their thoughts lead them in directions which make the link to the original topic hard to find. The chapters are relatively unstructured and mostly consist of only one long paragraph. Therefore, the following synopsis will not follow the, at times quite repetitive, structure of the text but rather offers a short overview of the main arguments that can be found in *Answer*.

Personal attack against Ramsay

The anonymous authors start their counterargument against Ramsay with an excerpt of an article from the Saint Christopher Gazette of Saturday, November 20, 1784, entitled "Extracts from the Marginal notes on the Reverend Mr. Ramsay's Essay, written by his only Friend" (AA i). Whether genuine or not, the extract comments on various pages of Ramsay's work, for example, "–Page 94. Weakness, wickedness, illnature, unjust, illiberal, untrue, absurd, egregious misrepresentation–" (AA i). This very much sets the mood of the rest of the text, which is largely a comment on a variety of quotations from *Essay* and the authors' personal rant against Ramsay's person. They carefully justify the spreading of negative rumours about Ramsay by explaining that, "We surely may be allowed the liberty of a few anecdotes in defence of an injured community" (AA 5). In general, they depict Ramsay as a traitor against the island community, writing only to please "those great men, whose prejudices to adopt is the ready road to future preferment 'his particular aim'" (AA 26). They further underline their argument with an anecdote from the American War of Independence, in which Ramsay allegedly collaborated with the French while the islanders valiantly defended the British Empire (cf. AA 6–11). On the one hand, they try to destroy Ramsay's credibility and professional reputation and are eager to point out,

> *That it is rather necessary for an author to understand something of a subject, before he presumes to write upon it.* Had the Author of the Essay now before us, measured his abilities by that standard, his production never would have seen the light. (AA 1)

Furthermore, they attempt to expose Ramsay's humanitarian concerns as bogus, explaining that "we know that our Essayist punished [his own slaves] with more severity than most" (AA 82) and that some planters used to frighten their slaves "with threatening to sell them to the parson" (AA 70).

Defending slavery

A large part of the *Answer* is, not surprisingly, taken up by the authors' arguments in defence of slavery. Four main strategies can be identified. The most important strategy for them seems to be a vindication of slavery on scriptural grounds, which is probably due to a similar trend in Ramsay's text. In this respect, it ought to be noted that the authors use the Bible as a historical source rather than a theological text. Most importantly, they quote the book of Genesis in order to prove that slavery not only existed among the Israelites but that it is a "divine permission, nay, command to purchase slaves of strangers" (AA 47). Accordingly, the authors are anxious to maintain that the responsibility for making Africans slaves lies not with the planters but with the slave himself since "it is his own law, not ours, that makes him a slave or free" (AA 47). They find further proof for the remaining of the slaves in their present position in 1 Cor vii 20ff:

> Let every man abide in the same calling, wherein he was called. Art thou called being a servant? care not for it, but if thou mayest be made free, use it rather. For he that is called in the Lord, being a servant is the Lord's freeman; likewise also he that is being free, is Christ's servant. (AA 54)

They also use Ephesians vi: 5–7, "Servants ... be obedient unto them that are your Masters" (AA 57) to show the wrongfulness of Ramsay's alleged attempts at urging the slaves to create unrest. Historical examples play an important role in their vindication of slavery. They use Ramsay's own assertion that "at Athens a slave was happier than a freeman in any other part of Greece" (52) to prove that "happiness is far from being confined to universal freedom" (52).

The most interesting strategy of the defence in respect of the topic of the present work is the rather outspoken justification grounded on the Africans' better adaption to hot climates and the inferiority of their natural capacities. The authors maintain that only "the negroes can work in the West-Indies without being affected by the heat of the sun" (59). The *Answer* frequently pretends to agree with Ramsay's plans for improvement and conversion. For example, they write about Ramsay's chapter on "general improvement of slaves" (94) that "no one can more sincerely wish this than the planter; but the means must be more judicious, than any which have been hitherto proposed" (94). However, they reject Ramsay's ideas as unrealistic dreams and point to the Africans being simply not capable of improvement since, ". . . they are utterly incapable, and obstinately stupid" (AA 75).

Downplaying Ramsay's account of cruelty

A huge concern of the authors' answer is to downplay Ramsay's account of the enormous cruelty against West Indian slaves. The authors try to present the *Essay's* report of the slaves' cruel treatment as a result of Ramsay's "private pique and malice", and are eager to maintain that "he [i.e. Ramsay] produces private anecdotes, not as casual enormities, that spring up in all communities, but as proofs of bad principles, peculiar to, and universally prevalent in this Island" (AA 3). Another strategy is to point out that the cruelties which Ramsay describes are so enormous that they cannot be true since:

> Were this really the case, our Islanders would be in a more savage and deplorable state than the wild Indians of America, or the brutal Hottentots of Caffraria: every planter would be a wild man: his hand would be against every man and every man's hand would be against him. (AA 61)

The whipping of negroes is, on the one hand, downplayed, where it is pointed out that, "three, four, or five strokes is the heaviest punishment allowed the Overseer to order" (AA 65) and, on the other hand, portrayed as a necessary evil in order to keep up the discipline just as on ships. Ironically alluding to Ramsay's profession, they ask:

> Did any of the best instructions of the most sensible and virtuous Sea-Chaplain ever operate so powerfully on the minds of a ship's company, as to supersede the necessity of corporal punishment? (AA 41)

All in all, the authors paint an idyllic picture of the slaves' life on the plantations, with free housing and healthcare, ample allowance, weekly dances and fields that furnish the slave "with peppers, greens, fruit; and his hogs and poultry with almost sufficient to fatten as well as rear them without expense" (AA 68). The overall argument is that African slaves in the West Indies "do possess advantages beyond a labouring man in England" (67). The authors even agree with Ramsay that free labourers would be cheaper, but "Nothing but their incapacity to work in these climes would prevent the 'self-interested planter' from preferring them [i.e. English labourers] to negroes" (66f).

Ramsay is infuriating the slaves against their masters

Another argumentative strategy of the text is to portray Ramsay's criticism of the situation in the West Indies as an attempt to provoke the slave population to rebellion. The *Answer* again paints an idyllic picture of the prevailing relationship between master and slave, pointing out that, "the esteem of slaves in general, their love for their owners at present is great, is almost enthusiastic" (44) and that "The slave looks on his master as his feeder, his protector, his father. They have often ventured their lives for each other;" (83). The authors then present Ramsay's false humanism as highly dangerous when they rhetorically ask, ". . . shall these bonds of society be broken by false pretences of humanity and unmeaning rant . . ."

(44) and "Would this author loosen the bands of society, and raise a spirit of enmity that would certainly be ruinous to both parties?" (83)

4.3.3 Ideology

First of all, it has to be stated that the anonymous authors' *Answer* is of course very much a reply to Ramsay's *Essay*. It contains about 120 direct quotes of Ramsay's text, which amount to about 6.75% of the total text. The whole structure of the *Answer* follows Ramsay's table of contents, since the anonymous authors have simply taken over Ramsay's chapter titles to structure their responses. All this points to the fact that the anonymous authors seem to have felt that Ramsay was writing from a hegemonic position, which also ties in with their self-representation as those who have been injured by Ramsay's unjust attack from the colonial centre. The fact that the anonymous author or authors write in the first person plural is a further indication that they feel the need to devise strategies to counter an opponent whom they seem to have perceived as overpowering. In an interesting rhetorical ploy, they turn Ramsay's superior position against him when they ask, "what entitled him to assume the dictator? by what authority, what superiority of rank, degrees, appointment did he presume to be a legislator" (AA 12). The political metaphor refers to the concept of the social contract, which implies the right to remove any legislator who does not act in the interest of those governed. To stick to the metaphor, in referring to themselves in the plural, the authors put themselves in the position of "the people" who are justly dissatisfied with a despotic Ramsay. The political metaphor also implies a certain threat, since the theory of the social contract did, of course, advocate a revolution in case the legislator does not act in the interest of the people. The emphasis on their loyalty to the British Empire during the American Revolution and that they clearly aim to contrast themselves with Ramsay who "wished no quarters to be given to the

Americans" (AA 19) also has to be understood as an implicit attack against Ramsay whom they present as uncritically speaking the colonial power's hegemonic position.

The anonymous authors again position themselves in a discursive proximity of the American Revolution when they write:

> 'Mr. Benezet of North America who wishes the West-India islands sunk in the sea rather than we should carry on the slave trade for their service, may possibly have the same kindness and good will to Great Britain, and may sincerely long to see the seat of empire travel Westward and the dominion of the Saints established in Boston.' This last conjecture has been since verified to our great national loss. (AA 31)

The passage follows a dual aim. On the surface, it allows the authors to present themselves as loyal citizens of the British Empire while vilifying the abolitionist Benezet as a revolutionary who wishes the West Indian colonies to sink in the sea. Thus, they consciously plant the image of colonial revolutions and the idea of breaking the social contract, which served the American revolutionaries as the argumentative basis for their explanation as to why it had become "necessary for one People to dissolve the Political Bands which have connected them with another" (*US Declaration of Ind.*). Portraying the national loss of the American Revolution as a result of the British Empire's inability to please its colonial citizens' demands strengthens their argument that a dictatorial position such as they blame Ramsay of assuming is indeed a serious threat to the British Empire as a whole.

As the *Answer* is a response rather than a standalone composition, it contains relatively little fundamental discussion of the relationship between the individual and society. The authors adhere to a conception of the human in which man in a state of nature is fundamentally lazy, as in their description of the free Caribs of St. Vincent, whose behaviour they describe as "a mixture of insolence and cruelty" (AA 42) and who:

> have by much the richest and finest part of the country, yet their whole cultivation consists of a little Indian corn, and such herbs and fruits as nature produces to their hands, without any assistance of art or care: they go a fishing in their canoes, make one gluttonous meal, and live the rest of the week upon stinking fish in lordly laziness and contented brutality ... no good usage, no instructions, no rewards can bring them to labour, or even society (AA 42f)

This passage clearly refers to a hegemonic concept of free labour built on reward rather than punishment. However, the authors do not agree with the universal character which Ramsay attributes to this when they point out that the Caribs do not fit into a capitalist system of free labour. They introduce what would become the stock pro-slavery argument, when they point out that Africans are better off as European labourers (cf. AA 67f) and call Ramsay's claim for universal freedom an

> enthusiastic rant of universal freedom: a freedom that would be as injurious to those poor creatures, for whose benefit it is pretendedly calculated, as detrimental to the rights of their owners, and destructive of the interests of society, and religion too; (AA 42)

The authors also advocate a static concept of society when they quote the Bible: "let every man abide in the same calling wherein he is called" (AA 54) and argue that

> Jesus Christ the Saviour of mankind and founder of our religion, left the moral laws and civil rights of mankind on their old foundations: his kingdom was not of this world, nor did he interfere with national laws: He did not repeal that of slaves, nor assert an universal freedom except from sin; (AA 29)

Accordingly, they accuse anti-slavery authors of threatening the harmony between masters and slaves with their "incendiary pens" (AA 49).

4.4 James Tobin's *Cursory Remarks* (1785)

4.4.1 James Tobin — Biography and Self-representation in the Text

James Tobin was born in London in 1736 or 1737. He was educated at Westminster School and took articles as a solicitor. From 1758 to 1766, he helped to manage his family's plantations in the West Indian island of Nevis. When he returned to England he married Elizabeth Webb, the daughter of a wealthy Nevis planter, with whom lived in Salisbury and had eight children. In 1777, he went back to Nevis in order to take control of his plantation. He was a member of the island council and negotiated the terms of surrender of the island to the French in 1782.

Tobin finally settled in Bristol in 1784 and established a successful firm of sugar factors together with his friend John Pinney. He is probably best known for being an active organiser of the West Indian interest. The publication of *Cursory Remarks upon the Reverend Mr Ramsay's Essay* in 1785 was followed by an extremely acrimonious and personal pamphlet war with James Ramsay until 1788. Ramsay even accused Tobin of having challenged him to a duel twice. In return, Tobin was attacked by many later abolitionist writers, the most prominent among them being Thomas Clarkson and former slave Olaudah Equiano.

In February 1790, the House of Commons called on Tobin to give evidence in their inquiry into the slave trade. Tobin testified that slavery was indispensable for the West Indian economy since Africans would not work without force and that populations could not be supported by "breeding". In his last pamphlet in 1792, Tobin defended the high price of sugar and called for the military protection of West Indian planters.

He died in Bristol on 6 October 1817. (cf. Small)

It is interesting that Tobin, too, writes anonymously. The conclusion to be drawn from this is that he either really feared reprisals for voicing his opinion publicly or that he wanted to present the abolitionists standing on the side of power which he rebels against. In any case, it creates a certain position of speaking and it poses the opinion of the abolitionists as the hegemonic one, against which it requires courage to speak out...

Also, the title of the work reflects on Tobin's desired self-image. Since 'cursory' means 'fast, rapid...' (OED), the title emphasises the distinction which Tobin is anxious to maintain between himself as a hardworking man and Ramsay as a kind of *bon vivant*, who is at leisure to pursue literary ambition. Tobin again aims at this kind of self-representation in the introduction. He writes of himself that he is convinced that "he runs no small risk of exposing himself to the censures of the different tribunals of periodical criticism;" (TC iii). What is meant by "tribunals of periodical criticism" is probably periodical magazines since Tobin further refers to them as "arbiters of modern literary reputation" (TC iv). He seems to accept them as a kind of authority whose judgement authors have to pass. He expresses his hope that his thoughts will change their hitherto positive view of Ramsay's work and recognise the "illiberal acrimony of his language [...] the striking inconsistency of his different assertions . . ." (TC iv). Tobin concludes his preface by once again recognising the authority of those who govern the discourse, explaining that "the ensuing pages are cheerfully submitted to the candid and judicious correction of superior leisure and abilities" (TC iv).

4.4.2 Synopsis and Argumentative Aim

The full title of Tobin's text is *"Cursory Remarks upon the Reverend Mr. Ramsay's Essay on the Treatment on Conversion of African slaves in the Sugar Colonies"* (TC i). Just as half of the title is actually taken up by the quote from Ramsay's text, the rest of Tobin's composition largely follows Ramsay's structure and is rather a response to Ramsay's Essay than a composition of its own. Tobin originally published his work anonymously, only informing his readers that the text was written "by a Friend to the West India Colonies and their inhabitants" (TC i).

Personal attack against Ramsay

Just like the anonymous Gentlemen of St. Christopher, Tobin personally attacks Ramsay. An interesting example of this is how Tobin deals with his opponent's self-critical account of how he dealt with his own slaves. He seems to really delight in presenting those passages of Ramsay's text to his readers, in which he orders his own slaves to be punished or sent off the island. Tobin triumphantly rests his arguments with the words "Indeed! Indeed! Mr. Ramsay, after all we can say for ourselves, the very best of us are but men!" (TC 136).

Freedom in "due time"

Nominally, Tobin supports the cause of freedom and states that he does not wis:

> to be ranked among the advocates of slavery; as I most sincerely join Mr. Ramsay, and every other man of sensibility, in hoping the blessings of freedom will in due time, be equally diffused over the face of the whole globe. (TC 5)

The crucial point of the passage is, therefore, the phrase "in due time". This argument that slaves have to be carefully prepared for emancipation would later be proposed by anti-slavery writers in the emancipation debate.

Slavery has always existed — it is not contrary to Christianity

Tobin presents Ramsay's discussion of the existence of slavery in various historical epochs as "acknowledgements, which some professed advocate for slavery may, probably, one time or other, be tempted to turn against the author" (TC 8f), not without mentioning that for his part, he had "already disclaimed so odious a province" (TC 9). He opposes Ramsay's argument that Christianity brought about a general emancipation of slaves in Europe around the 12th century. Tobin cites the "Christian boors of Russia, Poland, Livinia, Lithuania [who] continue to this day, in a state of the most abject slavery, constantly transferred, with the soil from the oppressions of one capricious tyrant to those of another" (TC 13), the "protestant peasants of Denmark and Norway" as well as the order of Pope Nicholas V. to "reduce all the infidel inhabitants [of the new world] into slavery" (TC 14).

Shifting the "national guilt" to the Portuguese and French

Another argumentative strategy of Tobin is to shift the moral obligation to other nations. For example, Tobin replies to Ramsay's lamentations that it was the Briton, John Hawkins, who started the slave trade by stating that other nations such as the Portuguese, the Spanish and the Moors had already started the trade long before. Tobin's little excursion into the history of non-British slave trade reaches a climax with the accusing question: "for what reason, then does Mr. Ramsay take such pains to load his innocent countrymen with the odium of being the first who embarked in such a disgraceful commerce?" (TC 18). In his discussion of the situation of French slaves, whom Ramsay presents as being better off than their British counterparts, Tobin's text follows a similarly apologetic strategy. The author tries to prove Ramsay wrong and points out that French slaves are, of course, worse off than their British counterparts. Tobin is eager to prove that the French treat their slaves with extreme cruelty and blames them for promiscuous intercourse with the slaves (cf. TC 27ff).

The British slave system is well regulated; slaves enjoy an idyllic life

In contrast to that, the system in the British colonies is portrayed as well-regulated one. Tobin employs a range of more or less subtle techniques to try to exculpate the British settlers in the West Indies and to weaken the power of Ramsay's accusations of ill-treatment and outright cruelty, attributing this to an "ignorance of the many unprinted laws of the different islands concerning slaves" (TC 25).

Generally, the text presents an idyllic picture of slave life in the West Indies. In what appears to be nothing less than an earthly paradise, the slaves "plant lime, lemon, plantain, banana, and calabash trees about their houses, which, by a quick vegetation, soon afford them both shade and fruit," (TC 94f) while the "wives (who are naturally much better caterers and cooks than the lower order of women in England) not only prepare the most nourishing, but also the most savory meals for their husbands and children" (TC 96). Tobin does not fail to mention that:

> ... mirth, festivity, music, and dancing, engross no small portion of [the slaves'] leisure: they have an ear for music and a graceful activity in dancing, far beyond the dismal scrapings, and aukward caperings of an English May-day, or a country wake. (TC 96)

Comparison of West Indian slave and British worker

In his comparison of the West Indian slave and the British workers and peasants, Tobin's text creates an anti-romantic image of the incredible hardships which British peasants have to suffer. He contrasts this image with the idyllic image he paints of the lives of the West Indian slaves. Thus, he describes British peasants as struggling

> ... through the years of their childhood ... half naked and half starved; equally exposed to the heats of summer, and the frosts of winter; ... their shoulders are bowed by a constant attention to the soil in which they delve; [and] if the natural bloom of health ... forces itself into the countenances of a few individuals, ... it proves but a transient gleam, which soon ... gives way to the fallow wrinkles of premature old age. (TC 85f).

After this, the author attempts to refute the argument that "all the hardships of the English peasant are softened by the idea of liberty" (TC 89) by pointing out that the peasants are "absolutely bound either to work or to starve" (TC 89) and that, therefore, "the liberty they are reckoned to possess, is truly nominal and *ideal*" (TC 89). Tobin refers to the situation of the labouring poor in Britain as wage slavery since "they are absolutely bound either to work or starve" and do not "in fact, enjoy the privilege of changing the scene of their labour" (TC 89).

Slaves would not work if not forced

Tobin then ets out to prove that slaves would not work voluntarily anyway. He points to the fact that freed slaves in the West Indies never take up a proper profession (cf. TC 116f) and asks Ramsay, in relation to Africans in England, if he "ever saw a single one employed in any laborious task? Did he ever meet with a black ploughman, hedger, ditcher, mower, or reaper in the country; or a black porter, or chairman, in London?" (TC 117). He rounds off this section with two further examples of communities of free Negroes in Jamaica and St. Vincent. Tobin presents them as being both equally lazy and uncivilised (cf. TC 119f).

African inferiority

It has to be noted, however, that apart from pointing to Africans' unwillingness to work, Tobin seems to avoid taking a stance on the topic of essential inferiority. He makes quite clear that he feels the question of Africans' inferiority is beside the point.

> Mr. Ramsay's fifth chapter is entirely employed in endeavouring to restore the negroes to that equality with the whites, from which many very ingenious philosophers have lately attempted to degrade them. This is a question totally unconnected with the design of these remarks; ... I cannot indeed consider the merits of this famous controversy of much consequence, even to the open and avowed advocates for slavery (if any such there are) as it has never been pretended, that the slaves either of the Jews, Greeks, or Romans of old, or the European and Asiatic slaves of modern times, were, or are, any way inferior to their masters, except in strength, policy, or good fortune. (TC 140f)

Although Tobin does not claim himself that Africans are inferior he describes the philosophers who do so as "ingenious". Tobin ends his essay with an attack on the poor quality of the clergy in the West, describing Ramsay as one of the people who, in Ramsay's own words, "flee to the church as their last refuge from poverty" (TC 146).

4.4.3 Ideology

It has already been pointed out that Tobin seems to perceive himself as writing against the opinion of the metropolitan British mainstream, asserting that "I shall not be so far misunderstood by the candid, and judicious part of mankind, as to be ranked among the advocates of slavery" (TC 5). He also writes that it is an "invidious a task it is, to take up the pen even in seeming opposition to a book of such apparent liberal tendency" (TC 3). Agreeing with Ramsay's fundamental assumptions but disagreeing in detail is a recurring rhetoric technique of Tobin. For example, he pays the usual lip service to an abstract concept of freedom when he states "I most sincerely join Mr. Ramsay, and every other man of sensibility, in hoping, the blessings of freedom will in due time, be equally diffused over the face of the whole globe" (TC 5). The same holds true for the concept of humanity. When Tobin calls Ramsay "the apparently benevolent advocate for the rights of human nature" (TC 2), he fundamentally subscribes to a positive concept of human rights only to blame Ramsay for having impure motives, calling him "ostensibly desirous of spreading the invaluable blessings of liberty and Christianity" while taking "the most illiberal and unchristian-like manner of doing it" (TC 2). Generally, however, the underlying concept of humanity in Tobin's text is not a positive one, just as he cites the laziness of free black communities in the West Indies (cf. TC 62f), he also writes of the British working classes that they "loiter away those hours of leisure which Sunday procures him ... in the dangerous indulgences afforded by some neighbouring alehouse" (TC 88f).

Thus, Tobin's true convictions remain rather elusive throughout his text. Tobin's main aim seems to be to disagree with Ramsay; therefore, one can never be sure if his statements are made from conviction or just for the sake of argument. Tobin does not want to promote any specific ideology in his text; he can best be described as an ideological eclectic who seems to be willing to use bits and pieces of literally any ideology which the overall discourse offers him to attack Ramsay. A good example for this is the passage in which he even styles himself as an opponent of slavery dealing with the Africans' alleged inferiority.

Ramsay discusses Fletcher of Saltoun's argument that "a sense of interest will prevent the abuse of power in the master" and comments "There cannot be a fairer deduction in theory nor is there one more false in fact" (22). Tobin, in wanting to present Ramsay's description of planters' cruelty against their slaves as implausible, strongly disagrees with this conclusion and points out that "Fletcher's conclusion [is far] from being false in fact, taken generally that a very slight acquaintance with human nature will be sufficient to establish the truth of it" (22f). Although the issue of self-interest is not what is primarily at stake in this passage, the general concept seems to fit into Tobin's overall ideology. He is more specific when he describes how "the love of plenty counteracts the love of ease and that is the main-spring which sets going the whole labour in the world, no man, who has studied the human nature ever so little will deny" (TC 80). Since he wants to build an effective argument against Ramsay, Tobin has to acknowledge the fundamentals of free labour; his evaluation of the concept, however, is a surprising one. He quotes Ramsay that "in a *free country*, a peasant in general, executes twice the work of a slave in the sugar colonies" (TC 82) and, later on, points out that the British peasants are:

> born to severe and hereditary labour ... They struggle through the years of their childhood, and the diseases and accidents attendant thereon, half naked, and half starved; equally exposed to the heats of summer, and the frosts of winter; and in a state of untutored ignorance. (85f)

It is quite remarkable how Tobin turns the argument around. Ramsay compares the amount of labour performed by free peasants and slaves in order to prove the higher efficiency of the first, while Tobin uses the very same argument to show that the slave is better off because he has to work less. Both arguments are equally valid. Tobin concludes his argument that it is merely the idea of liberty that is enjoyed by the British peasant. However, he shares with Ramsay the idea that the lower classes have to be somewhat controlled in order to keep the "impetuous dictates of unpolished nature" (TC 86) in check.

4.5 Thomas Clarkson's *Essay* (1786/88)

4.5.1 Thomas Clarkson—Biography and Self-representation in his Texts

Thomas Clarkson was born on 28 March 1760 in Wisbech, Cambridgeshire, the son of the Reverend John and Anne Clarkson and the eldest of three children. From 1779 to 1783, he studied for a bachelor's degree in Cambridge where he also partook in and won the Latin Essay Competition twice in succession. The topic of the second competition was *"anne liceat invitos in servitutem dare"* (is it lawful to make slaves of the unconsenting), which Clarkson won with his famous *Essay on the Slavery and Commerce of the Human Species*. After winning the competition and returning home, Clarkson experienced an often-cited moment of epiphany "in sight of Wades Mill" in Hertfordshire (cf. Clarkson, *History* 210), in which he decided to dedicate his life to the cause of abolishing slavery. After some initial hesitation, Clarkson then gave up his planned church career and became a full-time abolitionist. His first step was to translate his *Essay* into English, and on 22 May 1787, the committee for effecting the abolition of the slave trade was formally set up in James Phillips' London bookshop. All but three of the twelve original members were Quakers, providing an extensive network all across the country for Thomas Clarkson, who took on the role of a fact-finder for the cause. Clarkson travelled over 35,000 miles on horseback over the next seven years to gather information about the slave trade at Britain's main slave ports. Supported by the network of Quaker Friends, anti-slavery societies were started all over the country. Clarkson's findings, of course, greatly impacted his subsequent work, the second edition of *Essay on the Slavery and Commerce (1788)*, his *Essay on the Impolicy (1788)* and his *Letters on the Slave Trade (1791)*. Clarkson's brother, the naval officer John Clarkson, also joined the crusade against slavery, first as Thomas' secretary, then as a fact finder in Le Havre and finally through his involvement in the resettlement of American black loyalists from Nova Scotia to Sierra Leone. John was the first governor of the colony until his dismissal in 1793.

Thomas Clarkson spent five months in revolutionary France from 1789–90, attempting to persuade the National Assembly to abolish the slave trade. Despite his efforts, the abolitionist cause stagnated in the early 1790s, with William Wilberforce repeatedly failing to get his abolitionist bills through parliament and with the war against France changing national opinion. Eventually, Clarkson was forced to temporarily retire from the cause due to failing health. He returned to activism in 1804, when he again travelled extensively to collect new evidence and lobby sympathetic MPs. After the Abolition Bill was finally passed by Parliament in 1807, Clarkson published his substantial two-volume *History of the Rise, Progress, and Accompliment of the Abolition of the Slave-Trade*, by the British parliament, which has influenced the master narrative of the history of British abolitionism to the present day. In the years after the successful abolition, Clarkson sometimes took on the role of an unofficial ambassador for anti-slavery until he joined the effort to end slavery as such when, in 1823, the Antislavery Society was founded and he yet again travelled to rally support for the cause. Clarkson lent his voice to the cause of emancipation with his *Thoughts on the Necessity of Improving the Situation of the Slaves in the British Colonies*. He survived the emancipation of slaves by 13 years.

In his texts, Clarkson paints a picture of himself as an extremely modest person. Both *Essay* and *Letters* start with the assertion that he had to be persuaded by a third party to consider publication. In *Essay*, he writes that because he had concentrated on other studies, he felt that he lacked the critical knowledge of the English language necessary for the publication of such a text (CE xxi f). That these assertions are, at least to some extent, part of a carefully planned rhetorical technique to ensure the audience's goodwill becomes especially apparent in the beginning of *Letters*, when he claims that he had originally written them to "several gentlemen who expressed a wish to be informed ... of the Abolition of the Slave Trade" (CL v). Upon his return home from France, he "accidentally shewed what [he] had thus written to a friend" (CL v) who "was so struck with the answers [as]to desire [Clarkson] to publish them" (CL v). Keeping copies of the letters and "accidentally" showing them to a friend makes me suspect that Clarkson had at least some intention of publishing his composition in the first place. It is in tune with Clarkson's ostentatious modesty that he uses the voice of this friend to praise the quality of his composition.

In his *Essay*, Clarkson sides with James Ramsay when he explicitly names James Tobin as the author of *Cursory Remarks*. He describes this as rescuing Ramsay from "the cruel aspersions" and declaring that his fellow abolitionist had "explained himself to the satisfaction of all parties and has refuted him [i.e. Tobin] in every point" (CE xviii). Clarkson launches a counter attack against Tobin when he asks if an author "in attempting to silence a publication, attacks the character of the author, rather than the principles of the work itself, is it not a proof that the work itself is unquestionable, and that this writer is at a loss to find an argument against it" (CE xvii). Despite this affirmation, reputation as such seems to be important for Clarkson, as can be seen in his reference to authorities in the form of "human and worthy persons" (CE v, xii) or as "a gentleman of high consideration" (CT 34). Generally speaking, Clarkson styles the abolitionist cause very much as a fight of good against evil, in which he, of course, takes the side of universal values such as humanity, benevolence, generosity, etc. In his dedication of the *Essay* to William Charles Colyear, Clarkson refers to Britain as "that illustrious island, the very air of which has been determined upon a late investigation of its laws to be an antidote against slavery" (CE ii). Clarkson ties British identity to such positive values as "piety, morality and justice" 8CE xi). The slave trade, on the other hand, disgraces the national character (cf. CE xi) and is linked to negative principles such as "interest, violence and oppression" (CE xi). Clarkson's notion of an ideal British identity is perhaps most explicitly expressed when he corrects a fictitious African's misconceptions about Britishness due to the pernicious influence of the slave trade. "Their countrymen at home are generous and brave. They support the sick, the lame, and the blind . . ." (CE 126).

Although never converting himself, Clarkson had a life-long sympathy for Quakerism—he once remarked that he shared "nine parts in ten of their way of thinking" (ONDB Clarkson). Clarkson certainly ascribed a great moral importance to Christianity, describing it as "the most perfect and lovely of moral systems. It blesses even the hand of persecution itself and returns good for evil" (CE 125).

4.5.2 Synopsis and Argumentative Aim

Clarkson's *Essay* is a translation from his original Latin dissertation that won him the price in the Essay competition. Clarkson apologises that: "The reader will probably perceive the Latin idiom in several passages of the work, though I have endeavoured, as far as I have been able, to avoid it" (CE xxii). In 1788, Clarkson published a second expanded version of his *Essay*, which includes the facts from his research in the previous years.

History of slavery

Clarkson starts his composition with a first part on "The History of Slavery" (CE 1). The first six chapters contain Clarkson's account of the situation of slaves among "the ancients" (CE 4), especially among the Greeks and Romans. The conclusion which he draws from this is that the long existence of slavery "depressed their minds; it numbed their faculties; and, by preventing those sparks of genius from blazing forth, which had otherwise been conspicuous; it gave them the appearance of being endued with inferiour capacities than the rest of mankind" (CE 22). Clarkson continues his history of the slavery with the observation that after the people's migration, "as the northern nations were settled in their conquests" (CE 37) slavery seems to have been universally abolished in Europe, and he holds the introduction of Christianity responsible for this.

Fundamental arguments against slavery

The second part of the *Essay* contains Clarkson's central argumentation against slavery on philosophical grounds. He starts out with considerations about human societies in general and concludes "that mankind were originally free" (CE 56) and "government is a contract" (CE 66). Therefore, Clarkson argues, "liberty is a natural, and government an adventitious right" (CE 66) and "the grand object of the [social] contract, is the happiness of the people" (CE 68).

In the next chapter, Clarkson produces further fundamental arguments against slavery, such as that all possessions have to be inferior to the possessor and, therefore, slavery is repugnant to the fundamental equality of all humans, or that it would annihilate the natural authority of parents over their children (cf. CE 69ff).

Clarkson then deals with "the third order of involuntary slaves, 'to convicts'" (CE 76). He proves the injustice of slavery as a punishment on two grounds, firstly, because the crimes normally do not match the severity of the punishment and, secondly, because the enslaving of his own subjects by the African princes, whom the

"the Europeans . . . intoxicated . . . with their foreign draughts" (CE 81) is repugnant to the social contract since it only promotes his own happiness and not the "publick happiness" (CE 83).

In Chapter Seven, Clarkson deals with prisoners of war and argues the ancient right of capture to be conceptually wrong, and the principle of enslaving the opponents in a war on the principles of reparation and punishment is equally unjust since the injured party is always the state and no individual and the African wars are waged for the sole purpose of obtaining slaves and, thus, no just wars (cf. CE 83ff).

In the 1788 version, Clarkson added an eighth chapter in which he considers his fifth class of slaves, namely "such as the African traders breed for the purpose of selling to the Europeans" (CE88 68). Clarkson states that the principle of the offspring inheriting the servile status of their mother, as practised in ancient Rome, hinges on the assumption that their parents are brutes, which they are not. Clarkson concludes the chapter with the remark that "nature made every man's body and mind his own, so no just person can be reduced to slavery against his own consent" (CE*88* 69); therefore, the "sixth and seventh classes of slaves, consisting of those who have been reduced to a state of slavery in consequence of gaming and debt" (CE88 69f) need not be dealt with since, in the strict sense, they are "voluntary" (CE88 70) slaves.

Conditions on the Middle Passage

The 1786 version then only provides a more general description of the appalling conditions during the Middle Passage, drawing on such facts as the *Zong* incident (cf. CE 131). In the 1788 version, the treatment of the Middle Passage is expanded to a total of three substantial chapters. Clarkson's increased knowledge of the slave trade due to his investigations for the abolitionist cause enabled him to provide tonnages of slave vessels, the precise measurements of the accommodation of the Africans and further evidence of the cruel conditions of the transatlantic trade. Clarkson then provides a more detailed account of the various modes of sale of the slaves in the colonies, underlining the cruelty of this practice by giving examples of those being too sick or weak to sell being thrown overboard (CE*88* 102f)

Situation on plantations

Clarkson dedicates a whole chapter to the situation on the sugar plantations, including the period of seasoning, a typical day on a plantation, the cruel punishments inflicted and the general drudgery of plantation work (CE 138ff). He especially emphasises the arbitrariness of punishments and the absence of legal protection. The text concludes with a plea for the Africans' right to resistance, "those, whom they are under no obligations to obey, and whose only title to their services consists in a violation of the rights of men!" (CE 153)

Clarkson laments that in the case of the cruelties of the planters, "self-interest will be found but a weak barrier against the sallies of passion" (CE 156f), especially when combined with the drive to self-preservation in the face of a ratio of one master to fifty slaves, who "are retained in their present situation by violence; . . . perpetually at war in their hearts with their oppressors, and . . . continually cherishing the seeds of revenge" (CE 158).

An inferior link in the chain of nature

The last part of Clarkson's essay is concerned with what he calls "that other system of reasoning, which is always applied, when the former is confuted: 'that the Africans are an inferiour link of the chain of nature, and are made for slavery'" (CE 164). Clarkson, thus, sets out to appraise the capacities of Africans. He declares that in their original situation in Africa "their abilities are sufficient for their situation;- that they are as great, as those of other people have been, in the same stage of society" (CE 168) and in "mechanical arts, they do not discover a want of ingenuity" (CE 169). Clarkson's assessment of "African capacity" culminates with liberal arts and poetry. He uses Phillis Wheatley's poetry as proof that if Africans

> were unbroken by slavery; if they had the same expectations in life as other people, and the same opportunities of improvement, they would be equal; in all the various branches of science, to the Europeans. (CE 177)

Countering romanticised image of pro-slavery texts

Clarkson clearly rejects any comparisons of the situation of African slaves to British soldiers, and also the romanticised scenes of plantation life, such as the slaves' little plots for growing vegetables, their dances and their holidays, by the West Indians. Clarkson cites how suicides among Africans are frequent and that "They die with a smile upon their face, and their funerals are attended by a vast concourse of their countrymen, with every possible demonstration of joy" (CE 234) to prove such romantic representations wrong. His final proof of the slaves' miserable situation is demographic evaluations of the West Indian slave populations' failure to grow (CE 235f).

4.5.3 Ideology

Generally, Clarkson's ideas are very much indebted to the traditions of the European Enlightenment and humanism. The concept of the social contract is central to Clarkson's discussion of society and government. He develops the idea of the social contract from mankind's original situation of dissociation and independence in which government can only have arisen out of consent or is not based on compulsion. Government, for Clarkson, is a contract (cf. CE 66), the grand object of which is the happiness of the people (cf. CE 68). From the original equality of all men, Clarkson deduces that liberty is a natural right while government is an adventitious one (cf. CE 66). In his description of African societies, Clarkson attributes the emergence of a sort of anti-social contract to the corrupting influence of the slave trade on the African princes. He describes this as having led to a situation in which "the more abandoned the subject, the happier the prince" (CE 82f).

Personal liberty is another central concept in Clarkson's argument. He holds that "nothing is dearer than liberty to men" (CE 81). However, the liberty which Clarkson is thinking of is mainly the impossibility of the ownership of one human being by another. He is anxious to point out that sovereigns can never claim ownership over their subjects, such as African princes selling their people, since "their natures are both the same" (CE 73). Clarkson justifies the natural right of resisting those who take away one's liberty as only obeying "the dictates of nature" (CE 148). Despite this, the claim for personal liberty has an ambivalent function in relation to state authority. While clearly endorsing rebellion against tyranny, Clarkson also very much idealises the happiness and freedom of British subjects.

In the argument against slavery, Clarkson holds that the slave trade is primarily founded on "principles of antiquity" (CE 55f), and it is not "consistent with the laws of nature, or the common notions of equity, as established among men" (CE 55f). The author stands in the Enlightenment tradition in his criticism of traditional authorities (with the exception of Christianity) in favour of more universal concepts, such as "the laws of nature" (CE 55).

In his rejection of the argument that Africans are fundamentally inferior to Europeans, Clarkson thus follows two main lines of argument based on the suppositions that either the scriptures are true or false (cf. CE 179). Firstly, he takes a scriptural approach to prove that God has indeed created all men of one blood (cf. CE 188) and, secondly, he deals with the argument that Africans are an inferior link in the chain of nature (cf. CE 164). The competing narratives of world explanation are, on the one hand, provided by the Bible and, on the other, by natural history. For the sake of argument, Clarkson deals with both systems of reasoning equally. Despite his claim that the "present age would rejoice to find that the scriptures had no foundation" (CE 186), he finally declares his own sentiments on the truth of the biblical narratives "by asserting that they are true, and that all mankind, however various their appearances are derived from the same stock" (CE 186). Thus, nature seems to serve as a sort of ersatz-concept for a traditional theistic God. In a kind of compromise, Clarkson refers to God as "the author of nature" (CE 240) and attributes the existing differences in the human species as the result of natural influences.

Clarkson is a strong advocate of free labour, which he describes as better, faster, more efficient and more profitable than slave labour (cf. CE ix). Clarkson argues for a distinct difference between disciplining animals and human. While it is perfectly acceptable to control animals with the stings of hunger and the lash (CE 22, 151), humans, of course, have to be disciplined in a different way (cf CE 28f). Clarkson conceptualises that humans are by reward rather than by punishment:

> For what is it that awakens the abilities of men, and distinguishes them from the common herd? Is it not often the amiable hope of becoming serviceable to individuals, or the state? Is it not often the hope of riches, or of power? Is it not frequently the hope of temporary honours, or a lasting fame? (CE 165)

Already the title of the *Essay on the Slavery and Commerce on the Human Species* shows that Clarkson uses the belonging of all human beings to a common species as an argument for claiming the slaves' equality. He proves that "all men were derived from the same stock" (CE 184), both from scripture and based on "colour, and those other marks which distinguish them from the inhabitants of Europe" (CE 178). He argues that claiming superiority over those of a different colour is a ridiculous argument since it is evident that all humans are of same species as they can propagate. He then explains that mankind was originally of one colour—olive—and that the existing difference of complexion is merely due to climatic influence. Clarkson concludes his assessment by arguing that if Africans had been made for slavery, they would be devoid of reason (CE 214).

Already in the title of his work, Clarkson implies that the slave trade is immoral because it is the *human species* which is traded. His deliberate choice of words focuses the attention of the reader on this fact. Clarkson's species-ism (cf. Braidotti, *Posthuman* 71ff) is not without problems. The fundamental conceptual problem is that sameness is made a key argument for inclusion and participation, thus the possibility of the exclusion of 'Others' is implied, which makes the argument flawed. It is from this that the post-humanist criticism of static binary distinctions in favour of a "compassionate acknowledgment of [the] interdependence with multiple others" (Braidotti, *Posthuman* 100) no matter if they are anthropomorphic or not and their argument for a "zoe-egalitarianism" (Braidotti, *Posthuman* 103).

Although Clarkson repeatedly refers to different or distinct "species of men" (CE 178, 183, 184, 185, 187, 203), this is mainly replicating pro-slavery opinion. However, his perception of the Africans' blackness is such as to facilitate later racisms. Clarkson holds the notion that "The children of the blackest Africans are born white" (CE 203). In a footnote, he explains that:

> This circumstance, which always happens, shews that they are descended from the same parents as ourselves; for had they been a distinct species of men, and the blackness entirely ingrafted in their constitution and frame, there is great reason to presume, that their children would have been born black (CE 203 fn).

Considering the anatomical facts, this kind of reasoning has to conclude that the Africans' blackness is indeed "entirely ingrafted in their constitution" and, thus, that they are descended from different parents (radical Others?)

Clarkson stands in a tradition of classical humanism and Enlightenment; his texts posit humans as rational social beings who are accountable for their actions. The latter is one of the arguments against slavery. Clarkson argues (cf. CE 69f) that "there cannot be any property in the human species" (CE 70) because this would undermine the authority of parents and the duties of children and would remove the accountability of individuals for their actions:

> For if any one man can have an absolute property in the liberty of another, or, in other words, if he, who is called a master, can have a just right to command the actions of him, who is called a slave, it is evident that the latter cannot be accountable for those crimes, which the former may order him to commit. Now as every reasonable being is accountable for his actions, it is evident, that such a right cannot justly exist, and that human liberty, of course, is beyond the possibility either of sale or purchase. (CE 70)

Furthermore, Clarkson argues that ownership of human beings must necessarily reduce them to the inferior state of brutes (cf. CE 106).

The basic concept of the human in Clarkson's text is characterised by several binary distinctions: mind vs. body, feeling vs. thinking, man vs. animal, free man vs. slave, zoe vs. bios.

The mind-body dualism becomes evident, for example, when Clarkson reminds the slave traders that "you have the power only of alluding to the body: the mind cannot be confined or bound: it will be free, though its mansion be beset with chains" (CE 70). This dualism is also reflected in Clarkson's arguments which refer to the dichotomy between thought and feeling. Brycchan Carry has identified this kind of sentimental rhetoric as trying to appeal not only to the rational mind of the audience but also to make them feel the arguments (Carey 2). This dichotomy can furthermore be found on the level of society. Clarkson draws a sharp line between humans and animals, on the basis that the latter form larger social units. Clarkson's idea of the (modern European) human is one of social beings who gain their very aliveness from their social surroundings. He writes about slaves in classical antiquity,

> They were beaten, starved, tortured, murdered at discretion: they were dead in a civil sense; . . . Poor unfortunate men! . . . to be considered as dead in that state, the very members of which they were supporting by their labours! (CE 17)

Clarkson uses the belonging to one species as a central argument for the access to natural rights. He argues that slavery degrades "a part of the human species, and [classes] it with the brutal" (CE 6) since to own humans is to reduce them to the level of animals. Thus, it is important to note that in Clarkson's text, the opposite of "free men" is not "enslaved men", but slaves.

Clarkson argues that in a state of nature, "mankind were originally free, and that they possessed an equal right to the soil and produce of the earth" (CE 56). In Clarkson's text, this situation has a distinct positive tinge since he writes that, "Every man wandered where he chose, changing his residence, as a spot attracted his fancy, or suited his convenience, uncontrouled by his neighbour, unconnected with any but his family. . . . a state of dissociation and independence" (CE 57). It has been mentioned above that Clarkson adheres to a universal model of history based on three distinct stages. As he argues that, "in this dissociated state it is impossible that men could have long continued" (CE 59), they soon reach the "third situation of mankind a state of subordinate society" (CE 60). Based on a model of human progress, Clarkson develops a theory of social contract when he argues that:

> As empire then could never have been gained at first by compulsion, so it could only have been obtained by consent; and as men were then going to make an important sacrifice, for the sake of their mutual happiness, so he alone could have obtained it, (not whose ambition had greatly distinguished him from the rest) but in whose wisdom, justice, prudence, and virtue, the whole community could confide. (CE 62)

Just as mankind as a whole, the individual also has a historical dimension and the potential for progress. Clarkson argues that slavery prevents personal progress since the unfortunate Africans have no such incitements ... that they should shew their genius. They have no hope of riches, power, honours, fame. They have no hope but this, that their miseries will be soon terminated by death. (CE 164)

The concept of personal liberty is a central one for Clarkson's appreciation of the African slave trade. The author very much defines liberty as not being owned by others. In his overview of the history of human societies, Clarkson describes mankind's original state as one of "universal liberty" (CE 62); thus freedom is a natural right. The concept of liberty stands in relation with the concept of subordination. Drawing from human history, Clarkson describes all subsequent stage of human society as a progress from unbounded liberty to subordination (cf. CE 66). The liberty Clarkson proposes is intricately bound to state control, since one of his main arguments for personal freedom is founded on the question of accountability. Ownership by one subject of another is seen as an evasion from societal control since "the latter cannot be accountable for the crimes the former may order him to commit" (CE 70). Since liberty is a fundamental right, Clarkson describes government as a contract. In contrast to this, Clarkson refers to the human right to rule over animals as a natural right since they are brutes that are devoid of reason, which conceptually binds the right to liberty to the possession of reason.

Clarkson also links the idea of liberty to European and British traditions. He refers to "that general liberty at last, which, at the close of the twelfth century, was conspicuous in the West of Europe". Furthermore, he argues that the basis of British government is liberty (CE ix), and the text includes a dramatic adoration of "Immortal Alfred! father of our invaluable constitution! parent of the civil blessings we enjoy!" (CE 154).

4.6 Gilbert Francklyn's *Letters* (1789)

4.6.1 Gilbert Francklyn

Francklyn is the author of two better known pro-slavery texts, *Observations, Occasioned by the Attempts made in England to Effect the Abolition of the Slave Trade...*, which was originally published in Jamaica and reprinted in London in 1789, and the text which is dealt with in the present work, *An Answer to the Rev. Mr. Clarkson's Essay ... in a Series of Letters from a Gentleman in Jamaica to his friend in London*. In his text, the author claims to have written *Answer* in Jamaica between 1 October 1788 and 4 January 1789. His letters were then published in London in 1789. Although Francklyn's texts create the impression that he is actually a resident of Jamaica, the *Minutes of the Evidence Taken Before a Committee of the Whole House to Whom it was Referred to Consider the Slave-Trade* describe the witness, Mr. Francklyn, as "a native of England" who first "went to the W. Indies in 1766" (*Minutes* 18) and resided in Antigua until 1787, where he entered into a partnership with his cousin (cf. Francklyn, *Legacies*), Antony Bacon, and supervised "a number of negroes let by contract to government ... in order to attend the surveyors marking out the lands to be sold in the ceded islands [i.e. the Caribbean territories ceded from France to Britain in the treaty of Paris 1763]" (*Minutes* 18). He subsequently lived in Antigua from 1768 to 1770 and from 1774 to 1776, and from 1779 to 1789 in Tobago, where "he bought largely" (*Minutes* 19) and owned about 400 slaves together with his partner (*Minutes* 18). In 1788, he spent seven or eight months in Jamacia before returning to England until his death in 1799 (cf. Francklyn, *Legacies*). As already hinted at, he testified as a pro-slavery witness before the parliamentary committee on the slave trade. In contrast to most of his fellow pro-slavery writers, Francklyn did not publish his texts anonymously or under a pseudonym, but used his own name. David Brion Davis and Srividhya

Swaminathan refer to Francklyn as one of the more prominent West Indian apologists (Davis, *Revolution* 467; Swaminathan 198).

The text itself shows that Francklyn decidedly sympathises with the West Indian planters and the slave merchants. He criticises Clarkson's use of "the odious name of Receivers" to refer to the latter "…forgetting, sure, that among such purchasers are my Lords the Archbishops, Bishops, Noblemen, and Gentlemen, who are members of the Society for Propagating the Gospel in Foreign Parts" (FA 88). He, furthermore, blames Clarkson for branding the planters as being devoid of humanity (cf. FA 21), accuses the abolitionists of a "pretended zeal for the sacred interests of humanity and religion" (FA 6) and clearly sides with the "Gentlemen of St. Christopher" and James Tobin, whom he refers to as:

> a gentleman resident in England, but a native of the island of Nevis, appears to have been the first person who judged it proper to employ his pen in defence of his countrymen and friends, whom he conceived to be injured by the misrepresentations of the Reverend Mr. Ramsay. (FA 6)

Francklyn is generally anxious to portray the West Indian planters as the injured party and as gentlemen. The main opponents he refers to in the text are James Ramsay and Thomas Clarkson. His main argument against Clarkson's person is his youth and lack of knowledge about the details of the Atlantic slave system. He criticises the University of Cambridge for "having thought fit to offer a prize for the best Dissertation on Slavery, as a subject wherein to exercise the ingenuity and imagination of the junior members of that society" (FA 18). He calls Thomas Clarkson, the winner, "a young man of a fertile fancy" (FA 18). As Ramsay had personal experience of West Indian slavery, this kind of argument would not work. Thus Francklyn, like Tobin and the "Gentlemen of St. Christopher" before him, questions the moral and personal integrity of Ramsay, accusing him of:

having written his book at the expence of forfeiting those friendships which he had contracted by a long residence in the West Indies. Others say he wrote the book in question to shew his resentment against those people, with whom he had lived, and had, from his conduct, made almost the whole of them his enemies. (FA 166)

In Francklyn's text, we find the usual phrases of affected modesty, referring to his composition in apologetic terms, only offering it to the reader "unless some abler writer should think proper to stand forth in support of the injured reputations of the Planter and Merchant, and thereby render any further, feeble, efforts of mine, unnecessary" (FA 16).

Like other pro-slavery writers, he styles himself as writing against the prevailing public opinion at the time:

> In calling upon me to give you my opinion upon this subject, you put me upon a service of danger. The abuse so liberally bestowed on the West Indias, has been now so long and so often repeated, that many persons, in Britain believe it to be well founded. He who is hardy enough to oppose a popular and prevailing opinion [3], has little chance of obtaining a favourable hearing, especially if such opinion should be entertained by men of worth and virtue. I shall not, however, shrink from the task you have imposed on me . . . (FA 2f)

Francklyn seems eager to show his education and learning; the text contains over 250 references to textual sources, ranging from the authors of the Greco-Roman antiquity such as Homer, Plato and Ovid, to extensive quotations from the Bible, Mosheim's *Ecclesiastical History*, Shakespeare, the plays *Oronooko, the Royal Slave* and *Inkle and Yarico* and various accounts of African voyages, to contemporary anti-slavery writers, to name but a few. Francklyn's *Answer* is also the text of the corpus, which makes use of the greatest variety of languages. He extensively cites snippets of the languages used by the slaves, French, Latin, Greek, Hebrew and even Hindi.

4.6.2 Synopsis and Argumentative Aims

Like many of the other pro-slavery authors, Francklyn sought to portray himself as writing against the hegemonic opinion. The very structure of Francklyn's texts, as letters being written from Jamaica to Britain, seeks to base the argument on the claimed superior knowledge of a colonial position. Francklyn described himself as "Conversant, as I have long been, with almost all the British sugar colonies" (FA 178) in order to establish a superior position of knowledge and also concedes such a position to James Tobin (cf. FA 165):

> Mr. Ramsay, who knows something of the West Indies, acknowledges it. He says, 'it would be both inhuman and impolitic, to make a slave free who cannot earn an honest living.' He must know little of the generality of Negro, or any other slaves, who will suppose they will work without compulsion. It is for this very reason Mr. Ramsay himself seems to consider his scheme as an Utopian one. Mr. Clarkson, in proportion to his smaller degree of knowledge, is more positive, more violent, and more injurious in is expressions. [166] Mr. Ramsay's performance (notwithstanding Mr. Clarkson's assertions to the contrary) is certainly proved, by Mr. Tobin, to be replete with errors and exaggerations. (FA 165f)

The whole passage is the attempt of the colonial margin to write against the centre. Perhaps the tactics of the authors like Francklyn to rely on their arguments on their claimed superior knowledge of the colonies were doomed right from the beginning since they constitute a sort of self-marginalisation.

As in probably all argumentative texts, it is, of course, Francklyn's professed aim to tell his readers the truth, while blaming Clarkson for distorting it. When he discusses the question if "an author's private character being attacked" (FA 8) is justifiable in the discussion of slavery, he fundamentally agrees with Clarkson's critique of this, but only in "cases where the want of integrity in the author has nothing to do with the subject of the writings" (FA 9). Thus, he justifies an attack on the persons of the abolitionists in the case of the slave merchants and planters since they are the accused parties.

Francklyn's text is structured in a series of eleven letters written from Jamaica to a "friend in London" (FA i) who "desired his opinion of Mr. Clarkson's Essay on Slavery and the Slave Trade"

(FA iii), making Francklyn's position quite literally a West Indian one. In the preface to the letters, Francklyn explains that "the letters which are here offered to the public were written with intent to place in a proper point of view the attempts made to misrepresent the conduct of the merchant trading to Africa" (FA v f).

Abolitionism is an unfair attack against planters

Francklyn starts his first letter by calling the arguments of the abolitionists a mean and unfair attack against the innocent planters, who have not responded so far, which is a "proof of their conscious innocence" (FA 2). The author declares his wonder at the sudden change of public opinion about the slave trade when "very few years since the preservation and improvement of the trade to Africa was regarded as a matter of utmost importance to the British commerce" (FA 3). Francklyn wonders why the University of Cambridge chose the topic of slavery as a topic and points out that many people obviously and mistakenly consider Clarkson's *Essay* "not an academical dissertation but a real and true historical account" (FA 20).

Slavery has always been a general situation of life

Just like other pro-slavery writers, he uses the existence of slavery in the bible as proof of the antiquity of the practice (cf. FA 44f). Francklyn also suggests that "the Negroes are the descendants of Cush, the eldest son of Ham" (FA 31) and then points to the scriptural fact that "many of the descendants of Mizraim were slaves for several generations" (FA 35). He explores several possible origins of the Africans in the Bible and discusses whether the descendants of Canaan were black. The author agrees with Clarkson that they were not, but points to the fact that Canaan was sentenced to be "a servant of servants ... unto his brethren" and translates the original Hebrew phrase "Obed Obedim 'a slave of slaves'" (FA 38).

Francklyn also uses "the testimony of profane authors" (FA 46) to prove that slavery has always been a feature of mankind. Here, he refers to the existence of slavery as referred to by classical authors such as Homer and Herodotus to make his point, but also drawing the attention of the reader to the existence of slavery in China, East India and pre-Columbian America (cf. FA 50ff). Dealing with Clarkson's notion of a general emancipation of slaves in Europe around 1200 AD, Francklyn concludes that "religion had very little to do in the bestowing liberty upon slaves ..." (FA 77) since "Vassalage still subsists in many parts of France and Germany, and in Russia, Poland, Hungary, and Dalmatia. In many other parts of Europe it exists in all its rigour" (FA 82). Francklyn provocatively remarks that it would be more apt to link the emancipation of slaves "to the influence of the Mahommedan than to the Christian religion" (FA 83).

The author also argues that Clarkson malevolently misrepresents the slave trade in his descriptions and discusses Clarkson's notions about the "original state of mankind". Additionally, Francklyn quotes William Paley's *Moral and Political Philosophy* to show that "no social compact [sic!] was ever made in fact, [and] .... therefore no government in the universe began from this original" (FA 99). Francklyn then turns to the various classes of slaves Clarkson mentions and concludes with the assertion that Clarkson's sources are all at least 50 years old and that there have been great improvements in the manner in which the slave trade is carried on (cf. FA 111).

Africa and the slave trade

Francklyn writes that the slave trade has a distinctly positive effect on Africa. For this end, he relates several episodes of cannibalism and cruel religious practices in order to prove that the Europeans are actually doing the Africans a favour in taking them out of their country (cf. FA 116). Then he refutes Clarkson's accusation that the Europeans provoked African princes to go to war in order to obtain slaves as absurd since wars are never conducive to trade (cf. FA 119). The author maintains that, on the contrary, it has always been "the desire of the merchants, to make peace between the African nations" (FA 119). He contradicts Clarkson's theory that the Africans in the interior are now more civilised than the ones on the coast (cf. FA 124). Francklyn points out that frequent famines, such as one on the Gold Coast in the 15th century, and a more recent one in 1675 (cf. FA 150ff) often made the situation of the Africans so dire that "They not only [sell], but eat, their nearest relations; and the strongest, like wild beasts, preyed upon the weaker" (FA 151). Francklyn concludes that ending the slave trade would be to induce the "inhabitants to return to their old custom of sacrificing them on the graves of their masters … or of suffering thousands to die when a famine happens … " (FA 155). He generally describes the horrible climate, jungles and diseases of Africa in such terms as to show that it is far from a "Happy Country" (FA 218) to which slaves would ever want to return.

Cruelties not true

Franklyn brushes aside Clarkson's account of the Africans' sufferings during the Middle Passage by asserting that they are too extreme to be true. Francklyn asks what the infamous conduct of one individual like Collingwood of the *Zong* has to do with the planters in general (cf. FA 172). The *Letters* contain a series of relativisations, deliberately trying to give the cruellest actions a more humane appearance. For example, he writes in relation to the branding of slaves that "the place is immediately dressed with sweet oil. The operation is momentary. The pain cannot be half so considerable as a young lady must feel on having her ears bored" (FA 176).

Francklyn further explains that Clarkson's sources are too old and that this was like comparing the situation of "Russia, before the time of Peter the Great" with the present-day situation (FA 160). He argues that the English settlers at that time were "men of a fierce and military character" (FA 235) and that:

THE DISCOURSE ON SLAVERY 155

the extreme savage state in which the Africans then were, produced those severities, and a rigour of discipline on their plantations, nearly bordering upon that cruelty, which we of the present age, with justice, condemn, nor is now necessary, (if ever it was necessary) to be exercised upon the Negroes (FA 236).

However, the new generation of planters is much better educated and there is an increased number of Creole slaves (cf. FA 237). The text paints the usual idyllic picture of plantation life in order to show "in proof of the wealth and happiness of the Negroes in this country" (FA 238).

Comparison to British poor

The text also contains the usual comparison of the West Indian slave and the British worker. In the tenth letter, Francklyn again compares the Africans in the colonies to the British poor, who:

> are compelled to work by severe punishments; by stripes, by imprisonment: nor are they more goaded on to labour, by the fear of those stripes, and by that imprisonment, than by hunger, cold, and nakedness. They must work, or starve; unless they rather chuse to steal, which many do: witness the horrid public executions, and the numbers transported every year, for that crime! (FA 229)

Francklyn remarks that their freedom is just an empty name and asks if "that empty name [will] either feed or clothe them in health, or administer medicine, or comfort, to them when sick?" (FA 229). He then compares them to the negro in the colonies, who:

> ... lives in full enjoyment of his house, his family, his live stock, and his cultivated spot of ground, in safety; and in a climate congenial to that under which [230] he was born. His severest task is not equal to the daily labour of an husbandman in England. He has a sufficiency of clothing allowed him by his master; and if he had none, would scarcely suffer from the want of it, never having been accustomed to it in his own country. (FA 229f)

Asserts race as a static category

In his *Essay*, Clarkson states that the children of the blackest Africans are born white and only turn dark because of the climate (cf.

CE 203). In contrast to that, Francklyn sees ~~race~~ to be a static category when he explains that no matter what the reason, African children, although born with a lighter complexion, "soon acquire a more obscure [one] even without the aid of sunshine, or of smoak, though not sooner in the tropical than in colder countries" (FA 218f). Francklyn then explains that the Portuguese settlers in Africa turning black, which Clarkson describes as being due to the hotter climate, was the result of them mixing "with the black inhabitants of the country" (FA 218). As further proof of his theory, Francklyn refers the reader to the example of, "many young ladies, descendants of some of the first settlers in the islands, and now in England for their education, are of as fair and delicate complexion as any women in Europe" (FA 219).

Cultivation is not possible without slaves

Francklyn blames Clarkson for ignorance of West Indian agricultural practices when he explains that at the moment, there are about 10,000 free negroes in Jamaica, but these are mostly tradesmen and do not hire themselves out to work in the fields. Thus, the cultivation of the land would not be possible without slaves, although the planters would happily use free labourers if only they "could be hired in the colonies, at the same rate they are to be engaged in the dearest county in England" (FA 241).

4.6.3   Ideology

The author superficially agrees with the humane project of the abolitionists: "A tender regard to our fellow creatures, and an endeavour to promote their happiness, is certainly very commendable; and whoever can contribute to so desirable an end, ought to exert himself for that purpose" (FA 17). However, he is eager to divert the attention away from Colonial slavery back to metropolitan Britain when he argues that "the opportunities are innumerable and at the door of every man" (FA 17) and suggests that these humane endeavours rather be put into practice in Britain (cf. FA 17). Furthermore, Francklyn argues that the abolitionists act due to a "pretended zeal for the sacred interests of humanity and religion" (FA 6). This also supports his main argument that slavery is "a custom, sanctioned for so many thousand years, by the approbation and usage of all mankind" (FA 24) and thus a case "where the force of such custom pleaded so strongly against what [Clarkson] calls the feelings of humanity" (FA 25).

Francklyn believes in a society governed by strict authority and rules, and thus sees subordination as part of society. He explicitly describes society's "abridgement of natural liberty" (FA 242) and holds that "it is certain that, in civil society, every man is restrained of some part of his natural liberty, and is consequently, in some degree deprived of his freedom" (FA 14). He immediately turns this into a pro-slavery argument when he calls "every deprivation of freedom ... a species of servitude or slavery" (FA 14). Furthermore, he argues that servitude is even a Christian virtue since "there is a service which is perfect freedom" and to the pious Christian, "that yoke is easy and that burden light" (FA 14). Francklyn questions the concept of the social contract altogether when he cites William Paley's conviction:

> That no social compact was ever made in fact, and that it is to suppose it possible to call savages out of caves and deserts, to deliberate upon topics which the experience and studies and the refinement of civil life alone suggest; therefore no government in the universe began from this original. (FA 99)

When it comes to his conception of society, Francklyn's pragmatism borders on cynicism when he asks:

> ... where is the country where the weak are not oppressed by the strong? Much would that person merit who could effectually prevent it; till that is done, the man who depends on another's will or caprice for his daily subsistance, whether he be white or black, is in such a state of servitude as may justly be called slavery. (FA 164)

Francklyn also portrays the African princes as possessing less authority than Clarkson would like to have them when they sell their own subjects into slavery (cf. FA 110, 137f).

Francklyn states that an inquiry into "the rise nature, and design of government" "will afford us that general knowledge of subordination and liberty" (FA 96) necessary for a discussion of slavery. However, his conception of the state of nature is quite different from Clarkson's. Francklyn adheres to a much less romantic notion of the original situation of mankind, arguing that "men may, from vice, from accident, or misfortune, have degenerated into savages" (FA 98) "but that they could have been formed so, or have been placed in so miserable and helpless a situation, by their Creator, requires the credulity of an infidel to suppose" (FA 98). Referring to the concept of mankind's primordial equality, Francklyn states:

> As to the barbarous and savage hordes of people, their wants are few, and few slaves are necessary for their service; such people, therefore have generally no other slaves than their wives; but that they hold them in the severest state of servitude is so generally true, that we may defy those who are advocates for a perfect equality among mankind, and assert such an equality ever had existence in this world, to point out one savage nation where the women have not been treated as slaves. (FA 46)

The situation in Africa is, accordingly, not described as an idyllic one, and the idleness of the Africans is rather described in negative terms. In contrast to Clarkson who paints a picture of Africa as a natural Garden of Eden, Francklyn writes:

> as the fertility [150] of the land in such countries, when the seasons are favourable, renders very little labour sufficient to procure the inhabitants a redundancy of subsistence; and the warmth of the country, joined to the ease with which they can procure nourishment in common seasons, encourages the idleness, natural to persons living in an uncultivated state. (FA 149f)
> The oppression of the government does not a little to increase the natural indolence of the Negroes. They are at little pains to cultivate and improve their lands. They hardly till enough to supply their wants, but make up the deficiency by roots, fruits, and herbage; and hence we may perceive the reason, why they are afflicted with such frequent dearths and famine, of which the

Europeans beheld a dismal, but, to them, profitable instance in 1675, when fathers sold themselves, their wives, children, and connections, only for a small pittance of food, to relieve the immediate craving of hunger. (FA 151)

The hegemonic concept of freedom seems to pose a discursive problem for this pro-slavery author. Francklyn explicitly refers to the fact that Britain defined itself as free soil in the hegemonic discourse: "I know the risque I run of displeasing numbers of people in Great Britain, by daring even to hint, that any man in that country is not a freeman" (FA 238). Francklyn readily acknowledges the superiority of free labour when he states that if free labour was available in the Caribbean, the planters would immediately free their slaves (cf. FA 241). One can see that the author was conscious of the fact that it was not possible just to oppose the notion of freedom per se. Therefore, he applies various discursive strategies to come to terms with it. It has already been pointed out in the section about the social contract, Francklyn believes that "in civil society, every man is restrained of some part of his natural liberty, and is consequently, in some degree deprived of his freedom" (FA 14). He meets the anti-slavery strategy of linking Christianity and European freedom by stating that "the true business and professed end of Christianity were, to release from spiritual slavery" (FA 80). He also argues that freedom is not a Christian value per se, asking where in the New Testament the command to liberate slaves is to be found (cf. FA 56), before sliding into a discussion of abstract forms of freedom, writing that St. Paul, for example, only ever meant "spiritual freedom alone" (FA 57fn).

This is just one among many techniques of relativising the notion of freedom. Apart from arguing that freedom is a relative concept and different for each individual (cf. FA 14f), he quotes extensively from part of Cicero's *Paradoxa Stoicorum*. There, Cicero argues that slavery is not so much the becoming another's property but the blind obedience of those of "a broken and abject soul, lacking any judgement of its own," (Webb 33). Cicero concludes his argument by remarking: "who would deny that all unstable and ambitious people, and indeed all wicked people are slaves?" (Webb, 33).

Another strategy to circumvent the concept of freedom is Francklyn's reference to the alleged freedom of the British poor, about whom he writes:

> They must work, or starve; unless they rather chuse to steal, which many do: witness the horrid public executions, and the numbers transported every year, for that crime! Are these people entitled to boast of their liberty? And will that empty name either feed or clothe them in health, or administer medicine, or comfort, to them when sick? (FA 229)

Both pro- and anti-slavery texts rely on the explanatory discursive power of the concept of the Middle Ages as the formative period in European history. Anti-slavery authors portray the feudal bonds which characterise this period in a distinctly positive light. Francklyn, on the other hand, refutes Clarkson's argument that Christianity brought about a universal freedom in the West of Europe:—"religion had very little to do in the bestowing liberty upon the slaves when we find bishops, churches and monasteries" owning slaves (FA 76–77). He adds a long argument that people routinely surrendered their freedom to their feudal lords out of pure wretchedness (cf. FA 76) and portrays the feudal bond between lord and vassal strictly in terms of slavery, describing medieval ministeriales as "such as renounced their liberty, and became slaves in the strictest sense of the word" (FA 79). However, when it comes to the depiction of colonial slavery, Francklyn attempts to give the status quo in the West Indians a feudal tinge, which is endangered by the plans of the abolitionists

> Can any man believe, that, if those people were at this moment set free from all controul of their lords, and deprived of their cottages, and their present method of subsisting themselves, they would not be driven to pillage and devastation for their support? That such would be the consequence of giving a nominal freedom to the Negroes of the West Indies is most certain. (FA 204)

Francklyn additionally argues that harm is actually done to the Africans in the name of freedom and humanity, citing the example of the Sierra Leone Project and asking to let the slaves decide themselves "what it is which makes their own happiness" (FA 227)

Francklyn takes over Clarkson's references to the human species, mocking it as part of what he sees as misunderstood humanitarianism of abolitionists: "the African commerce, or (in the words of our Essayist) in *the commerce of the human species*" (FA 90). He also seems to question Clarkson's distinction between humans and beasts when he refers to "the assertion of Mr. Clarkson, that no man there can be sold like a beast; (a very figurative, pretty expression; as if a beast was sold in a different manner from any thing else)..." (FA 239).

Francklyn constructs the abolitionists' plans as "productive of the same scenes of slaughter and horror,—of the same impious sacrifices, and diabolical rites, which were heretofore so common in Africa" (FA vi). He also more generally blames the abolitionists for inciting the people to rebellion when, referring to the Gordon riots, he states that he shall not "wonder if the same conflagrations may take place in Liverpool and Bristol, as were experienced in London, under a pretended zeal for the Protestant religion in 1780" (FA 5).

When it comes to slave rebellions, Francklyn generally downplays the theme within the context of his attempt to counter the abolitionist accusations of excessive cruelties. He also uses this to argue for the improvements that he claims to have been made to the whole system. He cites the fact that "mutinies of the slaves on board are so much seldomer heard than formerly" (FA 210) as a sign of the better treatment of the slaves and also points out the insurrections in the islands are more a thing of the past (cf. FA 236).

4.7 Anonymous: *Observations* (1790)

4.7.1 The Anonymous Author

The anonymous author of the short text, *Observations on the Project for abolishing the Slave Trade, and on the Reasonableness of Attempting some Practicable Mode of Relieving the Negroes,* describes himself as resisting "popular tendency, proclaimed by petitions from every part of the kingdom". Thus, his self-image, of one who is writing against the mainstream opinion of his day, is very much in line with that of the other pro-slavery writers which have been dealt with so far. It is safe to refer to the author as a man since he frequently writes about himself using the masculine third person "he".

The writer further refers to himself as a "well-wisher to the empire" (AO 2). He writes that he does not want to appear to be the West Indians' "professed partisan" (AO 72) and even aligns himself with the humanitarian aims of the abolitionists when describing himself as "early and eager in his wishes, that the Negroes might be put on the best footing their situation and the state of things could possibly admit" (AO 5). However, he qualifies his own humanitarianism when suggesting that his humanity is one "regulated by reason, justice, and the public good, without defeating its own endeavours, by aiming at that which is either mischievous, or impracticable" (AO 72).

Concerning the other texts on the topic of the slave trade, the author admits that he "has read few of them, and those but very cursorily" (AO 5). The text contains no hints at any closer connections to the West Indies and does not draw on any personal acquaintance with the Caribbean. The author blames the "warm friends of abolition" (AO 36) for an undue passion, and boasts of his own objectivity when he describes himself as someone who has not the least connection with, or personal interest in, the plantation, or their trade; and it so happens, that, perhaps, no man who has in any degree lived in the world, can have less acquaintance with those who are immediately concerned in the question, than the writer of the present observations (AO 71).

However, he refers to his text as "approved by men of good sense, of good hearts, and of experience in the African trade, and who have resided many years in the West Indies" (AO 16).

As already suggested in the title of his publication, his aim is to suggest improvements to the condition of the Africans during the Middle Passage. This he describes as "an effort in the cause of humanity" and humbly remarks that if he could achieve this he should think his powers of persuasion and eloquence "most laudably exerted" (AO 36).

4.7.2 Synopsis and Argument of Observations

At only 10,537 words, *Observations* is quite a short text and its 72 pages are structured into 78 paragraphs, without any further chapters or sections. The author clearly limits the scope of his text by remarking that it is not necessary to enter a detailed discussion of how the Africans become slaves since it is surely not the European merchants themselves who enslave them (cf AO 15). As already mentioned in the section about the person behind the anonymous author, the text's argumentative aim is to remonstrate "against the inconsiderate and impracticable manner in which a great proportion of the community profess a disposition to relieve Negroes from slavery" (AO 1). The author, like other pro-slavery writers before him, describes it as an ungrateful task "to resist such a popular tendency" (AO 2).

The author blames the abolitionists for secretly wanting to bring about a general emancipation of slaves in the British Empire. He remarks on the change of the abolitionists' objective from emancipation to abolition, stating their aim is "an indirect and future abolition of slavery, and a direct and immediate abolition of the slave trade" (AO 51). He direly warns of "the consequences, glaring as they are, of turning loose 500,000 Blacks against a few thousands Whites, did not seem to create any difficulty to those who proposed such a measure" (AO 50f).

Improve the conditions of the trade

Thus, the author calls for a gradual approach "to relieve the unhappy Negroes on their passage from Africa to the West Indies" and declares it to be his aim to regulate the slave trade so as to "prevent, in great degree, the malpractices justly complained of in the manner of procuring and conveying slaves, and also the loss of seamen" (AO 17). In order to prevent the crowding of the ships, which he sees as the central problem, he proposes four measures concerning the size of the ships and the number of the human cargos (cf. AO 18).

The author cites the usual pro-slavery argument that in Africa the slaves are "at the mercy of their uncivilized master" (AO 34), so that their transfer to the colonies, where their "servitude is regulated by law" (AO 34), is actually a great improvement. The author further points out that the abolition of the slave trade would be counterproductive to the situation of the colonial slave, since the toil of the existing slaves would increase (cf. AO 47).

Colonial matters

As he argues that it is inappropriate for the British parliament to pass ineffectual laws, the author is anxious that it ought to be the governors of the West Indian islands who should be asked to "cause to be brought forward in the several assemblies, such laws and regulations relative to the Negroes as may best answer the purpose of humanity" (AO 8f). In other words, the author wants to see the question of slavery dealt with as a colonial matter.

The anonymous author concludes this argument with the not very subtle warning that "surely we have had enough of interfering with property, and of shutting ports in America" (AO 10) and while the loyal inhabitants of the West Indies "have not yet followed the examples which stare them in the face: but if we proceed, we shall force them to declare their rights" (AO 11).

Situation in the colonies

Concerning the treatment of the slaves in the colonies, the text's argument is the same as Francklyn's, namely that the abolitionists' information is by now obsolete. He points out that in the meantime, the negroes are as well protected by the colonial laws as those of white inhabitants and that they have a right to regular holidays (cf. AO 30). The author also points to the fact that at the moment in Jamaica, there are only eleven executions of Africans per year, which he describes as very little considering "the depraved character of these poor people" (AO 31). Concerning corporal punishment in the colonies, he states that it is certainly not possible to manage the negroes without some sort of chastisement. Although "Negroes are infinitely more manageable than Europeans would be [they] at present really are not prepared or fit for [freedom] and would not be capable of taking care of themselves" (AO 40).

The author is also quite clear in his conviction that there is no alternative to the use of African slaves in the West Indian sugar colonies. While he points out that work of Africans cannot be done by animals (cf. AO 46f), he also states that their work cannot be done by whites, since they cannot stand the climate and there are none available (cf. AO 48f).

Foreign merchants

Another argument in the text is that if the British Parliament actually passed legislation to stop the slave trade, it would simply be transferred to "foreign merchants" (AO13) and this kind of legislation could not "prevent English capitals from being employed in equipping foreign shipping" (AO 13), and such laws would simply be ignored as in Ireland. He later comes back to this argument, stating again that other European nations would gladly step in (cf. AO 52) and that Britain would be drained of capital (cf. AO 54f).

Christianising the Africans and marriage

Like the other pro-slavery authors, the writer of *Observations* seems to be somewhat reluctant regarding the Christianisation of the West Indian slave population. He backs this up with the usual argument that baptism must not be turned into an empty ritual if slaves are driven "by herd to baptism without examination" (AO 32). While he admits that it would be desirable to introduce the institution of marriage among the negroes to "restrain the liscentious intercourse between the sexes" (AO 33), he warns that this might be quite difficult, since the notion of marriage was averse to the Africans' "notion of the Rights of Men" (AO 33).

The essay is concluded by repeating the claim for a gentle abolition (cf. AO 68f). The author then expresses his confidence that the African merchants themselves "can best point out the proper means of preventing the unnecessary, abominable, and barbarous practice, of crouding slaves on board" (AO 70) and stresses that the planters similarly are the ones upon whom "a great deal depends" (AO 70). The last three paragraphs of *Observations* contain the assurance that the assemblies of the West Indian Islands will in due course "take every proper step to promote the happiness and civilization of the Negroes" (AO 71), the remark that, "The civilization of Great Britain required many centuries" (cf. AO 71) and, finally, the hope that the author too will not be seen as a partisan of the West Indians but rather a true friend of humanity.

4.7.3 Ideology

On a superficial level, the anonymous author feigns to agree with the humanity of the project of abolition. However, he criticises how the abolitionists "have declaimed against the slavery in our islands without prudence or moderation ..." (AO 56). The humanitarian claim resurfaces when he suggests that if the measures he proposes were followed, "other nations would soon, in a great degree, adopt our regulations and management, they being calculated to answer all the real purposes of humanity" (AO 25). While he agrees that the slave trade is abominable and that the cruel treatment ought not to stand, he also stresses that the slave trade is in the interest of the empire, and the property of British citizens ought to weigh more heavily than the abolitionists' "false humanity" (cf. AO 4f, and AO 62).

While the text does not feature any fundamental discussion of human nature as such, it relies heavily on the author's claim of the "real humanity" of his suggestions. When it comes to human rights, however, he seems to be anxious to reduce the universalism of the notion. For example, he implies that Africans have a different notion of their human rights from Europeans when he describes their reluctance to marry on the grounds that they consider the resulting restraint of their "licentious intercourse" as an infringement of their human rights (cf. AO 32f). Furthermore, he deliberately evades the discussion of the Africans' humanity when stating that:

> It is useless to dispute whether the human species of one part of the world is naturally more debased, and of weaker intellects, than that of another; but certainly education may do much even for the worst species of the Africans. (AO 42)

In line with this, the author concludes that his composition with the wish not to be seen as a "professed partisan" of the West Indian planters, but rather the "friend of humanity" (AO 72)

When, on the other hand, it comes to a discussion of freedom, the author resorts to the common argument that "the Negroes at present really are not prepared or fit for the state in which many seem desirous of placing them" (AO 40) and is anxious to point to the fact that the freedom of the British husbandman comes with a lot of duties and that a certain degree of dependence might even be preferable to this (cf. AO 44fn), perhaps to be preferred when looking at the situation of the negroes in the colonies.

His downplaying of the value of freedom is complemented by stressing the importance of strict discipline when he asks, "What would the armies and navies of Europe be, if not subjected to a strict discipline? The truth is, that the peasantry of a great part of the world has, at all times, been subject to a degree of arbitrary chastisement" (AO 38). This last part is in line with Francklyn's argument that slavery has always existed in the history of mankind, a notion that can also be found in Francklyn's writing. This author holds that slavery has always existed "and in the most enlightened times, even in a severe degree, and among the most civilized nations" (AO 56). One can see that the author's whole outlook on society is a rather authoritarian one when he writes that "An able minister should watch popular emotions, let the motives be ever so good and justifiable, that he may direct it in such manner as may not promote civil discord and prejudice to the country" (AO 7).

Furthermore, he seems to be quite critical of the French Revolution when he writes that:

> Little argument can be drawn from what may be said or done, at this time, by a neighbouring nation, which seems totally to have changed its character—a nation which has already abused, and may finally lose a glorious opportunity of founding an excellent constitution. The consequence of that country is, at least, suspended for the present, and for some, it will probably lose much of its former estimation and weight in the scale of nations (AO 53).

The only positive aspect he seems to see in the French Revolution is that it provides him with the comfort that "even in their wild career of extravagance" (AO 53), the French have not abolished the slave trade.

Observation is certainly a text which takes a strong counter position. The author points out that the "warm friends to abolition" (AO 55) endanger a cool and deliberate discussion of the issues by their undue passion in the name of humanity. He describes himself as a well-wisher of the empire, which, of course, implies that the measures proposed by the abolitionists are potentially detrimental to the imperial project. This becomes even more threatening in the passage which contains the thinly veiled threat of the West Indians starting a similar revolution as the American colonies 15 years before (cf. AO 11).

Another threat which the author refers to is the danger of slave revolts in the colonies if the Africans misunderstand the intentions of the abolitionists. Although the author had to admit that this has not happened so far, he nevertheless warns of the potential "insurrections and massacres, to which their intemperate declarations might have stimulated the Negroes" (AO 58).

4.8 Clarkson's *Letters* (1790)

4.8.1 Synopsis and Argument of the Letters

Clarkson's text is structured in a series of nine letters, dated between 20 December 1789 and 4 January 1790. Clarkson wrote the *Letters* from Paris, then the capital of revolutionary France, to "several gentlemen, who expressed a wish to be informed of the merits of the question of the Abolition of the Slave-Trade" (CL v). Upon his return to England, as Clarkson reports, he was persuaded by a friend to publish them as he found them useful to acquire a "just idea of the state of society in which the natives live" (CL vi). After the usual polite hesitation, Clarkson writes, he decided to publish such of his letters the contents of which had not "been given to the public in England in other works" (CL vi). At the beginning of his first letter, Clarkson declares it his aim to deal with the different methods of making slaves and with the state of society in which the natives lives (cf. CL 1). Letters I-V are concerned with the first topic while Letters VI-IX deal with the latter.

Clarkson's text can be seen as a reaction to the common pro-slavery claim that slaves are better off in the colonies and that since they are slaves in Africa anyway, their sale to the European merchants, therefore, has a legal basis. In his refutation at the end of the text, Clarkson then refers back to all the detailed information about

African society which he provided in answering the two above-mentioned questions.

After an overview of the various kingdoms and people shown in the map (CL 5f), Clarkson describes the "grand mode of obtaining slaves in these countries ... the Great Pillage, which is executed by the military at the command of their respective kings" (CL 6). The text also deals with ways in which African kings seize their own subjects and sell them into slavery (cf. CL 8ff). Clarkson remarks that the bulk of slaves is obtained in this way since (CL 12) private robbers only number a few as the kings would not tolerate anybody else stealing their subjects. Clarkson then turns to the prisoners of war, writing that in the African wars, only a "few people are either killed or taken" (CL 13). Another source of slaves he mentions are "real or supposed" (CL 13) crimes, as "there is no crime in this part of the world for which they are punished with death" (CL 13).

Clarkson's *Letters* then follow the Senegal River to "the kingdom of Oualo, and the isle of Bisseche" (CL 18). He gives a short overview of the political situation in these kingdoms, stating that Brac, the King of Oualo, is beholden the Moors and the ruler of the Island of Bisseche, a "Seignior, or Lord, who is called Bequio" again is beholden to Brac. Together, they provide 240 slaves each year. The slaves of Oualo are mostly criminals and some "are taken by the king in some kind of pillage" (CL 20). The slaves are provided by the Moors who live on the northern bank of the Senegal River and who make incursions into both the Kingdom of Oualo and the Island of Bisseche. Clarkson describes the cruel manner in which these people, whom he calls "barbarians" (CL 21), obtain the slaves they sell (cf. CL 20ff).

Clarkson continues his account further upstream the Senegal to a part of the country inhabited by the "Independent Poules" (CL 26). He provides a minute description of how "about five hundred slaves may be considered annually to come" from this country (CL 27). He states that the Moors, "these ruffians" (CL 27), obtain 300 of these slaves in the same way as in Oualo and Bisseche by crossing the river on horseback and ravaging the country (cf. CL 27). The remaining 200 slaves are stolen by their own countrymen. These "are in a state of continual warfare with one another ... they seize and plunder where they can [and] sometimes imitate the example of the Moors, and make incursions into Oualoff ..." (CL 28).

Clarkson continues still further up the Senegal River to the country of the "Dependent Poules", who are "are subject to one king" (CL 30). He first relates the story of the heroic usurper, Almammy, who not only stopped the slave trade in his dominion, but also blocked the transport of slaves through his country, causing the French considerable trouble in obtaining their slaves (cf. CL 30ff). Then Clarkson's text leaves "the river Senegal, and turn[s] to the right hand, or South . . . to go overland for two months journey to Bambarra" (CL 33). Clarkson describes "the mode of bringing down the slaves from Bambarra to Fort St. Louis, as it was previously to the year 1787 [i.e. Almammy's stopping the trade]" (CL 34). The author provides a detailed description, including illustrations of the wooden shackles and of how the slaves are marched from Bambarra to Galam by the Mandingoes (cf. CL 35ff), from whence they are transported to St. Louis by the Podor Fleet (cf. CL 38).

In his sixth letter, Clarkson starts dealing with "the state of society in which the natives of Africa ... may be said to live?" (CL 39). He confines his analysis mainly on the kingdom of Cayor, where he defines four social rankings: the king, the blood royalty, the people and their respective slaves. The text describes the king, who goes by the hereditary title, Damel, as the "absolute monarch" (CL 40), a country divided into provinces and villages which are each overseen by different officers of the king, whose orders are carried out by the military (cf. CL 40ff). Clarkson describes how the people of royal blood form a distinct social class and live across the country and must never be sold as slaves (cf. CL 43). Apart from that, he portrays an egalitarian society, in which "there is no distinction in point of rights" (CL 44) and where even the rich "are not considered forming another class" (CL 44).

Clarkson admits that there are slaves in African societies, "small as their numbers are" (CL 45). He divides them into two classes: "such as have once known freedom" and "such as are slaves by birth" (CL 45) and describes African "slavery less a distinction in reality than in the name" (CL 46). The author reports that the slaves share the lives of their masters and "their labour ... not more than the ordinary exercise which men should take" (CL 45). "As to whips, chains, or any other instruments of torture for slaves in these countries, they are totally unknown" (CL 46). Clarkson offers a few remarks on the religion of the country (CL 46ff), stating that the whole country is Muslim and that there are "whole villages, inhabited by the priests of Mahomet" (CL 46). However, "the bulk of the people .... seldom or ever assemble except for the circumcision [and] are little of Mahometans but by name" (CL 47).

Then Clarkson describes "the disposition and state of their villages, houses, lands, and property they possess" (CL 48). The text paints an idyllic picture of village life, in which the land is, for the most part, owned communally, with the exception of palm plantations and cattle. He concludes by pointing out the extreme attachment of the Africans to their villages (cf. CL 54), underlining this with an example of two villages the inhabitants of which had fled to the woods following their pillaging and waited there "for many moons" before returning and rebuilding the deserted village (CL 55) and "re-establishing themselves on their native spot" (CL 55). Clarkson goes on to outline "the different occupations of these people, or the various ways in which the inhabitants of these countries employ themselves in the course of the year" (CL 56). He describes the tools they use for the clearing of the land (CL 56F), how they cultivate their land in the course of the year (cf. CL 57f) and how the harvest is stored and distributed in the village (cf. CL 58f). The text emphasises the Africans' industriousness in an account of how boats are made far in the interior of the country and then carried to the shore due to the lack of good wood there (cf. CL 60).

It is only in the ninth and last letter that Clarkson sets out to use what he has written so far to refute the various main arguments from the pro-slavery side, namely that the slave trade was "a continual saving of human life" (CL 69) and that the slaves are mostly criminals in their own country. Clarkson then sums up the facts about life in Africa to show that the slaves are by no means happier in the colonies than in their native land. He also points out that the slave trade could easily be substituted for another trade with Africa in the light of what he has written about the Africans' spirit of commerce and their industriousness, as proven by the building of boats so far inland (cf. CL 78ff). Clarkson finishes his last letter with a favourable comparison of Africans as noble savages to Europeans:

> The Africans, on the other hand, though they have some bad laws and customs among them, may attribute them in a great measure to the Europeans. Notwithstanding the ignorance and barbarity with which we often charge them, they are not devoid of virtues. To the European master the African exhibits a noble lesson in the mild and gentle treatment of his slave. To the sovereigns of Europe the wise and virtuous Almammy sets a no less illustrious example in extirpating the commerce in the human race. (CL 80f)

4.8.2 Ideology

Clarkson's text is characterised by a tendency to classify things into a hierarchical structure. This is conceptually linked to a distinct mode of static analysis of a certain 'state of society' in which the natives live. This kind of analysis concentrates on static features rather than the lived experiences and processes at work in human life. In addition, the system of collective symbols used in the text implies a tendency towards classification. Clarkson speaks of different "branches of a subject", and the whole composition is structured in accordance with the two African rivers, the Senegal and the Gambia.

Another concept that informs Clarkson's text is the one of "nature". The text uses this to ascribe an inherent logic to the structure of text when he suggests that one topic naturally follows the other. On the other hand, the concept is also present in the form of 'human nature' in the form of what the OED describes as "The inherent power or force by which the physical and mental activities of man are sustained" or "The vital functions as requiring to be supported by nourishment" (OED 'nature' 10a.-b.). In Clarkson's example of an exhausted slave, "nature tells him that he is not sufficiently refreshed" (CL 73) and eventually this "nature is exhausted" (CL 75).

The African society which Clarkson describes in his text seems to fulfil the legitimising function of a primitive original which can attribute universality by the strength of the analogy with the earlier stages of development in a European master narrative. In the following passage, Clarkson portrays African societies as a simplified version of European states.

> The orders of the king are executed in this country, as in the others, by his military ... The king clothes all his military in uniform, giving to each soldier an orange-colored vest ... He feeds them also at his own expense, and makes them small presents of cloth and other articles from time to time. This is considered as their pay. There is no great variety of officers among them as in the European armies. The Laman is considered as one, the Gueraff as another, the Alcaide as a third. These, as commanding under the king in provinces and villages, are the commanders also of his troops, so that three or four hundred men are not broken into many little divisions, but are under the direction of one man.
> Though the people, who are thus employed as soldiers, are military in point of habit, there is little or no discipline among them. (CL 42)

It becomes evident that this kind of portrayal not only justifies a European status quo but also seeks to appropriate and make manageable African Otherness through mimesis: the military in the passage mimic a European ideal type, without fully reaching it. The soldiers do not have full uniforms but only a vest, and they have little discipline. This has a belittling and even a comic effect.

As for the common people in African societies, Clarkson ascribes a general egalitarianism to African societies. Although he describes most of the property as being owned communally by whole families, the author is also eager to point out that properties gained by the personal effort of industrious individuals are exempt from this. These "belong[s] exclusively to those who acquired them" (CL 54) and are then passed on to his next heirs. This certainly reifies the concept of free enterprise and promotes a capitalist concept of the individual worker as a free entrepreneur.

At the end of his *Essay*, Clarkson deals with a potential critique of the African system of government and replies that Europeans ought not to be too boastful about the situation in their own countries, mentioning that not too long ago there was the Bastille, that in "two kingdoms" the Inquisition still existed and that in Britain itself, how "almost impossible it is for the poor man to obtain redress from the injuries of the rich" (CL 78). This certainly has a decentring effect; however, it also promotes universalist notions of the human condition by suggesting a teleological model of progress.

The representation of African societies is ambiguous. Clarkson speaks of many of the African kingdoms having "a system of laws not only partial and wicked in itself, rendered still more intolerable by being interpreted and enforced by a despot" (CL 17). Thus, a European-style claim for liberty and resistance against despotism is transplanted to African societies. The moral impetus for intervention, which this implies, is made all the greater due to the fact, that Clarkson completely links this kind of corruption of the state of nature to the European influence via the slave trade. In the same manner, he describes the kings of Cayor, Sin and Sallum as absolute monarchs because they can pillage their subjects and are not "amenable to any laws" (CL 40) and are themselves the ultimate judges (cf. CL 40).

Other African societies are portrayed as living in a ruder state. However, Clarkson holds the pernicious effects of the slave trade to be responsible for such a more Hobbesian state of affairs. Writing of the "different tribes of the independent Poules" (CL 28) (who are thus called because they live without statehood), Clarkson states that they "are in state of continual warfare with one another", in which they "seize and plunder where they can" (CL 28).

On the other hand, Clarkson portrays African societies as proto-democracies embodying the idea of the social contract, where it fits his argument:

> In Africa every native in his own village is considered as a member of the community, and as a man. He knows no distinction of rank or privilege. He sees but one magistrate over him, and this person no otherwise more powerful than himself, than by being able to bring offenders to trial with the consent of the people. (CL 72)

It is in line with Clarkson's overall depiction of Africa that the dependent Poules, who are the people in his text living farthest upstream the Senegal River and thus least corrupted by their intercourse with the European slave traders, are the only ones whose ruler, Almammy, resisted the slave trade. Clarkson even recommends "the wise and virtuous Almammy" (CL 81) as an example for the European monarchs. Apart from Almammy, Clarkson emphasises the corrupting effect of the intercourse with the Europeans who seduce the various kings "by intoxication and bribery to subvert the just principles of government, and to become wolves instead of shepherds of their people" (CL 80)

Clarkson's fundamental conception of the human in *Letters* is again informed by a mind-body dichotomy when he explicitly writes that the slave trade only takes "possession of the bodies of men" (CL 22). Apart from this, Clarkson adheres to an inherent dichotomy of slave and free man in traditional societies. In this, he agrees with pro-slavery writers like Francklyn (cf. CL 45ff). He describes slaves—"small as their numbers are" (CL 45)—as one of the different ranks of life in traditional African society. While he clearly opposes the institution of slavery as an anachronism, he still acknowledges the long history of the fundamental dichotomy of slave and free (wo-) man.

He writes that the slaves in African societies "may be supposed not to be more disposed to vice than the former [i.e. free men] (for the mind cannot be so broken, where the state of slavery is neither burthensome nor degrading, as to lose all its virtue)" (CE 71). Clarkson implies that slavery as practised in the West Indian plantations does indeed break the mind of its victims and makes them more disposed to vices as free men, which shows that he presupposes a human who is fully accountable for their actions and that the absence of this prompts the critique of the institution of slavery. Consequently, Clarkson refers to the slaves in the colonies as "expunged from the rank of men ... a mere instrument of labour ... put upon a level with the brute" (CL 72).

Clarkson rejects the argument that "the natives of Africa have not the same faculties as other men; by which it is insinuated, that they were born, or at least are fit only for slaves" (CL 77) with references to the organisation of their states "under a regular form of government, with divisions and subdivisions of officers" (CL 77) and the fact that "We see also a certain system of jurisprudence instituted" (CL 77). The whole evaluation of Africans' humanity, of course, bears a distinct Eurocentric tinge: "the above observations on the systems of government, jurisprudence, revenue, and religion, to be found among the natives of Africa, are more than sufficient to establish their capacities as men" (CL 78). This shows that, firstly, it is the European writer who establishes their humanity and, secondly, the frame of reference used in the analysis is a markedly European one.

In his promise that it would not be difficult to substitute the slave trade with other forms of commercial intercourse, Clarkson is eager to present the Africans as *homines oeconomici* who could easily be included in European trading practices:

> They hold a continual intercourse with each other for the purposes of trade, and to such a degree has this spirit of commerce risen, that to procure a market for their commodities they will travel leagues with immense burthens on their heads, and be regardless of the weight. (CL 79)

Similarly, Clarkson describes the making of ships 30 leagues inland in the woods where the wood is good. He emphasises that the enormous effort of cutting down the trees and then transporting the finished boats for at least six leagues to the nearest waterway is accomplished by free men only (cf. CL 60).

> Notwithstanding the wonderful trouble and perseverance from the felling of the trees to the delivery of these boats upon the shore, they fell them at a price which would be hardly credited by an European. (CL 60)

In his description of daily life, Clarkson constructs clear-cut gender roles and work assignments for men and women (cf. CL 8). He also describes a differentiation of labour between male and female slaves in Africa. The men do "out of doors work, collect and bring in wood, and fetch water" and "cultivate the ground" (CL 45). The women, on the other hand, "pound millet, spin cotton, and do other things in the family way" and "do little more than gather cotton at the proper season of the year" (CL 45).

Polygamy is described as a common practice, and the punishment for adultery is being sold into slavery (cf. CL 13f). Interestingly, Clarkson only speaks of women being unfaithful to their husbands, not the other way round.

4.9 Anonymous: *Fugitive Thoughts* (1792)

4.9.1 The Anonymous Author

The author of *Fugitive Thoughts* declares himself to be the "most humble and devoted servant" of *"the MERCHANTS [sic] trading to Africa"* [the author's emphasis] (AF ii). He also writes that it is his aim to communicate "things that are imprinted on my memory, drawn from my own observations during a series of years spent in travelling" although he apologises for not having any journals for assistance (AF iii). Finally, the author considers it his duty against his country to speak up in favour against what he terms "an attempt …. to mislead government" (AF vi). As he describes himself as "a man totally unconnected with commerce, and unknown to any of the mercantile body" (AF vi), it is safe to say that the anonymous writer is male.

The author hints at a certain amount of education which he received when he asks, "Are we not compelled in our youth to very laborious tasks in literature, in order to curb our passions, that we may become useful members of society, and live happy?" (AF 56). Frequent referrals to military issues make me suspect that the author might be somehow connected to the military or navy.

4.9.2 Synopsis and Argument

On a formal level, the text is structured in an introductory dedication to the merchants to Africa, a preface and a main body of text without any chapters. All in all, the text has about 140 paragraphs. In the preface, the author states that he sees it as his duty to not just stand by silently, but warn the nation of the potential harm of the abolition of slavery (cf. AF iii).

The author starts the main part of the text by remarking that the petitions to Parliament are all worthless (cf AF 6f) and compares the momentary frenzy about abolition with the recent "rage for gaming", in which "the mob . . . took the law into their own hands and demolished many of the gaming tables" (AF 8). Describing the whole issue as an instance of "state policy …. in order to divert [public] attention" (AF 10), the author argues that "Grievances abound in these kingdoms, and call loudly for redress; before an attempt is made to abolish slavery abroad, let us look at home, and loose, from habitual shackles, all British subjects" (AF 10). He also ridicules the people who "in the frenzy for abolition, have rejected to use sugar" yet still use other products which "have been produced by the sweat of the negro's toil" (AF 47).

After some diversions to various topics ranging from the American Revolution to the Gordon Riots, the author, probably ironically, concludes his text by remarking that "the Spanish convention, and the French Revolution, have nothing to alarm us" (AF 66) as the people's attention is occupied by abolition and parliamentary reform.

The text again features the usual proslavery arguments. The author, for example, refers to the economic impact on Britain to lopping off "one of our arms" (AF 10). Carrying the argument somewhat further than other pro-slavery writers, he predicts that the economic downfall of the British port cities would lead to such a surge of emigration that eventually the same "short sighted would-be-thought philanthropists" would come up with yet another petition, "namely to enforce an act, to prevent mechanics from leaving the kingdom" (AF 11), which would effectively turn the British worker into a slave. Referring to the Dolben Act of 1788, which limited the number of slaves to be transported on British vessels, the author argues that it would undermine the authority of the British parliament if everything was changed again. Speaking of new vessels specially designed to meet the new requirements (cf. AF 46f), he brings up the topic of compensation for the planters and merchants (AF 46) which would burden the national budget, in addition to the losses for the manufacturing towns. He then argues that the cost of all this would necessarily lead to increased taxes, which would inevitably hit the poor and those in the military hardest (cf. AF 47).

Scriptural and philosophic arguments, however, are relatively absent from the text. It is only once that the author only briefly repeats the usual argument that "many learned writers have proved from the old and the new testaments" the legitimacy of slavery on religious grounds and that also the "church of Rome" (AF 14) approves of it.

Like other pro-slavery texts, this one argues that it is dangerous "to preach up liberty to people who knew not how to make use of it" (AF 29). Referring to the Somerset case, the author states that former slaves in Britain "not knowing the use of money, and being incontinently fond of liquor ... became so insolent and licentious, that their masters turned them out of doors, and the streets were infested with black mendicants" (AF 29).

The main argument of the text is an attempt by the author to relativise the suffering of the African and the allegedly cruel practices connected with the slave trade.

One part of this argument is the authors' explicit, strong focus on the cruelty of the African rulers, which supports the usual argument that it is Britain's duty to bring those "Pagans into a land of plenty, and mixing them with Christians, where their lives are secure" (AF 58). For example, the text contains an account of cannibalistic practices in Bonny and Calabar:

> they sacrifice them, cut them up, cook them, eat them, and drink the broth that is made of them in public boilers; nay more, they even drink their blood, and will not sell them to the ships for any price. (AF 37)

The text argues that "the slave trade has in some measure diminished these inhuman customs, by affording an asylum to those devoted wretches, where their minds may be enlightened, and their bodies beyond the reach of barbarous superstition" (AF 36).

Another technique which the author uses to relativise the inhumanity of the slave trade draws on the equally inhumane practices of metropolitan Britain. He downplays the "violent signs of grief and horror the negroes express when they are leaving their native land" (AF 15) and that "no one instance has been produced, that an African slave deserted from our islands or colonies, to return to his own country" (AF 15). Instead, the author recommends the "abolitioners [sic]" to "view an embarkation of troops, and behold the tear, reluctant stealing down the soldier's manly cheek, his wife and children wringing their hands on shore and suffocating with speechless grief" (AF 15).

The text also argues that the sending of convicts to penal colonies is nothing short of "buying, selling, and transporting christian white flesh to hostile pagan climes" (AF 6) and again suggests that this make a "more immediate impression on the feeling heart than the tales of foreign woe" (AF 11). Later in the text, the author asks, "Where is the distinction between perpetual slavery and transportation to Botany Bay?" (AF 41). Furthermore, he refers to "another traffic in human flesh, [which] is publicly carried on in these kingdoms, nearly atrocious with the former, that is, indenting servants, which they sell in the American markets" (AF 45). The author cites the instance of a vessel with "a vast number of women, the most part of them reduced to skin and bone by hunger and fatigue" (AF 45), calling the attention of the reader to what he explicitly refers to as the "white slave trade …. that prevails in all the sea ports in Scotland and Ireland" (AF 45).

Finally, referring to Clarkson's famous cross-section of a slave ship, he writes "this deception had the desired effect on the illiterate populace" (AF 58) and then explains that the Africans are "lying in the manner described" by their own will as "soon as they got into mild cool weather" (AF 58f).

A considerable part of the text consists of often quite obscure references to the infamous conduct of colonial officers. For example, the author dedicates a number of paragraphs to the conduct of "one of the king's officers who acted as governor in Africa" and who "treated the chiefs and principal negroes on the coast with the greatest cruelty, thereby, for a time preventing the garrison and the traders from the privilege of watering" (AF 17). He blames the British government for not putting a stop to this and thus to have encouraged "the lower class of adventurers in the African trade, seeing that ministry paid no attention to any complaints… to act as despots likewise, whenever they got beyond range of the cannon of an English fort" (AF 20). The text then lists further instances in which the British "government had not even reprimanded their own officers, who, from time to time, had repeatedly committed barbarities and depredations" (AF 25).

At one point the author asks, "What right has an English colony to set down at Botany Bay, and cultivate grounds they never purchased?" (AF 42). What first appears to be a critique of the imperial project is relativised when the author makes clear that he mainly wants to highlight the inconsistency in the abolitionist argument. This becomes more evident when he clearly criticises the British colonial policy after the Treaty of Paris in 1783, when so many islands were given up again—and stresses that now abolition would bring additional ruin to the West Indian colonies (cf. AF 50f).

While the racism in the previous pro-slavery texts is mostly hidden behind humanitarian pretences, the author of *Fugitive Thoughts* is surprisingly outspoken in his race-based justifications for Africans' slavery. For example, he explains how Africans' skin is different from Europeans':

> the vessels and fibres that convey sensation, are of a grosser texture in the blacks, they mind not in travelling through their thorny woods, if a branch should strike one, into their flesh an inch deep; without any seeming concern they will cut it out, and rub the wound with sand by way of styptic, some nations score their children's flesh with a knife .... (AF 28)

As far as the right of the Europeans to the service of the African slaves is concerned, he asks, "What right have negroes on the coast to make the large race of apes, pound corn and draw water for them, whilst they look upon them as a species of human beings?" (AF 28). He concludes the argument with a reference to the Bible, pointing out that God had condemned some nations to be servants (cf. AF 28f).

While the author does not explicitly denounce humanity of Africans, he also seeks to soften the distinction between man and the "brute creation" when he states:

> ... the sense of a negro can scarcely be distinguished from the sagacity of an animal, for, although he has the gift of speech, he dares not use it freely or inquisitively. The naturalists discover a reasoning faculty in the brute creation ... (AF 57)

4.9.3 Ideology

The author's concept of the human is informed by a notion of a fundamental inequality:

> the author of nature has thought fit to mingle, from time to time, among the societies of men, a few, and but a few, on whom he is most graciously pleased to bestow a larger proportion of the ethereal spirit than is given in the ordinary course of providence to the sons of men: there are they who engross almost the whole reason of the species, who are born to instruct, to guide, and to preserve, who are designed to be the tutors and the guardians of human kind. (AF 56)

As already mentioned above, the author deliberately praises the sagacity of some animals in order to blur the human-animal dichotomy, which allows him to ascribe a subhuman status to Africans (cf. AF 57).

Although the author does not deal extensively with the issue of personal freedom, he seems subscribes to the common notion, found both in pro- and anti-slavery texts, that liberty is something that requires a certain degree of maturity and moral disposition to make sensible use of. Writing of American slaves who thought themselves free at the beginning of the American Revolution, the author states that "this instance shews how dangerous it is to preach up liberty to people who knew not how to make use of it" (AF 29).

Generally, the author also uses the concept of humanity to signify positive values. For example, he refers to the slave trade as "the hand of humanity that plucked them from the grave" (AF ii). However, in tune with what has been written about the various diversion strategies in the text, the author again claims that "real" humanity rather ought to concern itself with more pressing issues. Probably in an attempt to mock the frequent allegorical uses of the concept of humanity, the author asks, "Was humanity in the Aurelia state and only now to be animated by the Wilberforcean heat of delusive eloquence, to flutter about, the gaudy butterfly of the day?" (AF 19).

The text puts relatively heavy emphasis on human sexuality as a fundamental drive and source of human motivation. He refers to it as "a passion implanted by nature, and sometimes too strong, for the most enlightened christian to control" (AF 31), showing the control over one's sexual drive is made a sign of enlightenment. Thus, the author describes the situation in Africa as promiscuous polygamy, in which the rich hold "a monopoly of any number of women that their estates can maintain" (AF 30) and outside the African villages "there [prostitutes] … who are obliged, for a stipulated fare, to indulge the passions of all ages and descriptions" (AF 31). In turn, he writes that African women "are by constitution lascivious, their dances express it by indecent gesticulation" (AF 30) and that they "cannot have their desires satisfied" by only one man, leading to frequent adultery, for which slavery is the slightest punishment (cf. AF 30).

Accordingly, he attributes the sentimental scenes at embarkation not so much to the pain of parting from friends and families, but to more carnal desires:

> Africans being the most lascivious of all human beings, may it not be imagined, that the cries they set forth at being torn from their wives, proceeds more from the dread that they never will have an opportunity of indulging their passions in the country to which they are embarking. (AF 15)

The author sees the same motive "when sailors impressed into our service, see an opportunity to regain the shore, and enjoy their wives or lasses" (AF 29).

The author is certainly critical of too much popular participation when he contrasts Britain and revolutionary France and praises the regulating function of the peers and the British monarch. He writes that if in France, the same popular frenzy for abolition had broken out, "the National Assembly must have acquiesced with the request of the people" since there is "no upper chamber of control … and majesty must have ratified an abolition" (AF 61) despite having a better judgement. Towards the end of the text, the author again expresses his hope that British bicameralism will prevent the nation from suffering any damage as:

> the members of the upper house, holding their feats independent of the people's suffrages, were not content with hearsay evidence, or flowery declamations in the house, they determined to examine upon oath, and decide accordingly, cool reason begins now to take place, and the fallacy of many accusations will be proved, which in the end must convince the public, that the enemies to the African slave trade, are not the friends of the public. (AF 60f)

The author is also cynical in terms of social class. While wondering why no one has yet stepped forward to propose a plan to stop the progress of vice, he supposes "that if the lower classes of the people were enabled by their industrious labour to bring up their children, and live at ease, we should not be able to recruit our army, or man our fleets?" (AF 13f).

It is an interesting feature of *Fugitive Thoughts* that it contains a substantial discussion of Native Americans. The title of the work already promises the text to be "Interspersed with Cursory Remarks on the Manners, Customs, and Commerce, of the African [sic] and American Indians" (AF i). The author constructs an image of Native Americans which serves as a contrast for Europeans and Africans alike, even styling them as a role model for the perfect ruler:

> The Sachems or chiefs of the Indians are always the poorest and worst clad, they are above the idea of keeping anything to adorn or make themselves comfortable, if a person of inferior capacity is in want within the village, it is not outward appearance or birth, that commands respect there. (AF 53)

He speaks of them as "a people endowed with every quality that adorns the human heart; having no wants but what spontaneous nature supplied, envy dwelt not amongst them, they had no emulation but in such arts as most tended to general welfare," (AF 52).

Human societies in the state of nature are thus represented in two forms in the text. While the Native American societies are portrayed in an extremely positive light, their African counterparts are described as living in a more brutal state. I have already shown above that the author puts a lot of emphasis on the cruel practices of African societies. On a more general level, he quotes Abbe Raynal remarking that "in all savage countries, the inhabitants cannot subsist in proportion to their increase, but must perish, or be put to death" (AF 36).

4.10 "Mercator": *Letters* (1807)

4.10.1 Biographical Note

According to Hogg's bibliography on British abolition, the author behind the pseudonym "Mercator" is John Gladstone (cf. Hogg, *Slave Trade* 184), a wealthy merchant and father of the later prime minister, William Gladstone. Gladstone was born in 1764 in Leith, the son of a local merchant. At the age of 13, he entered an apprenticeship with the Edinburgh Roperie and Sailcloth Company, after which he entered his father's thriving business. In 1786, he started a partnership with Edgar Corrie of Liverpool. The partnership soon traded in American grain and tobacco, upon which Gladstone's later fortune was based. After he ended this partnership 1801, Gladstone dealt in ship insurance, ship owning and Liverpool real estate. In 1803, he entered the West Indian trade and bought several estates, which eventually made him one of the largest absentee owners in the British West Indies (cf. Quinault, *Gladstone* 363), especially in Demerara. Although he never visited the West Indies personally, Gladstone became known as a stout defender of West India interests, especially in the course of a longer controversy in the *Liverpool Courier* with the anti-slavery writer James Cropper (cf.

Matthew, *Gladstone*; Davis, *Human Progress* 184). Upon the emancipation of slaves in the British colonies, Gladstone received a substantial compensation of £93,000 for the 2,000 slaves he owned (cf. Quinault, *Gladstone* 370). Furthermore, Gladstone is mentioned in the scholarly work on abolition for his ownership of Quamina and Jack Gladstone, who led the 1823 slave rebellion in Demerara (cf. Hochschild, *Chains* 328ff).

Gladstone's style of writing is characterised by the use of the inclusive pronouns "us" and "we" to refer to the reader. He clearly sides with the planters and merchants trading with the West Indies. He uses the pseudonym "Mercator"; however, this seems to be for different reasons than other pro-slavery writers had for using pseudonyms. Writers like Tobin and the anonymous "Gentlemen of St. Christopher" clearly wanted to hide their identity either because they really feared the damage to their reputation or because it was in line with the self-image of resisting an overwhelming public opinion. Gladstone's use of the Latin term for merchant seems to be an attempt to assume a position of speaking that is larger than life. It is not just John Gladstone of Liverpool who is writing these letters but the personified West-Indian merchant. The obscuring of his identity seems to be of secondary importance. While he also used the pseudonym in his controversy with James Cropper, the West India Association of Liverpool readily revealed his identity when they published *The Correspondence Between John Gladstone, Esq., MP. and James Cropper, Esq.* in 1824 (cf. Sheridan 249).

4.10.2 Synopsis and Argument of the Letters

Mercator's text is structured as two letters to an anonymous recipient only referred to as "Sir". The two letters are signed "Mercator". The text does not contain any background information about the setting or the motivation of the letters.

The first letter starts with a reference to the imminent discussion of a bill "for the immediate and total abolition of the slave-trade" (ML 3) at the next session of parliament. Mercator's first critique is the inconsistency of British legislature, which is about to harm the very people who "have only been the humble instruments of accomplishing the declared purpose of the British parliament … thereby adding to the wealth and strength of the British Empire" (ML 4). Siding with the planters' claim for indemnification, he censors the hypocrisy of stopping the slave trade on moral grounds while keeping the profits of it (cf. ML 5f). Mercator explains the constant need of "a constant supply of negroes from Africa" (ML 8) by pointing to the similarly decreasing population "in the manufacturing towns of England" (ML 7) to which is added in the West Indies "the ardent and uncontroled influence of the passions, where a promiscuous intercourse of the sexes takes place, where, consequently, fewer children are born, and where the climate is unpropitious both to health and longevity?" (ML 7)

Like so many before him, Mercator readily admits that, viewed in an abstract light, the slave trade is "irreconcilable to the principles of humanity and natural justice" (ML 8) However, he argues:

> having been so long established and acted upon, we are not now to consider the abolition of it abstractedly, but relatively, in all its bearings and consequences; or, in the excess of a blind though laudable zeal, we may occasion more mischief than we remedy, and injure the cause we mean to promote. (ML 9)

Furthermore, Mercator states that far from being forbidden by any religious precepts, "Slavery was expressly ordained by the law of Moses" (ML 9).

Next, he does away with the argument against the slave trade based on the rights of man. After pointing to the excesses in France in the name of human rights, he argues that "in the happiest communities, great sacrifices of the liberty of the individual are made for the general good" (ML 10). Mercator cites impressed seamen and the situation of the poor in England who "are as effectually doomed to labor in the parishes where they are born as the slaves in the West Indies are on the estates to which they belong" (ML 11). He then argues that the instances of cruel treatment of slaves have been "grossly exaggerated" (ML 12) and that "to argue from the abuse of an institution against the use of it is very unsound logic [since] no human institution can be free from abuses" (ML 13).

Asking how abolition will benefit humanity, Mercator points out that the result "of the abolition of the slave-trade, by Great Britain alone, will be the aggrandizement of foreign merchants and foreign colonies at the expense of her own" (ML 15). Furthermore, Mercator predicts that "Insurrections and massacres will be the consequence; the horrors of St Domingo will be renewed in our islands and the race of whites be speedily exterminated" (ML 16) since the Africans will "rationally conclude, that, if it be unlawful to make them slaves, it must be unlawful to keep them so" (ML 16). He then argues that if the colonies should "escape falling prey to revolutionary horrors, [they] will sink under the no less sure, though slower, operation of gradual decay, and the planters will emigrate from our own islands to foreign possessions, where their labours will be properly appreciated and rewarded" (ML 17). Mercator concludes his first letter by repeating his claim that, "The West-India planters and merchants ... must also be indemnified for whatever losses they may sustain by the prohibition of it ..." (ML 19). He adds the warning that "as a false philosophy lately deluged France with blood and revolutionary horrors, so a false philanthropy is preparing similar evils for Great Britain" (ML 20).

In his second letter, Mercator promises the anonymous addressee "a few observations on the subject as a measure of political economy, considering it solely as it relates to the inhabitants of Africa" (ML 20). Drawing on Mungo Park's travels, he points to the Africans' "aversion to regular labour" and their subsistence "on the spontaneous fruits of the earth, and such animals as they can either domesticate or procure by the chase" (ML 20f). This limited supply of food has the result that "the surplus of the population must either emigrate to some other country or starve" (ML 21). Mercator compares the population of Africa to rabbits in a field from which every year a "hundred pair" are removed to keep the "warren in good order" (ML 22). He points out that in a similar process, "the superfluous population of the barbarous nations in the north of Europe formerly overflowed in periodical eruptions upon their more civilised neighbours" (ML 25) and that, accordingly:

> The slave-trade, therefore, is now the substitute for famine and the sword; and the population of Africa is kept down to its necessary level, by the export of the superfluous numbers to the West Indies. (ML 27)

Thus, Mercator argues, the consequence of abolition in Africa would either be starvation or the revival of "the practice of putting prisoners to death" (ML 28). He then points to the origin of the "system of slavery which prevails in Africa .... probably in the remotest ages of antiquity, before the Mahomedans crossed the desert" (ML 29). For Mercator, these facts provided by Park, "completely exculpates the Europeans from the charge of having established a system of slavery in Africa" (ML 30).

He concludes the text by suggesting that rather than abolish the trade in Africans, the abolitionists should promote "their civilisation and instruction, and thus gradually bringing about the necessary alteration in their habits and manners" (ML 31) in order to "render their country capable of producing a much greater quantity of food, and of maintaining a much greater number of inhabitants" (ML 31).

4.10.3 Ideology

This author expresses criticisms of the Rights of Man. Writing of "new-fangled doctrines" (ML 10), he points to the horrors of the French Revolution, when he warns that "the conduct of their supporters in a neighbouring country should operate as a warning, not as an example" (ML 10). On the whole, Mercator seem to call for a more pragmatic view of human rights when he argues that even, "in the happiest communities, great sacrifices of the liberty of the individual are made for the general good, and something very nearly allied to slavery exists even in this just-boasted land of freedom" (ML 10). He asks "is the impressing of our seamen consistent with the rights of men or the liberty of the subject?" (ML 10).

Mercator constructs a fundamental categorical difference between free men and slaves: "These men were born to political rights and know their value. The slave was born a slave, without political rights, and is ignorant even of the meaning of the term" (ML 11). However, when it comes to slavery and individual freedom in Africa, he subscribes to a strictly contractual notion of human freedom. He quotes Mungo Park that in Africa, "there are many instances of free men voluntarily surrendering their liberty to save their lives". (ML 23) and also "the weak or unsuccessful warrior begs for mercy beneath the uplifted spear of his opponent ... gives up at the same time his claim to liberty and purchases his life at the expense of his freedom" (ML 28).

The usual abstract and allegorical notions of humanity can again be found in *Letters*. The author refers to the "altar of humanity" (ML 4) and allegorically describes humanity as "feel[ing] outraged" (ML 13). Thus, Mercator indeed acknowledges humanity as a universal value and even states, "as an abstract question, it must be admitted, that it is irreconcilable to the principles of humanity and natural justice" (ML 8). However, he argues that "one moral virtue is not to be trampled upon that another may be exalted .... [and] the votaries of humanity must not be the violators of justice" (ML 4f) and that "the cause of humanity will be injured instead of being benefited" (ML 15).

When Mercator discusses the origin of slavery, he writes that:

> The aversion to labour, so conspicuous a feature in the character of all uncivilized people, was probably the origin of slavery; as it induced those who possessed any superiority, either natural or acquired, to avail themselves of it, by compelling others to labour for them. (ML 27)

For the author, this is the crude foundation of society until "the laws of war were softened by civilization" (ML 28).

Mercator quotes Mungo Park, who laments "that a country, so abundantly gifted and favoured by nature, should remain in its present savage and neglected state" (ML 21). The Africans are described as living in a state of society in which "food is provided by the hand of nature, unless they add to the natural productions of the earth by labour and cultivation" (ML 21). Accordingly, if their number increases "the surplus of the population must either emigrate . . . or starve" (ML 21). Mercator subsequently compares the Africans to a warren of rabbits in a field of limited size (cf. ML 22) and writes that "Man, in a savage and independent state, scorns labour; considers it as degradation, and imposes it on those over whom he can exercise authority" (ML 23f).

While Mercator makes the abolition of slavery a sign of "civilized countries" however, he is anxious to point out there "the necessity of labour is impressed upon the minds of the whole, and actuates the conduct of the greater part of the community" (ML 25). He describes this highest state of civilisation as one in which "artificial wants, supply endless sources of occupation and keep up a constant circulation of property, which is diffused throughout all the members of the body politic, and provides every individual with the means of maintaining himself by the earnings of his own industry" (ML 25).

4.11 Wilberforce: *Letter* (1807)

4.11.1 William Wilberforce

William Wilberforce was born on 24 August 1759 in Hull as the third child of Robert and Elizabeth Wilberforce. After his father's early death, he lived with his uncle, William, at London and Wimbledon, where his aunt first acquainted him with evangelism, while his family temporarily managed to "distract him from such enthusiastic religion" (Wolffe). Wilberforce, however, was to return to evangelism after an "evangelical conversion experience" and to become a central figure of the Clapham Sect and leader of the group of evangelical saints among the MPs throughout his political career (cf. Wolffe).

Wilberforce was educated at St. John's College, Cambridge, where he took his MA in 1788. While still at Cambridge, he was elected MP for Hull in 1780 at the young age of 21. Wilberforce was to serve continually as MP for Hull, Yorkshire and, eventually, Bramber until his retirement from Parliament in 1825 due to failing health. It was at Cambridge that he formed a life-long friendship with the later Prime Minister, William Pitt the Younger. In his own words, Wilberforce's parliamentary life was characterised by a divine mission to deal with "two great objects, the suppression of the slave trade and the reformation of manners" (Wilberforce and Wilberforce, Vol 1. 149). The claim for the moral and spiritual renewal of the nation was expressed in his 1797 *A Practical View on the Prevailing Relgious System of Professed Christians in the Higher and Middle Classes of this Country Contrasted with Real Christianity*, which was widely read and exerted a considerable degree of influence (cf. Wolffe).

Due to a stress-related illness, which had forced Wilberforce to convalesce at Bath and Cambridge, he entered the parliamentary campaign against the slave trade somewhat belatedly with his first abolitionist speech on 12 May 1788. Despite various setbacks Wilberforce never tired of campaigning for the human rights of African slaves during the rest of his parliamentary life. The French Revolution and the war with France only proved to be temporary setbacks for the cause of abolition and Wilberforce finally managed to get his abolitionist Bill passed in the spring of 1807. Shortly before that, Wilberforce had summed up the state of evidence and argumentation in his *A Letter on the Abolition of the Slave Trade*. The feat of passing the Abolition Bill greatly enhanced Wilberforce's public standing.

In 1813, he repeated his earlier claim for the propagation of Christianity in India. In what has been seen as one of his most compelling speeches in the Commons (cf. Wolffe), Wilberforce urged people "to communicate to our fellow-subjects in India, the benefits of Christian light and moral improvement" (Wilberforce, *Substance* 81). The result of his efforts was the foundation of the Bishopric of Calcutta. Wilberforce strongly sought to include the abolition of the slave trade in the peace settlement after the Napoleonic wars and supported the Imperial Registry Bill for colonial slaves.

In the 1820s, Wilberforce renewed his efforts for the campaign to end slavery, supporting the Anti-Slavery Society by publishing his 1823 *Appeal to the Religion, Justice and Humanity of the Inhabitants of the British Empire in Behalf of the Negro Slaves in the West Indies*. Due to his failing health, however, he approached Thomas Fowell Buxton to become his successor in the parliamentary campaign against slavery. Wilberforce supported Buxton's efforts in parliament and took part in anti-slavery campaigns. In one of his last speeches in the Commons, Wilberforce spoke on the court martial and execution of the missionary, John Smith, at Demerara for allegedly exciting the slaves to rebellion. He called attention to the "colonial esprit de corps" (*House of Commons Debate* 11 June 1824) when he criticised how Smith had been tried by a military rather than a civilian tribunal, which prevented his appealing to a British court.

In early 1825, he finally resigned from Parliament, which seems to have been beneficial for his health after all, since he was to live for another eight years until 29 July 1833. He is buried in Westminster Abbey next to his friend, William Pitt the Younger.

Self-representation in texts

Wilberforce presents his own character very much within a context of piety and morality. For example, when he addresses his text to "all the inhabitants of the British Empire, who value the favour of God, or are alive to the interests or honour of their country—to all who have any respect for justice, or any feelings of humanity, I would solemnly address myself" (WA 1). He again creates an ideological in-group when he writes that slavery must shock "every liberal mind" (WA 56). The author, thus, also creates a British national identity based on a shared guilt when he writes of the slave trade as "a crime to which we cling in defiance of the clearest light" (WL 5) and states that:

> ... we are more criminal than the West Indians, for having suffered such a system to gain an establishment, and to grow to its present size; and we shall be still a thousand times more criminal than they, if, with our eyes at length opened to its evils, we suffer it to continue unreformed. (WL 175)

The text is characterised by a strong sense of national identity. The typical speaking position of "us" and "we" indeed was instrumental in the creation of a British national identity, as Swaminathan argues (11f). Wilberforce refers to Britons as "the most free, enlightened, any happy people that ever existed upon earth" (WL 42) and describes Great Britain as "free, just, and honourable" (WL 311). The Britishness the author constructs, however, is of a distinctly Christian type. He writes that the slave trade is "disgraceful to us as a Christian nation" (WL 43) and describes it as a gross absurdity that "in Africa, Christianity and Mahometanism appear to have mutually interchanged characters" (WL 43f).

4.11.2 Synopsis and Argument of the Letter

Wilberforce starts his text by dedicating it to his constituency, expressing that he aims to explain why he dedicated his efforts to the cause of abolition. *Letter* then turns to the various sources of information on the slave trade and to the difficulties of obtaining evidence (cf. WL 11). Wilberforce then points to the valuable evidence obtained before the House of Commons—despite intimidations of witnesses—and to the works of Winterbottom, Park and Golberry (cf. WL 11f).

In the next section of *Letter*, Wilberforce outlines the usual sources of slaves in Africa and the devastating effects the slave trade has had on African societies, prisoners of war, victims of "village breaking" and "predatory excursions" (WL 20ff). He refers the reader to the corruption of the administration of justice in Africa, and other reasons for enslavement in Africa, such as superstitions about witchcraft and insolvency or starvation (cf. WL 25ff). Wilberforce then describes the different effects of the slave trade on the coast and in the interior, creating an image of social harmony inversely proportionate to a pernicious European influence (cf. WL 34f).

Wilberforce heartily laments that through the slave trade, the Europeans have erected a barrier preventing "any rays of the religious and moral light and social improvements of our happier quarter of the globe might penetrate into the interior, and thus lock up the whole of that vast continent in its present state of wretchedness and darkness" (WL 41). The text points to the influence of Islam, which "has scattered a few faint beams of learning among these poor people" and cites Mungo Park in stating that "the Mahometan converts among them think but very lightly of our superior attainments in religious knowledge" (WL 45f) and "look upon us ... as little better than a race of formidable but ignorant Heathens" (WL 46).

He then turns to the alleged pro-slavery argument that the Africans are an inferior race (cf. WL 54) and to pro-slavery descriptions of Africans (especially Long and Edwards). Wilberforce refers to Long as a "commonly respectable author" (WL 56) and rationalises this author's hyper negative representations of Africans with the

> ... state of contempt into which the whole race had fallen, in the estimation of those who had known them chiefly in that condition of wretchedness and degradation into which a long continued course of slavery had depressed them. (WL 61)

Wilberforce contrasts this with the more recent accounts of the "negro character" by Park, Winterbottom and Golberry. He calls the description of the "negro character" in Mungo Park "a relief to the humane mind" (WL 65) as "Mr. Parke represents the Africans of the interior as naturally superior, both in their intellectual and moral endowments, to almost any other uncivilized nation" (WL 66).

The author then deals with what he refers to as the startling fact that "Africa, which contains nearly a third of the habitable globe, should never at any period have been reclaimed from a state of comparative barbarism" (WL 73). In order to illustrate how it is that "civilization and the arts grow up in any country" (WL 74), he offers the account of universal history tracing "the actual progress of human civilization from the very earliest times" (WL 74). Wilberforce's grand conclusion of this is that it could as well have been "the interior of Africa had been made by the Almighty the cradle of the world" (WL 80) and favourably compares Africa to the "state of Britain herself, when she was first visited by the Romans". This leads him to the assessment that the Africans are "at the very threshold of the full enjoyment of all civil and social blessings" (WL 84) if it were not for the negative impact of the slave trade.

Wilberforce then refutes the common argument that the enslavement of Africans is actually doing them a favour, first on the grounds "that we had no right to make men happy against their will" (WL 90) and by describing the "real state of the Africans" (WL 91) as "a species of feudal or rather of patriarchal vassalage" (WL 91). He describes the alleged cruelty of the African kings as similarly exaggerated as the argument that the unsold slaves would be massacred in the case of abolition (cf. WL 93ff).

The text then turns to the Middle Passage, the horrible conditions on board the slave ships (cf. WL 97) and the situation of slaves in the West Indies (WL 103ff). Concerning the first topic, Wilberforce cites the parliamentary action to improve this situation, especially the Dolben Act, despite which "many of the sufferings of these wretched beings are of a sort, for which no legislative regulations can provide a remedy" (WL 99).

Wilberforce then looks to the West Indies and deals with the "grand allegation of the West Indians that the stock of slaves cannot be kept up without importations" (WL 103). He first replies that he could "not believe that the prosperity of the West Indies must necessarily be built on a foundation of injustice and cruelty" (WL 104), especially since the "Negroes were said to be by nature peculiarly prolific" (WL 105). Since the increase in the slave population is at the moment not the centre of the planters' attention, he proposes a "breeding system" as opposed to the present "working down and buying system" (WL 117). This would remedy the fact that the West Indians are "importing a too small proportion of females" (WL 119). Wilberforce counters the pro-slavery claim for the continuance of the slave trade based on the need to keep slave populations stable, in three steps. He first argues that the abuses of the West Indian system are sufficient to account for a great decrease in population.

Among the vices of the West Indian system, Wilberforce sees "the Negroes, as a race, being sunk into the lowest state of degradation" (WL 127). He then cites various "Instances of Degradation" (WL 133) in the West Indies, such as that the slaves are insufficiently protected by the law in that West Indian proprietors are hardly punished for "wanton acts of cruelty" (WL 150). Wilberforce sees three further vices of the West Indian system as being responsible for this situation: absenteeship (cf. WL 177ff), pressure of time (WL 186ff) and speculations (cf. WL 190). After this Wilberforce states his second proposition, namely that despite the wretched situation of the slaves, the decrease in their population is not as big as expected (cf. WL 211ff), from which he infers his third proposition, that if the abuses of the slaves were corrected, the slave populations would rapidly increase (cf. WL 215f).

The author also deals with the claim of the pro-slavery lobby in Parliament that Britain ought to give the West Indian slaves and planters time to accommodate the change and that the situation of the slaves cannot be ameliorated without "the aid of such regulations as could only be enacted by the West Indian legislatures themselves" (WL 216). Wilberforce rejects this kind of playing for time in favour of direct intervention since the "Colonial Legislatures [are] neither able nor willing to effect the abolition, by regulations as to the detail of management of Slaves" (WL 222). He describes the colonial efforts at reform to be merely lip service to appease the abolitionists' supporters and points out the inefficacy of the French and Portuguese slave codes (cf. WL 232ff). He concludes the argument with a stern warning that the improvement of the slaves' situation is indispensable for preventing future revolts (cf. WL 235ff).

He then lists the positive effects of abolition, which he primarily sees as West Indians being forced to think harder about the introduction of "the breeding system" (WL 243). As whole communities would commit themselves to the better treatment of their slaves, the Africans would become more "susceptible of the restraints, obligations, duties, and comforts of the marriage state" (WL 246) and would "gradually and insensibly be transformed into a native peasantry" (WL 250).

After arguing that immediate abolition is preferable to a gradual one (cf. 254ff), Wilberforce deals with the accusation of inconsistency for not emancipating the slaves right away. He makes clear that the immediate freeing of the slaves would be like granting "the unconstrained enjoyment of his natural liberty to an unfortunate human being, who, by long imprisonment and severe treatment, had been driven into a state of utter madness" (WL 258). He also emphasises that the liberty he is speaking of is "the child of reason and law, the parent of order and happiness" (WL 258) and certainly not "the wild licentiousness of a neighbouring kingdom [i.e. France]" (WL 259).

Wilberforce then deals with the economic aspects of abolition both in the African and the West Indian branch of the commerce and argues that the present system is ruinous (WL 266ff) due to its highly speculative nature and to the fact that British capital is drained to the West Indies (cf. WL 271ff). Thus, the author argues that the abolitionists have saved the West Indians from financial disaster by stopping the importation of slaves into foreign colonies and into "those possessions chiefly in Guiana, which in the present war have been again conquered from the enemy" (WL 283), which would have put the ancient possessions at a disadvantage and led to their ruin (cf. WL 284f).

Wilberforce then considers the argument that other nations would simply take over the business, remarking that no one would at the present time of war be so mad as to invest their capital "out of the only country in which either person or property can now be deemed secure" (WL 307). He then points to the fact that the United States was already set to abolish the trade in 1808 as soon as their constitution allowed it to. He concludes by stating that slave trade would never stop if every nation waited for the others to end it— furthermore, Britain would most likely be looked up to by others as an example (WL 310ff).

The last chapters of the *Letter* contain Wilberforce's positive argumentation for abolition on the grounds of justice, religion and the danger of insurrections. Under the heading of justice, Wilberforce deals with the question of compensation for the planters but rejects the idea because this would be to suppose that the planters would suffer from this measure and that it would be "injurious to their interests" (WL 317). Concerning the religious side of the abolition debate, he argues "that Christ has done away all distinctions of nations, and made all mankind one great family, all our fellow creatures are now our brethren", therefore, Christianity clearly forbids keeping Africans "in a state of slavery" (WL 319). When it comes to the danger of insurrections, Wilberforce argues that abolition of the trade is indispensable for the security of the colonies for two reasons. Firstly, the constant importations from Africa aggravate the danger of insurrections by increasing "the disproportion between Blacks and Whites" (WL 322). Secondly, through the Haitian revolution, "almost with the visible horizon of our largest island, Negroes have been taught but too intelligibly the fatal secret of their own strength" (WL 324).

Wilberforce ends the *Letter* with a "summary view of the miseries produced by the slave trade" and points to one "instance of individual misery" (WL 340ff) in which he follows one African from some "some nightly attack on his dwelling" (WL 341) in Africa, to "a Negro's comfortless life" (WL 345) in one of the European colonies. Tellingly, Wilberforce concludes *Letter* by drawing a comparison with the downfall of the Roman Empire and issues a severe warning:

> ... if we are not blind to the course of human events, as well as utterly deaf to the plain instructions of Revelation, we must believe that a continued course of wickedness, oppression, and cruelty, obstinately maintained in spite of the fullest knowledge and the loudest warnings, must infallibly bring down upon us the heaviest judgments of the Almighty. (WL 350)

4.11.3 Ideology

Freedom vs. social order

Wilberforce's concept of freedom is one carefully balanced with the need for social order. In this, his text very much reflects what Davis has called the fundamental dilemma of Enlightenment thought (cf. Davis, *Revolution* 263). Wilberforce calls "true liberty ... the child of reason and law, the parent of order and happiness" (WL 258), and throughout his text, he advocates the rule of law and civil order against unrestrained freedom à la the French Revolution, which he describes as "wild licentiousness" and liberty's "perfect contrast, both in nature and effects" (WL 258f). His historical analysis is also informed by this when he asks:

> How is it that civilization and the arts grow up in any country? The reign of law and of civil order must be first established. From law, says a writer of acute discernment and great historical research, from law arises security; from security, curiosity; from curiosity, knowledge. (WL 74)

Thus, he also sees the merit of the ancient Romans mainly in providing "the established regularity and order of a Roman province" (WL 77) and "the blessings of civil order and security" (WL 81). Social subordination is also clearly the more important value for the author when he writes about the existing slavery in Africa:

> The existence of this milder species of vassalage may even facilitate the complete civilization of the negro nations, by having familiarized their minds to the gradations of rank, and by having accustomed them to submit to the restraints of social life, and to be controlled by the authority of law and custom. (WL 92)

This clearly infers that the emergence of European nations, and especially Britain, out of medieval feudalism was instrumental in creating the present political situation. Wilberforce writes about Britain:

> We enjoy a political constitution of government, eminent above all others for securing to the very meanest and weakest the blessings of civil liberty, of personal security, and equal laws yet we take the lead in maintaining this accursed system, which begins in fraud and, violence, and is consummated in bondage and degradation. (WL 42)
>
> But to all the foregoing considerations, add that new aggravation of the dangers of our West Indian colonies, that, almost within the visible horizon of our largest island, the Negroes have been taught but too intelligibly the fatal secret of their own strength. (WL 324)

Humanity

The concept of humanity seems to serve as an umbrella term for a secular set of moral values in Wilberforce's *Letter* since he refers on one occasion to "motives of Christian zeal as well as of humanity" (WL 45). He uses the term "humanity" 39 times; it most frequently collocates with the concept of "justice" (16 times), which also hints at it being a complementary concept to Christian compassion. I suspect that Wilberforce might have felt that arguing on purely religious grounds might not have been as effective with the British mainstream.

Wilberforce is clear about Africans belonging to the human species and paternalistically refers to them as "our fellow creatures" (17x), boasting that "Happily, the friends of these wretched beings have, at length, obtained the recognition of their human nature" (WL 287). However, Wilberforce clearly distinguishes between the natural qualities of men, which he in the case of the Africans highly praises, and the state of social improvement of both individuals and societies. While he explicitly argues that "it might scarcely be justifiable to withhold from the Africans the name of men" (WL 55), he seems to see it as far less problematic that authors like Long and Edwards describe them as, "manifestly inferior to the rest of the human species, both in their intellectual and moral powers" (WL 55). The only thing he criticises is that this inferiority be not seen in an essentialist way and that they cannot gain advantages "from an intercourse with polished nations" (WL 83), as he frequently hints at in his historical analysis. He holds the degrading treatment of the slave trade as being solely responsible for the degraded state of the slaves when he writes that, "their natural character must necessarily have derived a deep taint from the depraving effects of a long continued state of slavery" (WL 64). The dichotomy between the natural qualities and the degrading effects of their treatment becomes quite clear when Wilberforce describes the slaves as having been nearly depressed

> to a level with the brute creation, the negro Slaves instinctively adapt themselves to their level, and are immersed in merely animal pursuits. Hence it is, that those very Negroes, who in Africa are represented as so eminent for truth, so disinterested in kindness, so faithful in the conjugal and domestic relations, so hospitable, so fond of their children, of their parents, of their country, gradually lose all these amiable dispositions with the enjoyments which naturally arise out of them, and become depraved and debased by all that is selfish and mercenary, and deceitful, timid and indolent, and tyrannical. (WL 246)

It is in this context that Wilberforce strongly draws on Park's account of the Africans in the interior of the country which portrays them as noble savages: "Park represents the Africans of the interior as naturally superior, both in their intellectual and moral endowments, to almost any other uncivilized nation" (WL 66). Towards the end of his *Letter*, Wilberforce declares:

> I must once more raise my voice against that gross misconception of the character of the Negroes (an impeachment of the wisdom and goodness of their Creator no less than of our own), which represents them as a race of such natural baseness and brutality as to be incapable of religious impressions and improvements.(WL 247)

This shows that this kind of inclusion to the human ~~race~~ does not come without any strings attached. What the passage criticises is that the African is seen as "incapable of religious impressions and improvements" (WL 247), which clearly includes them in a very Eurocentric discourse of reform.

Self-interest

Wilberforce's conception of the human is, furthermore, informed by a capitalist belief in the merit of self-interest and clearly opposes the free labourer as a full human to the degraded situation of the slave. He regrets the effect of slavery that renders the colonial slave "as not capable of being worked upon by the ordinary motives of the hope of reward, or even the fear of punishment" (WL 144). Wilberforce envisions a capitalist utopia in the case of abolition:

> The Slaves in general will learn to feel the value of a good character, to covet the acquisition and drive for the maintenance of it. They will make it their study to gain a master's good opinion and confidence. With hope to animate, and gratitude to warm, how soon should we witness willing industry and hearty services. (WL 249)

He sees humans as being driven by self-interest and also praises the work of Adam Smith. However, he clearly puts moral and religious motives above mere self-interest when he expresses his hope that

"West Indian Proprietors would be prompted, not only by considerations of self- interest, but by motives of a still higher order, to pay some attention to the religious instruction of their Negroes?" (WL 126).

Nature and civilisation

Despite his portrayal of Africans in the interior of the continent as noble savages, it is interesting that Wilberforce does not use the term 'state of nature' but rather the image of polishedness. Apart from this, the text features the usual use of the concept in the form of "ties of nature" (WL 39), "the great Law of Nature" (WL 104), "the principles of human nature," (WL 222), "a sense of the dignity of their nature" (WL 236), "natural liberty" (WL 258) and "the laws of nature and morality" (WL 285).

Wilberforce's concept of the progress of human civilisation is characterised by an idea of cultural transfer. In this, he strongly advocates a Eurocentric master narrative with the biblical notion of Mesopotamia as "the original seat of the human race" (WL 74) which, together with Egypt, formed "the earliest seats of civilization" (WL 77) from whence civilisation spread across Europe. It is evident that Wilberforce posits one original source of civilisation when he writes that the "progress of the arts and sciences would probably be extremely slow, if a nation were not to import the improvements of former times and other countries" (WL 74). Thus, he reaches the following assessment of the situation in Africa:

> ... it has been the peculiar misery of Africa, that nations, already the most civilized, finding her in the state which has been described, instead of producing any such effect as might be hoped for from a commercial connection between a less and a more civilized people; instead of imparting to the former the superior knowledge and improvements of the latter ... instead of polishing (86) and improving, has tended not mereley to retard her natural progress, but to deprave and darken, and, if such a new term might be used where unhappily the novelty of the occurrence compels us to resort to one, to barbarize her wretched inhabitants. (WL 85)

4.12 Wilberforce: *Appeal* (1823)

4.12.1 Synopsis and Argument of Appeal

Wilberforce addresses his 1823 *Appeal* to "all the inhabitants of the British Empire, who value the favour of God, or are alive to the interests or honour of their country—to all who have any respect for justice, or any feelings of humanity" (WA 1). The text is not structured into any chapters and sections. Wilberforce's argument is that slavery is contrary to common morality and that its long continuance in the British Empire can only be explained by ignorance of its real nature (cf. WA 2). The text does not discuss the righteousness of slavery on a fundamental level anymore, but takes it as granted that it is contrary to "the clearest dictates of humanity" (WA 3) and "the sentiments and feelings produced in all generous and humane minds" (WA 8). In this context, Wilberforce also quotes Henry Dundas to show that even an advocate of the West Indies agrees in principle with the necessity of ending slavery and this not only for reasons of justice but also of expediency (cf. WA 4ff). Also, his reference to Edmund Burke as a moral and intellectual authority is aimed at establishing the hegemony of his position. He writes: "It scarcely needs be remarked, in how great a degree Mr. Burke was an enemy to all speculative theories" (WA 7).

At the same time, the author aims at establishing Britain hegemony over colonial voices. He claims a privileged position of analysis for the colonial centre when he writes, "though it is no praise to us, but to the good providence of God, we are exempt from the influence of the harsh prejudices to which they, in some degree by our concurrent fault, have been subjected" (WA 63). Thus, Wilberforce at the same time defends the idea at the centre of the imperial project and tries to appear sympathetic to the situation of the West Indians, who cannot be expected to "sympathise properly with them [i.e. the Africans] in their sufferings and wrongs, or form a just estimate of their claims to personal rights and moral improvement" (WA 43).

Wilberforce then lists what he calls the evils of the slave system. As the first of these, he mentions the degradation below the state of humans of slaves. In this context, he cites Long's *History of Jamaica* and its racist sentiments as still enjoying "the highest estimation among the West India colonists" (WA 12) so that the practical effects of its negative representation of the Africans can still be seen.

After mentioning the legal oppression of the slaves since "evidence of slaves is never admitted against white men" (WA 13f), he turns to the slaves' horrid working conditions under the whips of their overseers. For Wilberforce, this precludes any plans of "improving the condition of these poor beings, as rational and moral agents, while they are treated in a manner which precludes self-government, and annihilates all human motives..." (WA 16).

Wilberforce also strongly criticises the "the universal want of the marriage institution among the slaves" (WA 20), pointing to the "immoral and degrading effects" (WA 20) of the universal "promiscuous intercourse", (WA 18) which is not "confined to Negroes" but also common among the "single young men" (WA 21) who are commonly used as superintendents.

The authors next critique is that "the slaves ... are practically strangers to the multiplied blessings of the Christian Revelation" (WA 24), which he describes as "the most serious of all the vices of the West Indian system" (WA 24) and disgraceful for "a nation, which besides the invaluable benefit of an unequalled degree of true civil liberty, has been favoured with an unprecedented measure of religious light, with its long train of attendant blessings" (WA 25).

Wilberforce calls it a sad fact that as "low in point of morals as the Africans may have been in their own country, their descendants...who for several successive generations have been resident in the Christian colonies of Great Britain, are still lower" (WA 30f). He cites Park's and Golberry's positive representations of the Africans to show the contrast with the slaves: "in the West Indies [who are] the very opposite in all particulars; selfish, indolent, deceitful, ungrateful, and above all, in whatever respects the intercourse between the sexes, incurably licentious" (WA 32).

He then explains that the abolitionists did not aim at emancipation in the first place because "the effort was beyond our strength" (WA 34). However, the author also admits that: "We were too sanguine in our hopes as to the effects of the abolition in our colonies; we judged too favourably of human nature; we thought too well of the colonial assemblies" (WA 36), which leads him to the unwillingness of the West Indian assemblies to change the colonial laws. Because of this, Wilberforce argues that "the imperial legislature ought to consider itself bound to exercise the office of an umpire, or rather of a judge between" (WA 43) the slaves and the members of the colonial assemblies. Thus, he clearly opposes the pro-slavery argument that Britain ought not to meddle in colonial affairs and argues that the West Indians will never emancipate their slaves (cf. WA 48) and "a human and enlightened legislature" cannot "delegate its duties as to moral and religious reform" (WA 53f) to a society like the West Indian one.

Wilberforce then turns to a discussion of the African character. Firstly, he again expresses his enjoyment of the fact that the times are over when the Africans' oppression was justified with their "inferiority of intellect and incurable barbarity" (WA 64) and that "it may be confidently affirmed, that there never was any uncivilised people of whose dispositions we have received a more amiable character than that which is given of the native Africans by Park and Golberry" (WA 64). Wilberforce points to the British colony at Sierra Leone, where "the African character has been most effectually and experimentally vindicated" (WA 64). He writes that there, "these recent savages, having become the subjects of religious and moral culture, have manifested the greatest willingness to receive instruction, and made a practical proficiency in Christianity, such as might put Europeans to the blush" (WA 66). Always anxious about labour discipline, Wilberforce quotes Mungo Park "that the Africans, when prompted by any adequate motives, would work diligently and perseveringly both in agricultural and manufacturing labours" (WA 67).

Thus, Wilberforce argues that "while we are loudly called on by justice and humanity to take measures without delay for improving the condition of our West Indian slaves, self-interest also inculcates the same duty, and with full as clear a voice" (WA 68). He points out that "ultimately, the comfort of the labourer, and the well-being of those who have to enjoy the fruits of his labour, will be found to be coincident" (WA 70). Wilberforce stresses again that even the West Indians have to admit that if the slave trade "had continued some years longer, it must have completed their destruction" (WA 71).

Lastly, Wilberforce argues that only an improvement of the slaves' situation can "prevent the dreadful explosion that may otherwise be expected" (WA 72). In the author's utopia, he raises "these poor creatures from their depressed condition" and, quite significantly, teaches them "on the authority of the sacred page, that the point of real importance is not what is the rank or the station men occupy, but how they discharge the duties of life" (WA 74). Thus furnished, the emancipated slaves would "sustain with patience the sufferings of their actual lot" (WA 74) and soon turn into "a grateful peasantry" (WA 74).

Wilberforce concludes the *Appeal* with a serious warning of eventual divine retribution for the national sin, since it is only for having sinned in ignorance that Britain has so long been spared (cf. WA 74). However, he recommends that "we should treat with candour and tenderness the characters of the West Indian proprietors" (WA 76) since he believes:

many of the owners of West Indian estates to be men of more than common kindness and liberality; [only] utterly unacquainted with the true nature and practical character of the system with which they have the misfortune to be connected. (WA 76f)

This seems to be addressed to the West Indian interest in Britain rather than to the planters in the colonies. Wilberforce optimistically concludes:

Our ultimate success is sure; and ere long we shall rejoice in the consciousness of having delivered our country from the greatest of her crimes, and rescued her character from the deepest stain of dishonour. (WA 77)

4.12.2 Ideology

Wilberforce sees humans as "as rational and moral agents" (WA 16) and also advocates the "natural rights of human beings" (WA 7). His whole argument against slavery hinges on the belonging of Africans to the human species, which makes slavery irreconcilable with "the natural rights of human beings" (WA 7) and "their claim to the character, and privileges of human nature" (WA 12). Wilberforce's claim for the Africans' humanity, however, is charged in terms of power relations. He addresses what he deems the fair means of societal control over the individual when he describes the problem of slavery as being "subjected to the immediate impulse or present terror of the whip, and are driven at their work like brute animals" (WA 14f) instead of "the hope of reward, or the fear of punishment" (WA 14). This clearly contrasts the treatment of the slaves with an idealised relationship between capitalist master and labourer.

Thus, Wilberforce opposes the construction of an essential Otherness of Africans in the sense that they belong to a different species and are "creatures of an inferior nature" (WA 43) and expresses his conviction that the day is gone in which "the alleged inferiority of intellect and incurable barbarity of the African race were supposed to extenuate their oppression" (WA 63). He also criticises this kind of thinking in an act of the assembly of Barbados, describing slaves as "wholly unqualified to be governed by the laws, practices, and customs of other nations" (WA 11fn). For Wilberforce, it is only due to their treatment that "the slaves were systematically depressed below the level of human beings" (WA 11). It is clear that denying their fundamental humanity to Africans would make them unsuitable objects for the carrot and stick approach which Wilberforce envisions when speaking of controlling former slaves by the "the hope of reward, or the fear of punishment" (WA 14). Deciding power over the former slaves' humanity, thus, very much remains at the hand of the colonial centre, defining itself as the "land of liberty and humanity" (WA 60) and "the most moral and humane of nations" (WA 33). Wilberforce defends this brand of an explicitly British freedom when he calls any comparison of slave and British peasant "a proposition so monstrous that nothing can possibly exhibit in a stronger light the extreme force of the prejudices which must exist in the minds of its assertors" (WA 45).

Already the title of the text creates the fundamental opposition of humane Britons and suffering Africans. After all, the text explicitly is an appeal to the humanity of inhabitants of the British Empire on behalf of the negro slaves in the West Indies. The text also associates the concept of humanity almost exclusively with Europeans. Wilberforce writes: "we are loudly called on by justice and humanity to take measures without delay for improving the condition of our West Indian slaves" (WA 68). Africans are the mere objects of the humane efforts of "us"; however, "they" are not given a position of sufficient power to be "humane" themselves.

Wilberforce writes of the British settlement of former slaves in Sierra Leone: "But at Sierra Leone, they have resumed the stature and port of men, and have acquired, in an eminent degree, the virtues of the citizen and the subject" (WA 66). This shows that the text's claim for freedom is a carefully qualified one. Although Wilberforce opposes an unlimited "power of man over man" (WA 2), the slaves "should be gradually prepared for the enjoyment of freedom" (WA 54).

Also in *Appeal*, Wilberforce promotes the image of the noble savage. He almost quotes directly from *Letter* when he writes:

> the Negroes, who while yet in Africa were represented to be industrious, generous, eminent for truth, seldom chargeable with licentiousness, distinguished for their domestic affections, and capable at times of acts of heroic magnanimity, are described as being in the West Indies the very opposite in all particulars; selfish, indolent, deceitful, ungrateful, —and above all, in whatever respects the intercourse between the sexes, incurably licentious. (WA 32)

This conveniently justifies Wilberforce's explicit aim of "civilizing" the Africans (cf. WA 4). The image of the seeds of civilisation is again present in this text. Wilberforce writes that in Sierra Leone, the "first seeds of civilization .... were sown .... by the Christian philanthropy of Mr. Granville Sharpe" (WA 64). In the *Letter*, the seeds of civilisation only referred to the spreading of civilisation throughout the Roman Empire. Now he uses it to refer to the British civilising mission in Sierra Leone. Thus, it might be just to state the discourse on slavery, in turn, contained the seeds of empire.

I have already pointed out above that Wilberforce advocates a good measure of societal control over the individual. He seems distrustful of the voice of the people, especially in the West Indies, when he writes, "the cry of the mob, is always adverse to the humane and liberal principles by which the slavery of the blacks should be mitigated, and by which they should be gradually prepared for the enjoyment of freedom" (WA 54). Marriage also plays an important role in this context: Wilberforce describes it as "the source of all domestic comfort and social improvement,—the moral cement of civilized society" (WA 16f). Wilberforce thus criticises the notorious fact "that it has been the general policy to employ instead of married managers and overseers, single young men as the immediate superintendents of the gangs" (WA 21). Quoting Brougham's colonial policy, Wilberforce points out:

> The want of modest female society, the general case on the plantations remote from the towns, while it brutalizes the mind and manners of men, necessarily deprives them of all the virtuous pleasures of domestic life, and frees them

from those restraints which the presence of a family always imposes on the conduct of the most profligate men. (WA 53fn)

4.13 Bridges: *Voice* (1823)

4.13.1 George Wilson Bridges

George Wilson Bridges was born in 1788 to a wealthy family that was involved in banking and the corn trade (cf. Brennan). Due to the family's roots, Bridges' father intended George Wilson to become rector of Bruntingthore, Leicestershire. Accordingly, Bridges was educated at Trinity College, Oxford. In 1814, he toured Europe, after which he published *Alpine Sketches, comprised in a short tour through parts of Holland, Flanders, France, Savoy, Switzerland and Germany during the summer of 1814 by a member of the University of Oxford* (1814).

However, in 1815, during his first curacy, he brought scandal upon himself when he ran away to Gretna Green, a place just across the Scottish border, then notorious for runaway marriages, to marry the Jamaican-born Elizabeth Raby Brooks, said to have already been pregnant by him. This caused a split with his family, and no member of the Bridges family seemed to have been present even when the marriage was regularised in 1816. In the same year, Bridges left for Jamaica with his family to become rector and was responsible first of the parish of Manchester and later of St. Anne until 1837. A huge part of his generous income of £1,000 came from the money he received from slaves in return for thousands of baptisms he performed (cf. Brennan).

A convinced opponent of emancipation, he wrote his *A Voice from Jamaica; in Reply to William Wilberforce; Esq. M.P.* in 1823. Other publications include the two-volume *The Annals of Jamaica* (1828) and *Emancipation Unmask'd* (1835). *Annals* caused him some problems, giving rise to a libel case with anti-slavery activist Louis Celeste Lecesne (cf. Brennan). He sued Bridges for referring to him and his brother-in-law as "two French prisoners who had been confined for an attempt to revolutionise the island and who were impatient to sheathe their daggers in the breasts of its white inhabitants" (Bridges, *Annals* 372). Bridges' treatment of slaves also earned him some notoriety. In 1830, Henry Brougham raised a case in the Commons in which Bridges was blamed for having a servant of his, Kitty Hylton, "flogged so badly by servants … and … himself that her case was taken to the Council of Protection for St Ann in 1828 by one of Bridges' own colleagues" (Brennan).

In 1834, Bridges' wife left him and in 1837, he lost four of his daughters in a boating accident in Kingston Harbour. After his return to England in 1837, Bridges became interested in photography, gaining some fame for the photographic images which resulted from his travels in the Mediterranean between 1846 and 1852. Bridges died on 20 September 1863 (cf. Brennan).

Self-Representation in Texts

Bridges frequently emphasises that he is "a clergyman of the Church of England" (BV 3) and clearly takes the side of "the friends of these colonies" (BV 7) and "our unfortunate planters" (BV 15). He frequently refers to himself using the first person pronoun "I" in the text and also addresses Wilberforce directly as "you". For example, he does so at the beginning of the text when calling himself "the feeble advocate of a Church Establishment, whose domestic as well as foreign institutions, you [i.e. Wilberforce] appear to take every opportunity of impugning" (BV 4).

His position is an interesting one: on the one hand, he refers to himself as "a voice from Jamaica" in the title of his work and clearly takes a West Indian position in expression like "our local Legislature," (BV 17) or when referring to "our laws … our habits, our religion, our common sense" (BV 19). On the other hand, however, he seems anxious to stress his Britishness and to show off his education at Oxford using 13 Latin and 14 French original quotes. He lays claim to first-hand knowledge about the situation of both British paupers and colonial slaves when he boasts that:

> I, Sir, have served cures in the Counties of Essex, Norfolk, and Hampshire, and in London, and will be bold to say, that I have never, during my subsequent residence of seven years in this island, with a population of sixteen thousand negroes under my charge, witnessed such absolute misery, or such cruel abuse of authority, as I have seen in the conduct of parish officers towards paupers, or in the hovel of the wretched husbandman, to which my painful professional duties have led me, in England. (BV 39)

Bridges refers to the observations he has made during his Grad Tour when he asserts that the conditions of the colonial slaves "will bear comparison with the most favoured condition of the working classes which I have beheld in the south of France, and in various other parts of Europe" (BV 12).

Thus, the main argument which he bases on his biography is his claim to a superior degree of personal knowledge in contrast to Wilberforce. He declares it the goal of his composition that "I shall from my own personal experience, and the professional opportunities of observation and research, which lie within my reach, endeavour to correct your statements" (BV 8). Bridges writes of himself:

> When I tell you that I came hither seven years ago, biassed by as great an abhorrence of the very name of slavery, as ever haunted an educated mind; and ... possessing as much respect for you, its opposing champion, as ever enthusiast felt, you will perhaps be induced to give me credit, at least for the pure motives which alone dictate this letter (BV 8)

He contrasts his lived experience with Wilberforce's book knowledge when asserting that instead of gaining first-hand knowledge, Wilberforce instead sits calmly in his library, composing speeches and writing books on countries he has never visited (cf. BV 24f) and describes him as "sitting by your own fire-side four thousand miles off" (BV 27).

Instead, Bridges asks Wilberforce to "let the Established Clergy here do their duty" (BV 28) and counters the anti-slavery claim for religious instruction of colonial slaves by priding himself that, "I have actually baptized 9,413 negro slaves" (BV 27).

At the end of his text, Bridges styles himself as a saviour of the empire, in referring to Wilberforce's publication as "a pamphlet, the mischievous tendency of which threatens to involve these most valuable possessions of the Crown in indiscriminate ruin" (BV 48). He personally attacks Wilberforce as too old when he states that,

> I have looked in vain for that expansion of mind, or vigour of intellect, by which your former exertions in the sacred cause of humanity were eminently distinguished, and find only the dying embers of a distempered imagination, brooding unceasingly upon one object (BV 48).

4.13.2 Synopsis and Argument

Bridges refers to his composition as "a letter to William Wilberforce" (BV 3) and starts the text with the typical pro-slavery trope expressing the expectation of probably appearing in a negative light for entering into a controversy with an author writing for "a cause, [4] which, if *abstractedly* [my emphasis] considered, is doubtless that of degraded humanity" (BV 3f). Bridges goes on to blame Wilberforce for wanting to attach both abolition and emancipation to his name instead of leaving emancipation for coming generations (cf. BV 4).

It is interesting that Bridges refers to Wilberforce's text as "Appeal" under quotation marks throughout his composition. It has to be noted that he refers to the compositions of other authors without the inverted commas. The only other publication which is thus referred to is "the African Society's Report", which Bridges calls "a publication which has been so repeatedly convicted of gross inaccuracies" (BV 41). Thus, these are clearly scare quotes which aim at questioning the seriousness of Wilberforce's text and the sincerity of motives.

He points out that Wilberforce, instead of allowing "the slow yet certain progress of time" prematurely urges the cause of emancipation (cf. BV 6). Pointing to St. Domingo, Bridges asks Wilberforce, "... where are your boasted results of emancipation to be traced, but in the appalling features of a barbarous revolt" (BV 7) and expresses the "anxious wish to avert an impending blow, which, if now inflicted, will deluge these unhappy islands with blood, and consign them to utter desolation" (BV 8). He repeatedly blames Wilberforce for never having been to the West Indies and not having "viewed the habits of negro life in its indigenous state" (BV 8).

Bridges then scrutinises Wilberforce"s assertion that slavery has "a natural tendency towards the maximum of labour and the minimum of food and other comforts" (BV 11). He plainly rejects any comparison between colonial slaves and British labourers due to the fact that "a negro's habits are such ... that two of the most effective of them would not turn over as much ground in your garden in one day, as your own gardener does, ceteris paribus, in half that time" (BV 11). Bridges emphasises the material security of the slave over the European working classes, stating that, at night, the slave:

> returns to his family, secure of finding them, not cold and hungry, clinging to his knees, and crying for food he cannot give them, but around a good fire, happy and contented as himself; and that, in a warm house, he passes the night, secure of the same provision for the morrow. (BV 12)

The author denies Wilberforce's accusation that the slaves are being denied a jury of their peers and blames him for malevolently selecting old material. Bridges cites an incident in 1821 in which the magistrates who failed to try a slave, who was sentenced to death before such a jury, were severely punished and the power of life and death put in the hands of the governor alone (cf. BV 14ff).

Bridges then deals with Wilberforce's use of Edward Long's infamous comparison of "Hottentots" with orang-utans (cf. Long 364f). He first accuses Wilberforce of using this "long-forgotten, and degrading estimate of the negro race" (BV 17) only to infuriate the public against the planters. He then argues that Wilberforce misinterprets Long's original argument, which was only to show that "in the inanimate and inferior parts of the creation, so even up to man, there are conjoining links in the great chain of nature, the lowest of which, in the human species, seems to be the Hottentot" (BV 17).

He then warns that admitting slave evidence in the present situation would to "sign our own death-warrants" (BV 21) since they "are numerically ten to one against the whites" (BV 20). The author urges to first "build up the sacred wall of Christianity" (BV 20), once again calling to mind the "the bloody independence, of St. Domingo" (BV 21).

Bridges meets Wilberforce's appeal to abolish the whip as punishment with agreement, writing that "the desire of every possessor of slaves: and by many of them it has been abolished" (BV 21). However, he acts surprised that Wilberforce seems to forget the use of this instrument "in the army, navy, and courts of justice at home, where its use is infinitely more humiliating and severe" (BV 21). Bridges assures Wilberforce that the drivers on plantations are selected because of their good conduct and if they treat the slaves badly they are reduced to the rank of slave again, which guarantees "their not abusing the temporary power confided to them" (BV 22).

Bridges counters Wilberforce's charge that no attempts have been made to introduce the institution of marriage among the slaves by boasting to have personally married 187 couples (cf. BV 22f). Being a minister, Bridges acknowledges the importance of spreading Christianity and boasts of having personally baptised 9,413 Africans. However, he criticises Wilberforce for supporting what he calls "Christian Missionaries" instead of letting the established clergy do their work (cf. BV 27f).

The author then challenges Wilberforce's positive representation of Africans in their own country, quoting Bosman's *Voyage de Guinée*, he points out that the Africans are extremely lazy, only work when forced to, love hard liquor and practice polygamy (cf.

BV 30ff). What Bridges seems to oppose here is the notion that the depravity and degradation of the Africans is the result of slavery. While he takes the Africans' degradation and barbarity for granted, he offers a quite different explanation. For Bridges, the reason that after 20 years "in these Christian isles" the Africans are still savages is "the very rough materials on which we have to work" and the "constitutional barbarity of such a people" (BV 31ff).

> Bridges accuses Wilberforce of repeating the same untruths and (cf. BV 36ff) turns to Wilberforce's unfavourable comparison of the British peasant and the African slave to offer his own more favourable estimation of their respective situations. The author argues that the slave can rely on a "constant supply of all the necessaries of life; the best advice and assistance in sickness; perfect reliance on the future support of themselves and children ... warm houses, freedom from all restraint during fourteen hours of relaxation out of every twenty-four" (BV 36f). He contrasts this with "our own English workmen, whose o'er-wearied slumbers are too often broken by the agonising thoughts of the future or by vain attempts to sooth the heart-rending cries of their hungry helpless children" (BV 36f). Bridges adorns his romanticised depiction of the situation of West Indian slaves with a little anecdote in which slaves even loan a substantial amount of money to their master, who is in financial difficulties. (BV 38). He argues that it is not the slaves but actually the "the free negro and coloured population of these colonies" (BV 39f) who deserve sympathy. The author charges Wilberforce's sudden plea for emancipation with inconsistency in the light of the fact that for 27 years, "he has been constantly vindicating [himself] from the charge of wishing to make the slaves free" (BV 40f). Bridges then warns about the economic consequences and of violating the principles of British faith "on which the merchant has advanced his capital in these distant isles" (BV 45).

At the end of his text, Bridges turns to what he calls the tendency of *Appeal* "to inflame dormant passions, and excite rebellion amongst our yet peaceable negroes" (BV 45). He argues that Wilberforce's text is "little short of treasonable sedition, and actual murder!!" Bridges concludes by expressing his faith that "there is still, in the British Empire, a characteristic principle of intelligence, justice, and good faith, which will see through the wretched artifices, and reiterated misrepresentations, so unceasingly employed to mislead the judgment" (BV 49). He appeals to Wilberforce: "Pause then, Sir, before you further risk the lives, and ruin the fortunes, of so many thousands of your countrymen in these distant isles" (BV 49).

4.13.3 Ideology

Bridges acknowledges freedom as a universal value, speaking of "the sweet fruits of freedom, harmony, and peace" (BV 7). However, as has been pointed out above, he proposes a longer period of transition. Writing of the miserable situation of the "free negro and coloured population" (BV 39), he calls this the "the wretched production of premature liberty" (BV 40). Furthermore, he blames Wilberforce for not thinking of the consequences of his proposal "so long as they are but free, and owe their freedom to your interference, may afterwards cut each other's throats if they like" (BV 44). In this context, it is especially the religious education of the slaves which forms the prerequisite for them (BV 27).

There is little discussion of philosophical fundamentals in the text. The only passage which offers some insight into Bridges' ideas about the state of nature is when he discusses Long's *History* and seems to agree with him that creation is ordered as "conjoining links in the great chain of nature" (BV 18).

Just like all the other authors, Bridges uses "humanity" as a universally positive concept. He acknowledges that Wilberforce deserves "the honour which the relieved sufferings of humanity can bestow" (BV 4) for achieving the abolition of the slave trade. However, when it comes to emancipation, he blames Wilberforce for wanting to "monopolize both these philanthropic objects, to attach them to your own name" (BV 4).

He also accuses Wilberforce of exploiting the sacred claims of humanity for the interest of the East India lobby when he asks: "let the sacred claims of humanity rest on their own broad foundation, and not depend upon the weak adventitious aid of temporary intrigues and rival interests" (BV 5). In contrast to this, he styles his own intentions as pure when writing of "the impartial justice and humanity of my purpose" (BV 8).

The main threat in the text is that of slave rebellion. It has been pointed out above that Bridges goes to some length when portraying the horrific effects of Wilberforce's attempt to "to inflame dormant passions, and excite rebellion amongst our yet peaceable negroes; to raise once more the horrid war-whoop, which would doom us, and our helpless families, to certain destruction" (BV 45). It is especially the Haitian revolution which serves an easy way for Bridges to conjure up before the reader the "deluge of blood" (BV 6) and "scenes of carnage and desolation" (BV 48) in the aftermath of emancipation.

4.14 Clarkson: *Thoughts* (1823)

4.14.1 Argument and Synopsis of Thoughts

Clarkson starts the preface of the text by informing the reader that *Thoughts* was first published in the periodical *The Inquirer*. The author states that since then and based on new information, he has come to realise that he has overrated any improvements since abolition. Thus, in retrospect, he would have changed "those parts of his essay which speak of the improved condition of the slaves in the West Indies" (CT ii).

Clarkson then sets out to allay any fears due to the term "emancipation" and refers to Henry Dundas—"a Friend to the planters" (CT ii)—using the term as early as 1792.). Clarkson emphasises that he desires such emancipation only as is "compatible not only with the due subordination and happiness of the labourer, but with the permanent interests of the employer" (CT ii). This sets the main theme of the text. Clarkson concludes his introduction by acknowledging that a huge amount of property is at stake on the planters' side, weighing this with the liberty of 800,000 slaves (cf. CT iii).

Clarkson starts the main part of his *Thoughts* by remarking that "a mitigation of the slavery, with a view afterwards to the emancipation of the Negroes" (CT 1) would equally serve "humanity and justice, as well as public and private interest" (CT 1). He then repeats the common story of how abolition was seen as taking the axe to the root of the evils of slavery, forcing the West Indians to improve the situation of their slaves and eventually "pass them to . . . . the rank of Free Men?" (CT 2). However, despite some positive effects concerning the individual treatment of slaves, the system as such has unfortunately not been changed, according to Clarkson (cf. CT 3f). Thus, he then states it is the duty of the abolitionists to continue their efforts, since the situation of the Africans is still unacceptable and they "may be tortured, nay even deliberately and intentionally killed without the means of redress ... so long as the evidence of a Negro is not valid against a white man" (CT 5).

The text then discusses the question of whether it is legitimate for the British parliament to interfere with colonial matters. Clarkson does not shy away from confronting the West Indian legislatures when he suggests that "an entire new code of laws" be introduced in "our colonies" (CT 5). Clarkson expresses his conviction that "we can have not reasonable expectation from that quarter [i.e. the West Indies]" (CT 6) since the colonial laws have remained the same for the last 150 years and the West Indians are too prejudiced against their slaves "to become either impartial or willing actors in the case" (CT 6). Accordingly, he refers to the British parliament as "the source of all legitimate power" (CT 7) which ought to interfere on behalf of the slaves "by subjecting the colonial laws to the revision of the Legislature of the mother country" (CT 8). Clarkson rejects any arguments drawn from the charters of the West Indian colonies:

> Let the West Indians then talk no more of their charters; for in consequence of having legislated upon principles, which are at variance with those upon which the laws of England are founded, they have forfeited them all ... the

Colonial system is an excrescence upon the English Constitution, and is constantly at variance with it. (CT 14f)

After this Clarkson turns to the main topic of *Thoughts*, which is showing

> that however awful and tremendous the work of emancipation may seem, it is yet practicable; that it is practicable also without danger; and moreover, that it is practicable with the probability of advantage to all the parties concerned. (CT 16)

In order to do so, he provides "six or seven instances of the emancipation of African slaves in bodies" (CT 16). The first three of these are larger bodies of former black soldiers in the British army, which were made free after their service. Clarkson writes of them that they "found in the British army a school as it were, which fitted them by degrees for making a good use of their liberty" (CT 20). The fourth example are captured Africans in Sierra Leone, who "were taken out of slave-ships captured at different times from the commencement of the abolition of the slave trade to the present moment, and that on being landed they were made free" (CT 18). Clarkson writes that these "have now fallen entirely into the habits of English society" (CT 18f). Clarkson admits that these examples can, of course, not provide absolute certainty that the colonial slaves "would pass through the ordeal of emancipation without danger to their masters or the community at large" (CT 21). However, he expresses his confidence that emancipation is safely possible since "there is a peculiar softness, and plasticity, and pliability in the African character" quite in contrast to "the unbending ferocity of the North American Indians and other tribes" (CT 21).

Clarkson's fifth example are "the slaves of St. Domingo as they were made free at different intervals in the course of the French Revolution" (CT 22). It is, of course, a rhetorical feat that Clarkson uses the very example which pro-slavery authors only refer to as the "horrors of St. Domingo" (ML 15) to make his case for emancipation. Clarkson first provides a historical overview of slave revolts after 1791 and the Haitian Revolution (cf. CT 22ff). Clarkson then proceeds to "inquire how those who were liberated on these several occasions conducted themselves after this change in their situation" (CT 24) and is happy to report that:

> the Negroes continued their labours, where there were any, even inferior, agents to guide them; and on those estates, where no white men were left to direct them, they betook themselves to the planting of provisions; but upon all the plantations where the Whites resided, the Blacks continued to labour as quietly as before. (CT 25)

According to Clarkson, it was only when the French attempted to reinstate slavery that "a scene of blood and torture followed ... though planned and executed by Whites" (29). Clarkson largely excludes any massacres, only to point out "in the year 1804, Dessalines was proclaimed emperor of this fine territory" (CT 29). He concludes his discussion of this case by asking his readers to remember that "the island at this juncture was prey to political discord, civil war, and foreign invasion at the same time" (CT 32). He argues that compared to that, the gradual emancipation at "a time of tranquillity and peace" (CT 32) which is proposed for the British colonies, would be nothing.

Clarkson provides a sixth example of liberated slaves in "the newly-erected State of Columbia" (CT 33) under General Bolivar, who also "conducted themselves well without a single exception" (CT 34).

The seventh example is a substantial discussion of the experiments of Joshua Steele in 1789 on his plantations in Barbados. Clarkson states that Steele based his experiment on "the practice of our Anglo-Saxon ancestors in the days of Villainage" (CT 37) and "erected his plantations into manors" and "registered in the manor-book all his adult male slaves as copyholders" (CT 38). Steele introduced a system of wages and rent, with the result that the slaves "were to work 260 days in the year for him, and to have 48 besides Sundays for themselves" (CT 28). Clarkson draws two conclusions from the example of Joshua Steele. Firstly, that "emancipation is not only practicable, but that it is practicable without danger" (CT 42) since "the Negro character is malleable at the European will" (CT 42). Secondly, Clarkson states that Steele himself greatly profited financially from the introduction of task work and renting out the provision grounds to his slaves (cf. CT 43f). Apart from the financial gain, Clarkson also refers the reader to the increase of the slave population on Steele's plantations, quoting Steele's statement before the Privy Council (cf. CT 46). Clarkson concludes with "an old maxim... confirmed by Dr. Adam Smith, and all the modern writers on political economy, that the labour of free men is cheaper than the labour of slaves" (CT 47). Thus, Clarkson's argument for the introduction of free labour is that:

> the slaves in the West Indies do much more work in a given time when they work for themselves ... having all their earnings to themselves, they have that stimulus within them to excite industry, which is only known to free men. (CT 50)

Clarkson cites the assertions of pro-slavery authors such as Francklyn and Tobin that "no Negro works like a day-labourer in England" (CT 52) to emphasise that the planters themselves would profit most by emancipation (cf. CT 53f).

Clarkson then argues that there might have been a time when it was necessary to break the spirits of the slaves. However, he maintains that no argument can be produced for "the continuation of a barbarous discipline" (CT 57) now that "the great majority of the Negroes were become vernacular, born in the island, naturalized by language, and familiarised by custom" (CT 58). Clarkson concludes his *Thoughts* by addressing the planters directly, justifying the right of the British people to interfere on behalf of "the liberty of your slaves, seeing that you hold them by no right that is not opposed to nature, reason, justice, and religion" (CT 59). However, he stresses, "the people of England have no desire to interfere with your property, but with your oppression" (CT 59).

The negotiation of power relations within the British Empire was certainly a central issue in the debate about slavery. I have pointed out above that part of Clarkson's argument against slavery is that it is contrary to the natural rights of all humans. Making the case for colonial intervention based on natural rights puts considerable discursive power into the hands of the colonial centre. It must have substantially influenced later British colonial policy that the negotiation of civil liberties happened in this antagonistic form against the background of a West Indian plantocracy. This probably resulted in a lasting stigma for colonial administrations per se. However, it might not have been inconvenient to create a kind of scapegoat by emphasising the difference between the corrupt colonial elites and the pure intentions of the imperial centre. For example, Clarkson puts the blame entirely pm the colonial subalterns when he defends the virtue of Elisabeth I in portraying the beginnings of the slave trade as an act of delusion on the side of Captain Hawkins (cf. CT 12). We find the same technique in Wilberforce's *Appeal*, when he attributes the continuance of slavery exclusively to the ignorance of the British people.

4.14.2 Ideology

Also in *Thoughts*, Clarkson sees liberty as a natural right of all humans: "every man's liberty is his own property by the laws of Nature, Reason, Justice, and Religion?" (CT iii). However, just like Wilberforce, Clarkson does not advocate unbounded freedom, but carefully qualifies the concept to meet the need for social order. For example, he proposes that "debt and crime have been generally admitted to be two fair grounds, on which men may be justly deprived of their liberty for a time" (CT 10). He also stresses that the advocates of emancipation "wish for no other freedom than that which is compatible with the joint interest of the master and the slave" (CT 41). Thus, he proposes that the slaves "should be emancipated by degrees, or that they should be made to pass through a certain course of discipline, as through a preparatory school, to fit them for the right use of their freedom" (CT 32). The cautious nature of the gradual approach is perhaps best reflected by the full name of the anti-slavery movement, which was founded in 1823: The Society for the Mitigation and Gradual Abolition of Slavery Throughout the British Dominions (Harmer, *Companion* 76).

Clarkson's discussion of Joshua Steele's experiments on free labour again shows how he balances the need for labour discipline with the claim for emancipation: "he kept up discipline on the plantations, without lessening authority on the one hand, and without invading the liberty of individuals on the other" (CT 31). Steele's experiment was, of course, a very cautious one. Seymour Drescher referred to it as "a modest experiment in quasi emancipation" (Drescher, *Experiment* 111f). Clarkson writes that Steele's aim was only that "the slaves should be led by degrees to the threshold of liberty, from whence they might step next, without hazard, into the rank of free men," (CT 35) and also "that they should be attached to the plantations, and made, though free labourers, a sort of adscripti glebae for five years" (CT 31). The maxims of prudence and foresight are central to Clarkson's utopia of upholding labour discipline after slavery: "they [i.e. the former slaves] must have been made to look beforehand, to think for themselves and families from day to day, and to provide against the future, all which operations of the mind are the characteristics only of free men" (CT 41).

This cautious approach to freedom also informs Clarkson's claim for the Africans' humanity. He once refers to Africans and Creoles as "those, whom we have so abundantly proved to be men" (CT 10), which shows that the claim for humanity constitutes distinct power relations. The fact that "we" prove "their" humanity clearly leaves the deciding power over humanity with "us". Clarkson's basic concept of the human serves the needs of capitalist modes of production. He writes: "Self-interest is a leading principle with all who are born into the world" (CT 21). This serves him to naturalise the concept of wage labour, He contrasts its "natural, efficient, and profitable reciprocity of interests" (CT 47) to "the unnatural and destructive practice of forced labour" (CT 55). He states that it is "confirmed by Dr. Adam Smith, and all the modern writers on political economy, that the labour of free men is cheaper than the labour of slaves" (CT 47). Clarkson's approach to labour discipline, however, is informed by the assumption that "that labour is not agreeable to man" (CT 50) and that the only stimulus is the "hope of gain [and] ... the knowledge, that what he earns is for himself and not for another" (CT 50).

While he clearly emphasises the need for discipline, Clarkson challenges the mode of keeping a workforce in check. He advocates the exploitation of the workers' self-interest for that end. Contrasting West Indian and East Indian sugar production, he cites Mr. Botham: "Let it be considered how much labour is lost by the persons overseeing the forced labourer, which is saved when he works for his own profit." (CT 49f).

Sierra Leone serves Clarkson as a sort of model case to prove the universality of his concepts and, thus, the feasibility of the utopia. He reports of its inhabitants:

> The people there have now fallen entirely into the habits of English society. They are decently and respectably dressed. They attend divine worship regularly. They exhibit an orderly and moral conduct. In their town, little shops are now beginning to make their appearance; and their lands show the marks of extraordinary cultivation. Many of them, after having supplied their own wants for the year, have a surplus produce in hand for the purchase of superfluities or comforts. (CT 18f)

Clarkson reassures any doubters that the Africans could easily be fitted into a system of capitalist wage labour, asserting that:

> There is, as I have observed before, a singular pliability in the constitutional temper of the Negroes, and they have besides a quick sense of their own interest, which influences their conduct. I am convinced, that West India masters can do what they will with their slaves; and that they may lead them through any changes they please, and with perfect safety to themselves, if they will only

make them (the slaves) understand that they are to be benefited thereby. (CT 42)

The text contrasts the projects of gradual emancipation and colonial reform with the spectre of a slave rebellion. The threat of rebellion was certainly tangible in 1823 since the British colonies saw repeated uprisings of slaves in Jamaica (1815), Barbados (1816), Belize (1820) and Guiana (1823). Even in his treatment of the Haitian revolution, Clarkson avoids the topic of the massacres, only writing that "the emancipated Negroes never abused their liberty, from the year 1793 ... to the present day, a period of thirty years" (CT 29) and that they "continued to work" (CT 25, 26, 27). Clarkson's reasoning clearly denies agency to the Africans when he writes that the abolitionists "undertake the cause of the Negroes" (CT 5). The unspoken but logical alternative, namely that the Africans undertake their own cause, would mean rebellion, which Clarkson is so anxious to avoid.

Another dimension of Clarkson's claim for the Africans' humanity is his Christian conviction that "Every man who is born into the world, whether he be white or whether he be black, is born, according to Christian notions, a free agent and an accountable creature" (CT 10). The importance of this for Clarkson lies in the fact that it is the "revealed will of God, that all men, without exception, must be left free to act, but accountable to God for their actions" (CT 11). In consequence, slavery is "contrary to the laws of God" (CT 54) since it puts too much power in the hands of the master:

> if the master has the power, a just, and moral power, to make his slaves do what he orders them to do, even if it be wrong, then I must contend that the Scriptures, whose authority we venerate, are false. (CT 11)

Furthermore, he asserts that the ownership of the children of slaves is ridiculous since "They can have surely no natural right to the infant, who is born of a woman slave. If there be any right to it by nature, such right must belong, not to the master of the mother, but to the mother herself" (CT 10).

4.15 Hampden: *Commentary on Clarkson* (1824)

4.15.1 Biographical Note

In her introduction to Hampden's text, Debbie Lee suggests that Hampden is a pseudonym which possibly alludes to the 17th-century British politician of the same name (cf. Lee, *Slavery* 145). The original John Hampden challenged the authority of King Charles I before the English civil war and his arrest was instrumental in sparking the outbreak of the war. He was famously put pm trial for refusing to pay the ship-money tax which Charles I attempted to raise without the approval of parliament. The use of this pseudonym possibly serves the author to create a position of speaking for himself in which he is the lone opposition against an absolutist exertion of power, in this case of Britain over the colonies. It juxtaposes the interference of power-hungry metropolitan Britain in colonial affairs with the tyranny of an absolute monarch. This fits the author's blaming of Clarkson as a tyrant when he asks:

> ... who but someone possessing the spirit of a tyrant would choose to accomplish his purpose by means of compulsion, which are not only injurious to the feelings, but ruinous to the interests of men, in preference to those methods of kindness and conciliation which are at once more effectual to the attainment of our object, more congenial to the inclinations and the interests of all parties. (HC 187)

Whoever hides behind the pseudonym Rev. John Hampden implies that he has local knowledge of the colonies when he writes of "others, less qualified by local information" (HC 147). In the appendix, he relates that he had "been in the Island of Tortola, and observed the market crowded by negroes offering for sale veal, pigs, poultry, vegetables and provisions of every kind" (HC 201). Throughout the text, the author's standard self-reference is a "we" which claims to be speaking for the larger interest of the West Indian planters and proprietors. Apart from this, the text offers little information as to the identity of the author. The use of a male pseudonym, however, suggests that it is a male writer; thus, I will refer to the anonymous author as "he".

4.15.2 Synopsis and Argument

At the beginning of the text, the author explains that he has selected Clarkson's text because it "has disappointed our expectations, [and] may impose upon others, less qualified by local information, to appreciate the doctrines developed in this pamphlet, and to expose their dangerous tendency" (HC 147). Hampden also criticises Clarkson's public agitation for the cause of emancipation as manipulating the public and, thus, parliament. As he puts it: "petitions can never be received as the spontaneous or unbiassed expression of public sentiment" (HC 150).

Hampden feigns complete incomprehension of Clarkson's disappointment at the failure of abolition to improve the condition of the colonial slaves. He asserts that "the general condition of the slaves, and the established system of treatment have been considerably improved within the last few years; which is no doubt, in a great measure, the effect of the abolition" (HC 151f).

Hampden replies to the accusation that the colonial slave laws have not been amended, that "the theory or code, and the practice of the slave system, are sometimes found to be in an inverse ratio" and argues that laws never give a just representation of real conditions (HC 152). Hampden ironically writes that it is the failure of the planters to bring about their own ruin which serves Clarkson to make the case for the massive intervention of metropolitan Britain by forcibly amending the colonial laws (cf. HC 153). Hampden refutes Clarkson's argument that the planters have no just right to their slaves based on the sacredness of private property (cf. HC 158).

The text then turns to the main part of *Thoughts*, consisting of the various instances of proving that emancipation is possible without danger. With regard to former soldiers in Trinidad and Sierra

Leone, Hampden states that they contain too small a number to prove anything and quotes Clarkson himself who suggests, "all the four cases together prove nothing" (HC 164). Hampden then deals in more detail with Clarkson's use of the revolution in St. Domingo. Contrary to the positive lesson which Clarkson draws, Hampden refers to it as:

> ... exhibiting the most awful warning that could be recommended to our notice in the midst of such speculations. It must be admitted by the most infatuated admirers of the name of liberty, that it is purchased too dearly at the price of so much blood, by the dreadful excesses of human wickedness and misery, which, in the Kingdom of Hayti, have erected a monument to the disgrace of human nature. (HC 164)

Hampden then turns to Joshua Steele's experiment. He starts by arguing that this also does not allow for any conclusion since "these slaves perfectly understood that although their master did not exercise despotic power, he still possessed it" (HC 170). He then quotes a local witness to show that the alleged prospering of Steele's plantation is based on "an unfair comparison between the three years preceding, and the like number of years which followed the change" (HC 172). He argues that the island was hit by frequent droughts and vermin in the years before Steele took over the affairs of his estate himself, which changed after 1780 and lead to a general increase in profits in the colony (cf. HC 173). Hampden cites his witness calling Steele's experiment "a system fraught with persecution and petty tyranny" (HC 174). Additionally, he quotes a further local authority to show that:

> Kendal estate was, during Mr. Steele's direction of it, under the worst cultivation; the net returns were uniformly less in proportion than its neighbours; the system was unsuitable to the habits and feelings of the negroes, who decreased in number; and the ultimate consequence was the ruin of the estate. (HC 175f)

Thus, while not fundamentally challenging Clarkson's reasoning that free labour is cheaper than forced one, Hampden questions the practical applicability of Clarkson's reasoning on the West Indian system. He asks for understanding that the planters will not "surrender their affairs at once into the friendly hands of Mr. Clarkson, without one lingering scruple or misgiving" (HC 178). He also denounces Clarkson's argument that the planters would be indemnified for their loss in slaves by the increased value of their estates as visionary (HC 178). He points out that slaves would, of course, not use their own time as diligently if it were not a scarce good since they "would be physically incapable of a continuance of such exertion" (HC 182). Thus, he describes the result of Clarkson's colonial policy as "the sunset of British light, and influence in these regions of the western hemisphere, and the protracted reign of darkness, vice, and barbarism" (HC 184).

Therefore, Hampden warns that Clarkson's plans are not as harmless as they might seem since the call for metropolitan intervention might antagonise the planters and thus "challenge the hostility of those who are capable of being our most formidable enemies" (HC 186). He also blames Clarkson for not proposing any definite plan for the emancipation (cf. HC 188f). Furthermore, Hampden criticises Clarkson for paying too little attention to the religious instruction of the slaves without which "any attempt at emancipation would be dangerous to the interests of the master, would be injustice and cruelty to the slave" (HC 191). Hampden then elides into typical pro-slavery considerations of abstract freedom and Christianity, asking why Clarkson and "every other romantic lover of the word emancipation" (HC 191) are content with emancipating the slaves "from the bondage of sin and ignorance; to prepare and to qualify them by that service which alone is perfect freedom, for the enjoyment of an immortal inheritance?" (HC 191f).

Hampden then argues that "we are in truth and sincerity what Mr. Clarkson professes to be, friends to a system of emancipation, consistent with a due regard to the claims of justice, or the rights of private property, with the true interests of liberty and humanity, with national faith and the spirit of the British Constitution" (HC 196). He suggests an even more gradual approach to emancipation when he proposes to just let "the progress of civilization" (HC 196) run its course so that the slaves would "advance progressively in the road of improvement, and arrive at the enjoyment of freedom, precisely at the moment when they are fit for it" (HC 196).

In his conclusion, Hampden repeats his main arguments that great improvements have already been made, that the slave laws do not, of course, represent the actual situation of the slaves since they "are not only obsolete in practice, but abhorrent to the public feelings" (HC 199). He ends his text by stating that the treatment of the slaves is actually:

> highly honorable to the character of the Colonies ... therefore any foreign interference, even directed by the enlightened counsels of Mr. Clarkson, would only interrupt the tide of progressive improvement, and instead of introducing into this portion of the British dominions liberty, peace, and social order, the light and inestimable blessings of the Christian religion, threatens to inflict upon us the horrors of rebellion and bloodshed, the ruin of thousands, and the final alienation of our Colonies. (HC 200)

The text contains five appendices, in which the author presents miscellaneous information about the situation of the slaves in the West Indies. These consist of extracts from colonial slave laws (cf. HC 201f), examinations of witnesses on the slavery in Barbados (cf. HC 202ff), discrediting facts about Clarkson's source, Colonel Malenfant (cf. HC 208ff), additional facts about emancipation in Columbia from the communications of a "Joseph Rafael Revenga, to James Dick, Esq. of London" (HC 211) and a negative appraisal of the character and conduct of slaves in 1823 (cf. HC 213ff). Hampden's final appendix contains a comparison of the production of St. Domingo before and after the revolution to prove that "the country in general presents a scene of desolation" (HC 215).

The main conflict of interest, which the text addresses, is the one between the colonial centre and periphery. Hampden blames Clarkson for disenfranchising the colonial assemblies by his suggestion of introducing "an entire new code of laws into our colonies" based on the premise that "nothing in the way of improvement" is to be expected from the colonial assemblies. He doubts the obedience of the colonies to "a code forced upon them by the British Parliament" (HC 156f). The author calls Clarkson's plan for amending the colonial codes an "unconstitutional invasion of their rights ... founded on the principle, that power constitutes right; a doctrine which, we conceive, is not the most salutary that could be suggested to the mind of the Colonist, and perhaps is not better calculated to make him a loyal subject than a merciful master" (HC 157).

Hampden warns that such a "tyrannical invasion of chartered rights" (HC 194) would provoke "the hostility of those who are capable of being our most formidable enemies," (HC 186). He predicts that this kind of policy would "draw after it a similar train of horrors and disasters" (HC 195f) as in St. Domingo. The last sentence of the text again contains a severe warning that this kind of metropolitan intervention "threatens to inflict upon us the horrors of rebellion and bloodshed, the ruin of thousands, and the final alienation of our Colonies" (HC 200).

4.15.3 Ideology

Hampden criticises Clarkson's concept of liberty, calling the abolitionists "the most infatuated admirers of the name of liberty" (HC 164) who labour in the name rather than the cause of liberty (cf. HC 150). On the other hand, Hampden refers to the pro-slavery lobby as the true and sincere friends of "a system of emancipation, consistent with a due regard to the claims of justice, or the rights of private property, with the true interests of liberty and humanity ..." (HC 196)

Hampden contests Clarkson's universal conception of man as a capitalist subject which is best motivated by wage labour. He writes:

> It is the effect of slavery to render men indolent and improvident, but happily at the same time to make their habits frugal and their wants few; if they are strangers to the gratifications of refinement, they are strangers also to its artificial wants; the only luxury which they know, is indolence and ease. If then they would not labour to acquire wealth for themselves, shall we be persuaded, that they would labour still more to secure that benefit for others? 'Credat Judaeus.' (HC 182)

However, the author also posits a fundamental categorical difference between free individuals and slaves. In disproving the validity of Joshua Steele's experiment for a discussion of emancipation, he writes that "the whole plan was perfectly consistent with the interests of humanity, justice, and prudence" (HC 171) since Steele's "Negroes still were, and still are slaves, transferred through the reigns of several successive masters; they, or their descendants, are living at this day in peaceable and contented subjection" (HC 171). Hampden argues that slavery is the only possible way of running plantations, calling the present case "a question between free and slave labourers, but between slave labourers, or no labourers at all" (HC 177fn). While Steele led the slaves "to the very threshold of freedom", he predicts that the "step must be irrevocable, and may be fatal" (HC 171).

Apart from this, Hampden describes it as contrary to human nature for the planters to make sacrifices for an emancipation the outcome of which is problematical anyway (cf. HC 153).

As in the other texts, humanity serves as a positive value which is abstract enough to be employed by both sides of the argument. Hampden makes use of the usual phrases, such as "the great cause of humanity" (HC 148), "motives of humanity" (HC 151), "the interests of humanity, justice, and prudence" (HC 171) and "the true interests of liberty and humanity" (HC 196).

The female gender is strikingly absent from Hampden's text; he only explicitly refers to it three times throughout the whole text, and the first two instances are only minor allusions to femininity in footnotes (cf. HC 155fn and 195fn). In the appendix to his work, Hampden cites communications about the general conduct of slaves in Tortola. It is there that he dedicates the only full sentence of the text to females: "The females are dependent chiefly on slaves for their support; they seldom cohabit for any length of time with the same husband" (HC 213).

4.16 Heyrick: *Immediate Abolition* (1824)

4.16.1 Elizabeth Heyrick

Elizabeth Heyrick (née Coltman) was born to a dissenter family in Leicester in 1769. In her youth, the family was visited by the theologian John Wesley and in 1785, the family home was plundered by a machine-breaking mob. Anecdotes about her childhood depict Elizabeth as a saintly child giving spare pennies to a beggar (cf. Grundy). In 1789, at the age of 19, she married John Heyrick. Originally the Leicester town clerk, John soon joined the 15th Light Dragoons and the couple lived in English and Irish barracks thereafter. John died in 1797. They had no children.

As a widow of an officer, Elizabeth received a pension, which she was anxious not to spend on herself but rather to devote it to charitable ends. She rejoined her family. In Leicester, she became a member of the Society of Friends and began her life-long devotion to social issues, anti-slavery and the protection of animals. In 1809, she famously ended a bull-baiting by buying the bull (cf. Grundy). Heyrick anonymously published more than 20 books and pamphlets on various issues, the best-known of which is probably *Immediate, not Gradual Abolition, or, An Inquiry into the Shortest, Safest, and most Effectual Means of Getting Rid of West Indian Slavery* (1824).

However, Elizabeth Heyrick died somewhat disillusioned in 1831, aged only 61. Hochschild cites a letter of Heyrick to her fellow anti-slavery activist Lucy Townsend: "Nothing human can dispel that despairing torpor into which I have been plunging deeper and deeper for many months past" (qtd. in Hochschild 328).

Heyrick's work is referred to frequently in the scholarly debate on the slave trade and animal rights. Davis refers to her as a militant British Quaker and quotes her conviction that abolitionism was a "holy war,—an attack upon the strong holds, the deep intrenchments [sic] of the very powers of darkness" (Davis, *Human Progress* 145). He calls her text "an inflammatory pamphlet, that denounced the principle of gradualism, attacked the government for conspiring with slaveholders, and called for a massive consumers' boycott of slave-grown produce in order to achieve immediate, unconditional emancipation" (Davis, *Human Progress* 183). Hochschild describes her as "A blast of fresh air, [who] unlike virtually every other writer on the subject roundly criticised the mainstream anti-slavery figures for their slow, cautious, accommodating measures" (Hochschild 324). He highlights that Heyrick "was openly sympathetic to the black insurrections in the West Indies" (Hochschild 325) and compared them to the "heroic and meritorious" (HI 22) resistance of the Greeks against the Ottoman Empire. He further notes that Heyrick did not black out domestic social problems in favour of the suffering of the slaves abroad. He mentions that unlike many other anti-slavery writers, she did not see the need to contrast the image of the slave with that of the happy British peasant and worker:

> Her feeling about slavery were of a piece with those about all injustice. The poor in England suffered because the rich treated them 'with the spirit of the slave trade'; a man could be hanged for petty theft, while society did nothing to punish 'robberies en masse which impoverish millions'. (Hochschild 325)

Moira Ferguson takes a somewhat more critical approach towards Heyrick's commitment to animal rights. She writes that Heyrick "circulated a gender-based discourse about cruelty to animals that renegotiated a formerly totalising view of Englishness. Heyrick established a sense of female power" (Ferguson 325). In her analysis of Heyrick's *Bull-Baiting: a Village Dialogue between John Brown and*

John Simms, Ferguson argues that this dialogue between two working class characters turned the discourse on cruelty into "a discourse against class insurrection. It inscribed a horror of violence and labouring people" (Ferguson 325). Ferguson, furthermore, argues that Heyrick, by intervening on behalf of the bulls in her pamphlets against the working-class pastime of bull baiting (Ferguson 328), invoked the image of John Bull, the symbol of Englishness (Ferguson 329). Finally, Ferguson remarks that Heyrick's "use of statistics, eyewitness accounts and factual data contrasted sharply with the anti-slavery poems and tales of the 1780s and 1790s" (Ferguson 341). It is quite remarkable that while most other female anti-slavery writers made use of these genres, Heyrick appropriated the predominantly male genre of the argumentative essay.

In her article on women and early abolitionist movements, Rycenga calls *Immediate Abolition* "the first widely circulated assertion of 'immediatism'" (Rycenga 37) and points out that Heyrick's example gained a wide following among women's anti-slavery organisations, which "explicitly followed Heyrick's immediatism and rejected the gradualism of their male coadjutors" (Rycenga 40). Faulkner stresses Heyrick's devotion to the free labour doctrines of Adam Smith (cf. Faulkner 381) and highlights her impact on both sides of the Atlantic (cf. Faulkner 381).

Self-representation

Heyrick published her *Immediate Abolition* anonymously, and, accordingly, there are no references of a personal nature in the text. The only passages that allow a glimpse at her person are those in which she tries to persuade her readers to join the group of "the true friends of justice" (HI 4).

She uses the first person plural pronouns "we" and "our" frequently. In contrast, especially to pro-slavery writers, she thus tries to persuade the reader to identify with the values around which she creates an in-group "whose moral perceptions are unblinded by interest or prejudice,—whose charity is unwarped by partiality or hypocrisy" (HI 22). Heyrick's "we" attempts to include the British people as a whole, making the emancipation of the West Indian slaves a question of collective morality and its omission a sign of shared national guilt. She makes it a matter of national prestige to live up to the moral obligations connected to the successful abolition of the slave trade. She argues that emancipation would increase the weight of British influence, "Then, and not till then, we shall speak to the surrounding nations with the all-commanding eloquence of sincerity and truth,—and our persuasions will be backed by the irresistible argument of consistent example "(HI 3).

Calling for consumer action against West Indian sugar, she tried to install in the British public a consciousness of their power as consumers and at the same time promised a sort of moral purity—"we shall have clean hands,—and the Divine blessing may then be expected to crown our exertions for the redemption of other captives" (HI 23).

4.16.2 Synopsis and Argument

Heyrick starts her argument for immediate emancipation by stating that now the truth about the situation of the West Indian slaves is out, and it would be immoral for the public not to take sides (cf. HI 3f). She writes: "the whole nation must now divide itself into the active supporters and the active opposers of slavery; there is no longer any ground for a neutral party to stand upon" (HI 4).

Thus she calls for an "ABSTINENCE FROM THE USE OF WEST INDIAN PRODUCTIONS [her capital letters]" in order to "give the death blow to West Indian slavery" (HI 5). She argues that by doing so, both slave and planter would ultimately be benefitted, since it would only force the planters to follow the principle of self-interest. "This potent and active principle ... would compel the planter to set his slaves at liberty" (HI 5).

Heyrick's radical stance shows when she argues that even if emancipation were injurious for the planters, it would still have to be carried through based on the basic human rights of the slaves (cf. HI 6). She calls for an immediate emancipation, calling slavery "the detaining our West Indian slaves in bondage, is a continued acting of the same atrocious injustice which first .... robbed them of that sacred unalienable right" (HI 8). Heyrick literally describes gradual abolition as the work of Satan (HI 9f), arguing that the devil himself, "by a train of most exquisite reasoning", has brought "the abolitionists to the conclusion, that the interest of the poor, degraded and oppressed slave, as well as that of his master, will best be secured by his remaining in slavery" (HI 10). She admits that it is understandable that the slave owners should argue against immediate emancipation based on their (fallacious) argument that the slaves "would rise in a mass, and massacre all the white inhabitants of the islands" (HI 13). However, she presents it as absurd that abolitionists would have "caught the same infection" (HI 13), that "the friends of humanity,—the wise and the good" (HI 13) should fall victims to the same delusions as the slave holders.

Heyrick argues that emancipation is perfectly safe:

> Should the wretched African find the moment for breaking his own chains,—and asserting his own freedom,—he may well be expected to take terrible vengeance,—to push the law of retaliation to its utmost extreme. But, when presented with his freedom,—when the sacred rights of humanity are restored to him, would that be the moment for rage, for revenge and murder? (HI 14)

She radically asserts that "the interests and the prejudices of the West Indian planters, have occupied much too prominent a place in the discussion of this great question" (HI 14) and demands that "compensation be first made to the slave, for his long years of uncompensated labour, degradation and suffering" (HI 16).

She then continues to argue for the superiority of immediate over gradual emancipation, urging that the topic of slavery be considered less in the light of interest but rather "with regard to the broad and palpable distinctions between right and wrong, virtue and vice" (HI 18). Heyrick states that unsuccessful attempts at emancipation actually worsen the situation of the slave (cf. HI 19), concluding that "an immediate emancipation then, is the object to be aimed at; it is more wise and rational—more politic and safe, as well as more just and humane, than gradual emancipation" (HI 19).

The text has an appendix dealing with the Demerara rebellion. Heyrick argues for the slaves' natural right to rebellion, comparing them to the Greek rebels (cf. HI 22f), whom "we deem it an act of virtue,—of Christian charity, to supply ... with arms and ammunition, to enable them to persist in insurrection" (HI 22).

4.16.3 Ideology

It is self-evident from the very nature of Heyrick's basic argument for immediate emancipation that freedom is a prominent concept. She asks to "give the slave his liberty,—in the sacred name of justice, give it him at once" (HI 8). Thus, she is also quite outspoken in her conviction that freedom is a natural right when she states that "the slave has a right to his liberty, a right which it is a crime to withhold" (HI 5). It is only through the parenthetical addition "until forfeited by crime" (HI 6) that Heyrick qualifies the "birth right" (HI 6) of liberty.

In her immediatist approach to emancipation, Heyrick also rejects the common anti-slavery promise of only emancipating the slaves when they are fit for it. She argues that,

> We have no right, on any pretext of expediency or pretended humanity, to say—'because you have been made a slave, and thereby degraded and debased,—therefore, I will continue to hold you in bondage until you have acquired a capacity to make a right use of your liberty.' As well might you say to a poor wretch, gasping and languishing in a pest house, 'here will I keep you, till I have given you a capacity for the enjoyment of pure air' (HI 8)

Heyrick cites Clarkson's account of the Haitian revolution to dissipate fears of massacres in pointing out that "no instance has been recorded in these important annals, of the emancipated slaves (not the gradually, but the immediately emancipated slaves) having abused their freedom" (HI 7). She even describes the idea as absurd that the slaves, when set free, would take part in massacres. Heyrick incredulously asks: "... when the sacred rights of humanity are restored to him, would that be the moment for rage, for revenge and murder?" (HI 14)

Despite her commitment to immediate freedom, the safety of emancipation is, of course, an issue for Heyrick. The subtitle of her text refers to her plan being, "THE SHORTEST, SAFEST, AND MOST EFFECTUAL MEANS OF GETTING RID OF WEST INDIAN SLAVERY" (HI 2).

Apart from what has been pointed out above, Heyrick follows further strategies to assuage any doubts about her radical plans. She expresses her strong belief in societal means of control when stating that emancipation does not "imply emancipation from law [and] the same laws which restrain and punish crime in the white population, would still restrain and punish crime in the black population" (HI 13).

Heyrick declares her solidarity with black rebels; she even juxtaposes them with the Greek freedom fighters of her day (cf. HI 22f) and thus argues that rebellion has universal motives. Seeing a universal human love for freedom as the reason behind slave rebellions, rather than portraying them as irrational massacres is an attempt of depicting black violence as manageable and thus less threatening.

Heyrick has been described as an avid follower of Adam Smith (cf. Faulkner 381), and her utopia of post-slavery society certainly confirms this. She is convinced that boycotting West Indian products would force the planters to mind their own interests (HI 6) and eventually "the over-laboured, crouching slave is converted into a free labourer,—his compulsory, unremunerated toil, under the impulse of the cart whip, exchanged for cheerful, well recompensed industry" (HI 19f). The very idea of a consumer boycott indicates a strong belief in the regulating power of the market,

> The market, though shut to the productions of slave labour, would still be open to the productions of free labour and the planters are not such devoted worshippers of slavery as to make a voluntary sacrifice of their own interests upon her altar; they will not doom the soil to perpetual barrenness rather than suffer it to be cultivated by free men (HI 5)

Heyrick thus reminds the British consumer of their power and asks all doubters to "reflect, that the grandest objects of human observation consist of small agglomerated particles; that the globe itself is composed of atoms too minute for discernment; that extended ages consist of accumulated moments" (HI 23).

Heyrick's text is characterised by the prevailing dichotomy between full human and slave.

> As long as a human being is bought and sold,—regarded as goods and chattels,—compelled to labour without wages,—branded, chained, and flogged at the caprice of his owner; he will, of necessity, as long as the feeling of pain, the sense of degradation and injury remain, he will, unless he have the spirit of a Christian martyr, be vindictive and revengeful. (HI 13)

However, as part of her immediatist approach, she has a somewhat more optimistic outlook on human nature when she asserts that "independent of such considerations, the oppressed and miserable, corrupt as is human nature, do not naturally become savage and revengeful when their oppressions and miseries are removed" (HI 13). She contrasts humans as moral agents to the brute creation, writing of "every principle of virtue which distinguishes the human from the brute creation" (HI 21).

Heyrick also uses the header "humanity" as a generic positive value, which seems to be associated with emotion rather than rational intellect, when she refers to "every feeling of humanity—in every bosom" (HI 21). She writes of "those who have any claim to humanity" (HI 7), "friends of humanity" (HI 7), "sacred rights of humanity" (HI 14), "inherent rights of humanity" (HI 15) and "every principle of humanity and justice" (HI 17). As has been referred to above, Heyrick warns that "the father of lies" (HI 10) has deceived the "the wise and the good ... by the humanity of the arguments propounded for gradual emancipation" (HI 10), introducing a concept of wrong humanity. She generally contrasts the divine and the human, for example, when she refers to "justice, divine or human" (HI 15). Thus, she argues that the misguided gradualism of mainstream anti-slavery could have been avoided "had they depended more upon divine, and less upon human support" (HI 18).

Heyrick's text features a distinct notion of human progress. In a longer passage, she describes this progress as possessing a certain inevitability:

> It is absurd to imagine that the progress of humanity, of moral and political improvement, is to be arrested, because some individual perquisites, derived from institutions of brutal ignorance and barbarism, would be curtailed. A great deal more reasonably might the industrious artizan, whose daily subsistence depends on his daily labour—whose only property is his labour—and who, in many cases, has no means, like the West Indian capitalist, of transferring it from one channel to another; with a great deal more reason might he exclaim and cry out for protection against all mechanical improvements, which diminish labour, which deprive thousands of the labouring classes of their wonted resources, and drive them to beggary. (HI 16)

The latter part of the quote is especially interesting against the background that, in her youth, Heyrick had experienced the plundering of her family's house by a machine-breaking mob (cf. Grundy). Her argument seems to be that not even the "industrious artisan" can demand the arrest of progress and even less so the West India planter, since "it is absurd to imagine" (HI 16) that human progress would heed individual hardships. Thus the author expects both the West India planter and the British artisan to bow to inevitable progress.

4.17 Conclusion

Anti-slavery authors mainly argue against slavery at a fundamental level, the main argument being that human beings cannot be sold or owned. Clarkson argues that slavery is contrary to humanity and reduced slaves to the level of the brute creation when they ought to be considered as human beings. Also, Ramsay describes slavery as an obstacle to the improvement of the slaves, since it is an "unnatural state of mankind" (RE 102). This argument returns even more prominently in the emancipation debate. Elizabeth Heyrick makes personal freedom the distinguishing mark between human and brute creation (cf. HI 21) and Wilberforce argues that slavery is irreconcilable with the "natural rights of human beings" (WA 7) who have to be disciplined by hope and fear rather than by brute force like animals (cf. WA 17). Therefore, these authors make the mere absence of slavery the definition of freedom (cf. WA 66) and construct reformed slaves who are "free agent[s] and accountable creature[s]" (CT 10) but also capitalist subjects. The descriptions of the suffering of slaves have to be seen within this context; they serve as proof of their inhuman treatment. Also, the racial dimension of abolitionist discourse is motivated by the fundamental logic that to enslave a human being is to deny their humanity. Within this context, anti-slavery authors set out to "prove the Africans to be men" (cf. CE 137f, CT 6). This is also backed up by the religious argument that God has created all humans of the same blood and that all mankind was derived from the same stock (CE 184). Thus, the anti-slavery argument contrasts the slave with the human of European modernity who has to be fully accountable for their actions (cf. CL 72).

On an ideological level, anti-slavery discourse is clearly torn between its claims for individual freedom and the desire for a well-ordered society. This results in a quite distinct concept of limited personal freedom, a kind of "true liberty", as Wilberforce calls it (WL 258f), which is contrasted with the excesses of the French Revolution. Despite this, Britain is very much defined as free soil; Ramsay, for example, calls it "a country where liberty is the established birth-right of the lowest member of the community" (RE 43).

Anti-slavery authors oppose the pro-slavery claim that the slave trade is actually doing the Africans a favour in taking them to the European colonies. They portray it as a paradox that the improvement and civilisation of African societies is inversely proportionate to the degree of European influence. Thus, they try to include Africans in a universalist discourse of progress which is based on a Eurocentric notion of civilisation springing from a singular origin in Mesopotamia (WL 74ff).

In the emancipation debate, the focus shifts to the colonial slave populations, which authors include in a similar discourse of improvement in order to transform slaves into "a grateful peasantry" (WA 74). This would ultimately be in the interest of the planters according to the Smithian logic that "the labour of free men is cheaper than the labour of slaves" (CT 47). In addition to that, the topic of slave revolts, of course, receives more attention. The emancipation debate argues that freeing the slaves is actually a question of safety in order to prevent "the dreadful explosion that may otherwise be expected" (WA 72).

At this point, the question of slavery also increasingly becomes a negotiation between the colonial centre and the colonial periphery. Although anti-slavery authors, with the notable exception of Elizabeth Heyrick, are always anxious to appease the colonial interest, they also argue for metropolitan intervention (cf. CT 7ff). Clarkson explicitly calls the British Parliament the "source of all legitimate power" (CT 7) and argues that the West Indian assemblies ought not to be depended upon to bring about change. Generally speaking, a centrist worldview manifests itself at several levels of the discourse on slavery: humanity stems from a singular origin, there is only one source of civilisation and, finally, metropolitan Britain is the one source of power within the empire.

The arguments of pro-slavery authors are necessarily more varied since they are the ones who are attacking a hegemonic position. They have to use various techniques in order to subvert the anti-slavery position. Perhaps the most obvious of these strategies is attacking the personal integrity and authority of anti-slavery authors. The most prominent examples of an attack against the person of the author are the responses to Ramsay's *Essay* by James Tobin (cf. TC) and the anonymous authors from St. Christopher (cf. AA). With authors like Clarkson and Wilberforce, pro-slavery authors could argue that they lacked first-hand knowledge of the West Indian plantation economy. This played into the hand of various evasive strategies, which range from the claim that the depictions of cruelty are either exaggerated or isolated cases that are not representative of the West Indian colonies as a whole (cf. AA 16, FA 172ff). Generally speaking, pro-slavery authors are anxious to represent the West Indian sugar economy as a well-regulated system and slavery as a kind of benevolent despotism of a distinctly feudal kind.

Another frequent argument of these authors is the existence of slavery in the Bible (cf. AA 47) and the rejection of Clarkson's argument that it was primarily the spread of Christianity in Europe which put an end to slavery. Within this context, pro-slavery authors like to contrast the alleged ease of the West Indian slave with the hardships of both European peasants and factory workers (TC 89, FA 229). Arguing that the situation of slaves in Africa is, of course, more miserable than in the British colonies, pro-slavery texts point out that the slave trade is actually a blessing for the Africans (cf. AF 15, FA 116) as it rescues the surplus population from certain death (AF 41). The miserable situation is sometimes underlined by instances of cannibalism (cf. AF 37, AO 34). In addition, they argue that it is not the Europeans who make slaves out of the Africans, as they are slaves already when they are bought (cf. TC 18).

Pro-slavery authors, of course, claim that the whole question is a strictly colonial matter and no concern of the British Parliament. In this context, they blame their opponents for interference, inciting the slaves to rebellion (AA 44), massacres (ML 16) and negative economic impacts on the colonies (AF 10). While they superficially agree with the humanitarianism of the anti-slavery project (AO 50f), pro-slavery writers tend to propose an even more gradual approach in an attempt to simply delay emancipation ad infinitum. Bridges, for example, asks to just let the slow progress of civilisation run its own course (cf. BV 8) until the slave will gradually be fit for freedom at the right moment.

The anti-slavery writers' lack of first-hand experience becomes even more salient in the emancipation debate when pro-slavery authors tried to argue along the lines that it was simply not possible to work slaves without the whip. Bridges cites the existence of corporal punishment in the army and navy to prove this point (BV 21). The same author argues that Africans are inherently lazy (cf. BC 11) and Hampden similarly challenges the anti-slavery utopia of introducing free labour in the colonies as illusory (cf. HC 178).

The two sides of the discussion propose quite contrasting conceptions of the human being. While anti-slavery texts construct a human being who stands in binary distinction to "the brute creation", the pro-slavery argument favours a more gradualist approach. Still, in 1823, Bridges argued that "the great chain of nature" is formed of "conjoining links" from "the inanimate and inferior parts of the creation, so even up to man ... the lowest of which, in the human species, seems to be the Hottentot" (BV 17).

5 The Image of Africans

5.1 Vocabulary for Africans — A Quantitative Approach

A short appraisal of the most frequent vocabulary used in order to refer to "Africans" introduces this part of my work. Because of the quantity of texts, this is restricted to an analysis of nouns and pronouns.

5.1.1 Nouns

The table below lists the most frequent nouns in phrases coded "Africans". The code "Africans" not only includes words referring to Africans directly, but has also been applied in such a way as to cover whole phrases referring to Africans. For example, if an author writes about "their condition" with "their" referring to Africans, the whole phrase has been coded in order to represent the immediate linguistic environment in which Africans are referred to. The four parts of the table list the most frequent nouns of all texts, anti-slavery texts, pro-slavery texts and pro-slavery texts outside of quotations. Some pro-slavery authors extensively quote from the texts they write in response to, so these texts often contain a substantial amount of what is actually anti-slavery text. The rightmost part of the table, therefore, takes into account only the parts of the text which are not quotes from any other authors.

252 'MALLEABLE AT THE EUROPEAN WILL'

Nouns in Phrases Coded "Africans"

	All texts			Anti-slavery			Pro-slavery			Pro-slavery outside quotations		
rank	freq	word	%	freq	word	%	freq	word	%	freq	word	%
1	1624	slaves	3,82%	1102	slaves	3,81%	522	slaves	3,85%	382	slaves	3,56%
2	668	negroes	1,57%	302	negroes	1,05%	366	negroes	2,70%	328	negroes	3,05%
3	394	slave	0,93%	276	slave	0,96%	120	negro	0,88%	115	negro	1,07%
4	294	negro	0,69%	174	negro	0,60%	118	slave	0,87%	85	slave	0,79%
5	228	people	0,54%	166	africans	0,57%	86	people	0,63%	65	people	0,61%
6	220	africans	0,52%	142	people	0,49%	54	africans	0,40%	44	africans	0,41%
7	159	men	0,37%	118	men	0,41%	43	children	0,32%	31	children	0,29%
8	140	children	0,33%	97	children	0,34%	41	men	0,30%	29	men	0,27%
9	92	natives	0,22%	71	natives	0,25%	35	women	0,26%	29	prisoners	0,27%
10	87	inhabitants	0,20%	66	man	0,23%	33	prisoners	0,24%	28	women	0,26%
11	87	man	0,20%	64	inhabitants	0,22%	28	population	0,21%	20	population	0,19%
12	77	persons	0,18%	64	persons	0,22%	23	inhabitants	0,17%	19	inhabitants	0,18%
13	76	women	0,18%	60	king	0,21%	21	natives	0,15%	15	natives	0,14%
14	74	king	0,17%	51	creatures	0,18%	21	man	0,15%	15	numbers	0,14%
15	70	population	0,16%	43	family	0,15%	21	blacks	0,15%	14	man	0,13%

16	59	creatures	0,14%	42	population	0,15%	19	numbers	0,14%	14	blacks	0,13%
17	58	family	0,14%	41	women	0,14%	15	family	0,11%	13	family	0,12%
18	56	prisoners	0,13%	34	subjects	0,12%	14	king	0,10%	11	subjects	0,10%
19	53	blacks	0,12%	32	blacks	0,11%	14	subjects	0,10%	10	king	0,09%
20	49	numbers	0,12%	30	numbers	0,10%	13	persons	0,10%	10	persons	0,09%
21	48	subjects	0,11%	23	prisoners	0,08%	8	creatures	0,06%	5	creatures	0,05%

Fig. 10: Nouns in phrases coded "Africans"

It is hardly surprising that "slave/slaves" and "negro/negroes" are the most frequent nouns in both anti- and pro-slavery texts. It has to be noted that plural forms are more frequent than singular ones. The percentage of the racially defined term "negroes" is slightly higher in pro-slavery texts. Generally speaking, plural nouns outweigh the singular ones in both discourses, which indicates that the discourse on slavery is a discourse on human multiplicities. The appearance of "inhabitants", "population", "numbers", "natives" and "subjects" as items also suggests that the discourse on slavery is rather a discussion of whole populations of Africans than of individuals. However, it is interesting that there is hardly any difference between pro and anti-slavery texts in the use of the term "Africans". Both sides use "negro/es" much more frequently. The high overall frequency of the word "Africans" is mainly caused by Thomas Clarkson's frequent use of it in his *Essay*, which accounts for almost 40% of the total occurrences. This hints at the relevance of an ethnic/racial dimension to the discourse as a whole. Still, pro-slavery texts make use of this race-based representation of Africans to a higher degree than anti-slavery texts. The contrast is even greater in segments coded "Africans" outside of quotes (3.05% in pro-slavery texts vs. 1.05% in anti-slavery).

The frequent representation of Africans as slaves by both pro- and anti-slavery writers further helped the creation of a distinct image of Africans that was very much "the Other" of what Hall describes as the Enlightenment subject (cf. Hall, *Cultural Identity* 275). The negative connotations linked to the image of the slave are shown by the OED's definition for the adjective "slavish," namely "of a submissive, unmanly disposition, ... vile, mean, base, ignoble, [and] servilely imitative; lacking originality or independence." (OED 'slavish'). The last part of the definition, in particular, describes a lack of the Enlightenment subjects' "capacities of reason, consciousness and action" (Hall, *Cultural Identity* 275). It will, therefore, how far Africans are represented as fully human individuals in the debate on slavery will have to be investigated.

The frequency with which "master/s", "treatment", "labour", "work" and "gang" occur is probably the result of the discourse's concern with master-slave relationships in the West Indian colonies, which has an impact on the image of the African as slave. "Man/men/women", "persons", "creatures" and "beings", on the other hand, reflect the discussion of the Africans' claim to a common humanity. It has to be noted that those words implying a common humanity of Africans, such as "man", "men", "person", "persons", "creature" and "creatures", constantly appear in anti-slavery texts to a higher degree than in their pro-slavery counterparts. The contrast is even stronger in the pro-slavery sequences outside quotations.

The more frequent use of the term "prisoners" in pro-slavery texts is part of their justification strategy based on the argument that the Africans are prisoners or slaves in their country anyway. In turn, anti-slavery texts use the term "labourer" much more frequently than the pro-slavery ones, the reason for which is probably the anti-slavery utopia of transforming the former slaves into wage labourers.

5.1.2 Pronouns

In his introduction to critical discourse analysis, Siegfried Jäger comments on the importance of analysing the pronouns of discourse fragments (cf. Jäger, *Einführung* 183). The chart below compares the frequencies in percentage terms of the 16 most common pronouns in phrases coded "Africans" in all texts (red), in anti-slavery texts (grey) and in pro slavery texts (orange) with the overall frequencies of these pronouns in the whole text corpus (blue).

256 'MALLEABLE AT THE EUROPEAN WILL'

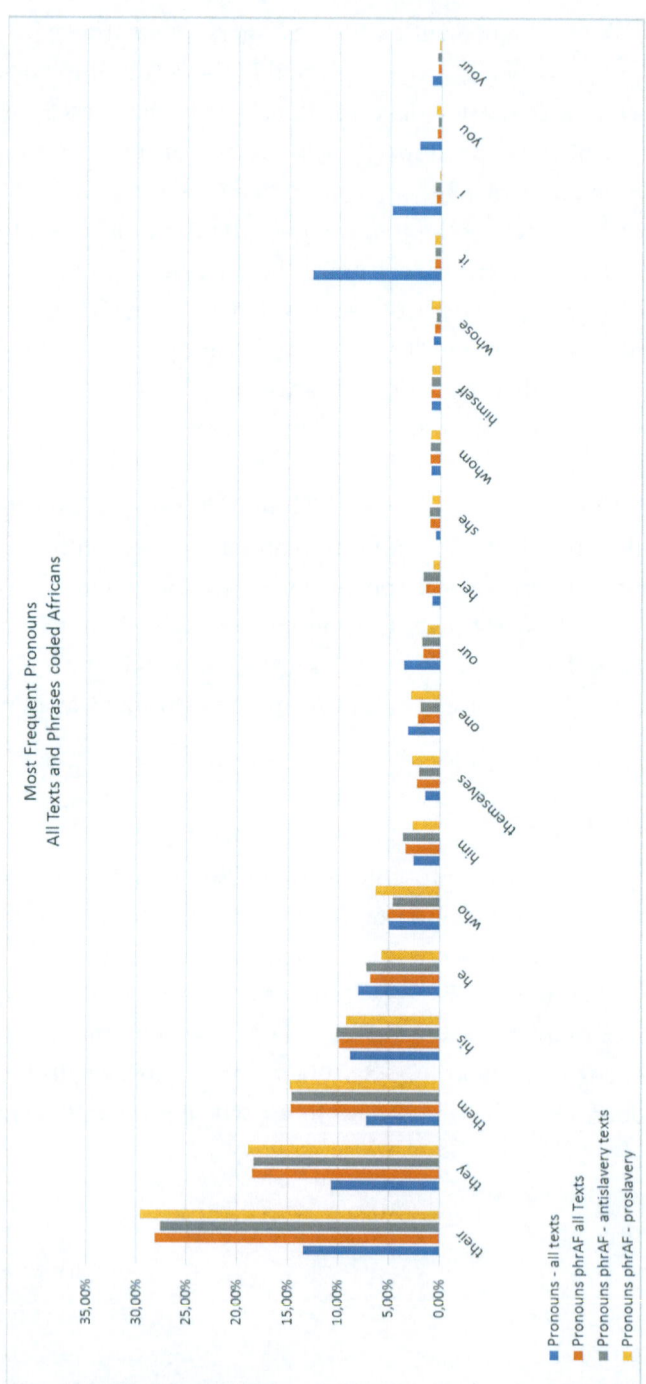

Fig. 11: Most frequent pronouns

The first result of an overview of the texts' pronouns confirms what has already been observed with the nouns, namely that Africans are represented in the plural. The three most frequent pronouns are "their", "they" and "them". The difference between the frequencies of these pronouns in all texts and phrases referring to Africans gives additional evidence to the fact that, unsurprisingly, "Africans" in the text seems to be plural beings rather than single individuals. Furthermore, the prevalence of "he", "his" and "him" over "her" and "she" suggests that if Africans do appear in the singular, they are predominantly male.

The dominance of the plural possessive "their" is perhaps the most striking feature of the pronouns used for Africans, which is more striking if compared to the overall frequency of the pronoun "their". It speaks of a tendency to literally attribute properties to "them". The collocations of "their..." will be further analysed below.

There seems to be no huge difference between pro- and anti-slavery texts. However, pro-slavery authors use plural possessive and object pronouns a bit more frequently than anti-slavery ones. On the other hand, the male singular pronouns "he", "his" and "him" appear a bit more frequently in anti-slavery texts, which might be the result of passages which portray Africans as individuals.

That it is the third person plural which is most frequently used to refer to Africans along with the relatively low percentages of "I", "our" and especially "we" show that Africans are portrayed as Others rather than as belonging to what the authors perceive as "us". The few instances of "I" are mostly contained in narrative passages in which Africans are speaking in the first person. In the other cases, in which a first person pronoun is referring to an African, it is most frequently the possessive plural, "our", which results from such constructions as "our slaves".

The contrast in the overall frequency of "you" and "your" and the frequency of these two pronouns in segments coded "Africans" results from Africans not being the addressees of these texts.

The high frequency of the possessive plural certainly merits further scrutiny. The table below compares the most frequent clusters of two to three words, starting with "their".

Two- and Three-Word Clusters starting with "their"

	All Texts		Anti-slavery Texts		Pro-slavery Texts
Rank freq	cluster	freq	cluster	freq	cluster
183	their own	118	their own	65	their own
111	their slaves	77	their slaves	34	their slaves
84	their masters	55	their masters	29	their masters
39	their present	25	their children	15	their present
35	their children	25	their situation	14	their own country
33	their situation	24	their present	10	their children
32	their own country	21	their condition	9	their lives
28	their lives	19	their lives	8	their master
24	their condition	19	their respective	8	their native
23	their native	18	their labour	8	their owners
21	their country	18	their own country	8	their situation
21	their fellow	17	their country	7	their being
20	their freedom	16	their fellow	7	their freedom
20	their labour	15	their native	7	their present state
20	their respective	14	their work	6	their negroes
19	their work	13	their freedom	6	their passage
17	their liberty	12	their liberty	6	their wives
17	their present state	12	their little	5	their duty
16	their being	11	their families	5	their fellow
16	their little	11	their minds	5	their former
14	their master	11	their parents	5	their liberty
14	their minds	10	their lands	5	their subjects

Fig. 12: Two- and three-word clusters with "their"

The most frequent cluster with "their" in all three groups of texts is "their own", which again frequently collocates with "country", "slaves", "people", "interest", "masters" and "time". The high frequencies of such clusters as "their own country" "their country" and "their native country" shows that the discourse on slavery did in part negotiate the situation of the Africans in "their state of nature" and that the identity of Africans is also constructed in terms of geographical provenance. The clusters "their own interest" and "their own time" again hint at the preoccupation of these texts with the issue of labour discipline and the project of universalising wage labour as opposed to slavery. The clusters typically appear in passages like Thomas Clarkson's *Thoughts*, "they have besides a quick sense of their own interest," (CT 42), and discuss the possibility of granting the autonomy of a capitalist subject to former slaves, which is also reflected in expressions like "their freedom" and "their liberty". The lower frequencies of "their labour" and "their work" in pro-slavery texts also gives evidence to the preoccupation of anti-slavery authors with the issue of labour discipline and the inclusion of former slaves in a system of wage labour.

The high frequencies of the clusters "their slaves" and "their masters" shows that Africans are frequently referred to indirectly in both pro and anti-slavery texts. A further characteristic of the discourse is reflected by the frequent use of the clusters "their present", "their condition", "their state" and "their present state". The main strategy of anti-slavery texts for countering (alleged) racist arguments of their opponents was to attribute any alleged negative features of Africans completely to the effects of slavery. Thus, we find these clusters in passages like, "their present state of ignorance and dependence" (RE 87). In addition, the preoccupation with "their state" also speaks of a distinct form of static social analysis, which wants to render living humans and human societies as unmoving objects of a scientific observation.

The appearance of the cluster "their minds" speaks of the concern, especially of anti-slavery authors, with "the improvement of their minds" (RE 99) before emancipation. The different frequencies of "their own country" seem to suggest that a discussion of the Africans' condition "in their own country" seems to be more important for anti- than for pro-slavery authors. This is hardly surprising considering the discursive power, connected to the state of nature, of a discussion of basic societal concepts, such as the freedom of the individual or the emergence of state power.

5.1.3 Adjectives

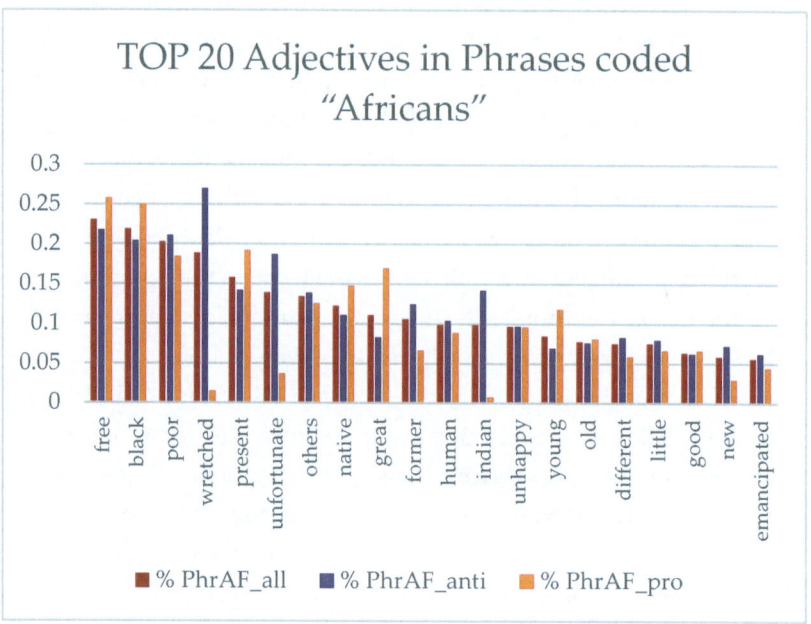

Fig. 13: Adjectives in Phrases coded "Africans"

The graph compares the 20 most frequent adjectives in phrases coded Africans in all texts, in anti-slavery texts and in proslavery texts. The most frequent adjective are "free" followed by "black" and "poor", which is hardly surprising given both the topics of abolition and emancipation. The fact that pro-slavery authors refer more frequently to "free" Africans than anti-slavery ones might be explained by their increased concern about the behaviour of freed slave populations after a possible emancipation. "Black", on the other hand, suggests a ~~racially~~ defined representation of Africans which seems to feature more prominently in pro-slavery than in anti-slavery discourse. On the other hand, a representation of Africans as "poor", "wretched" and "unfortunate" characterises their representation in anti-slavery discourse to a higher degree. How far this is the result of a distinct image of Africans as unfortunate wretches in anti-slavery discourse will be analysed below. Finally, the more frequent use of the adjective "little" in anti-slavery texts hints at tendencies of belittling Africans which are slightly more present in anti-slavery texts than in pro-slavery ones.

5.2 Africans in Africa — Qualitative Analysis

5.2.1 Knowing Africa

The way of how these texts know Africa is an exclusively indirect one. In contrast to the West Indies, none of the authors had actually been to Africa. Thus, it is only through additional sources that knowledge about Africa enters the discourse. Edward Said aptly outlined how the images and analyses of the Orient in European discourses were informed by a desire "to dominate, to have authority over it" (Said, *Orientalism* 32). A similar thing can be said of the image and the knowledge of Africa, especially in anti-slavery discourse. It must be kept in mind that it was, of course, the anti-slavery claims for freedom and improvement which encouraged a more direct colonial intervention and the building of the British Empire in Africa (cf. Drescher, *Capitalism* 165; Davis, *Human Progress* 363). Also, Carey addresses the problematic nature of European knowledge about Africa when he writes that abolitionist authors created a pseudo-Africa inhabited by pseudo-Africans (cf. Carey 4). The constructions of Africans and the African continent are, therefore, projection screens of the respective ideology of authors.

Some of the more frequently quoted sources about Africa are Willem Bosman's *A New and Accurate Description of the Coast of Guinea* (1705), William Snelgrave's *A New Account of Some Parts of Guinea and the Slave* (1734), Thomas Astley's *A New General Collection of Voyages and Travels* (1745), William Smith's *A New Voyage to Guinea* (1744), Mungo Park's *Travels into the interior Districts of Africa* (1799) and also to some degree Long's *History of Jamaica* (1774) to name just a few.

Since both pro- and anti-slavery authors were faced with the same textual basis, the divergent images of Africa and the Africans in pro- and anti-slavery texts are largely the result of a process of different interpretation and selection. The example of Mungo Park can show how the same author is used by both sides of the discussion to serve their respective ends. Wilberforce cites Park to show that he,

> ... represents the Africans of the interior as naturally superior, both in their intellectual and moral endowments, to almost any other uncivilized nation. He speaks in high terms of their powers of ingenuity and invention, of their quickness and cheerfulness; of the value which they set on the learning within their reach, and the price at which they are willing to acquire it for themselves, or their children; of the skill which they display in several arts and manufactures. (WL 65)

Pro-slavery author Mercator quotes the same author to confirm a more negative image when he writes that,

> it was not possible for me to behold the wonderful fertility of the soil, the vast herds of cattle, &c. without lamenting, that a country, so abundantly gifted and favoured by nature, should remain in its present savage and neglected state. (ML 21)

Also, Thomas Clarkson's *Letters* is essentially a collection of accounts by French authors about various African states. The very structured way in which Clarkson describes African societies creates a distinct form of knowledge about and, thus, discursive power over Africans, while anti-slavery authors attempt to create a knowledge about Africans that establishes authority and European power over them. Some pro-slavery authors try to distance themselves from claiming too much knowledge about the 'Dark Continent'. They argue that the whole discussion of the state of Africans in Africa is beside the point. For example, the anonymous author of *Observations* points out that,

> It is not necessary for the present purpose to enter into a long enquiry how the Negroes become slaves in Africa. It is known that a great part are born so, that in some parts they are bred, as we do cattle, for sale; for we must not suppose that vast extent of country is all in the same state, or under the same regulation. (AO 15)

What both pro- and anti-slavery texts have in common is the idea that Africans are less civilised than Europeans and live more or less in a state of nature. It has been shown above in the section about history that the state of nature was a powerful argumentative tool in the discourse of the European Enlightenment. In the tradition of thinkers like Hobbes and Rousseau, the original situation of man played an important role in the negotiation of the just society. The difference between pro- and anti-slavery texts lies mainly in the interpretation of the state of nature, which will be shown below.

5.2.2 Anti-slavery: Corrupted Harmony

Anti-slavery authors often emphasise the destructive effects of the slave trade on African societies and thus argue that, on the coast, the natural harmony has been destroyed by a European influence. Wilberforce, for example, writes that:

> ... the countries on the coast are in a state of utter ignorance and barbarism, which also are always found to be the greatest where the intercourse with the Europeans has been the longest and most intimate;- while the interior countries, where not the face of a white man was ever seen, are far more advanced in the comforts and improvements of social life. (WL 86f)

The stock image of the negative effects of slavery is that of the corrupted African ruler who is tricked by the European merchants into selling his own subjects. Wilberforce describes this in his *Letter*:

> But it is not to kings or chieftains only, that the Slave Trade holds out strong temptations. The appetite for spirituous liquors is universal. European commodities are coveted by all. Whether for attack or defence, fire-arms and gunpowder are most desirable. (WL 35)

According to the author, this creates the paradoxical situation described above, which could, of course, conveniently create a moral impetus to "take up the white man's burden". Both Drescher and Davis link anti-slavery ideology to the British imperial project. Drescher, for example, states that anti-slavery ideology was a justification for British imperialism before and after the fact (Drescher, *Capitalism* 165), and Davis points out that this ideology encouraged a more direct British colonial intervention in Africa (Davis, *Progress* 363). That these anti-slavery authors see the corruption of African societies on the coast as an invitation or justification for greater European interference in the post-slavery era becomes quite evident when Wilberforce laments that:

> The very channels through which alone, according to all human calculation, Africa might have hoped to receive the blessings of religious and moral light, and social improvement, are precisely those through which her miseries flow in upon her with so full a tide. (WL 41)

Whenever African societies are described in terms of a state of nature, however, anti-slavery texts tend to view the situation in Africa as a more idyllic one. Clarkson contrasts the lives of Africans in their native countries with the hardships of colonial slavery, when he writes that Africa is "producing almost spontaneously the comforts of life, and requiring for its cultivation none of those hours, which should be appropriated to sleep" (CE 229). Also, Wilberforce creates a distinct contrast between the Africans in their state of nature and in a state of slavery:

> Hence it is, that those very Negroes, who in Africa are represented as so eminent for truth, so disinterested in kindness, so faithful in the conjugal and domestic relations, so hospitable, so fond of their children, of their parents, of their country, gradually lose all these amiable dispositions with the enjoyments which naturally arise out of them, and become depraved and debased

by all that is selfish and mercenary, and deceitful, timid and indolent, and tyrannical. (WL 246)

Being confronted with negative accounts about Africa by what Clarkson once refers to as "a writer of the highest reputation" (CE 159), of course, created a problem for anti-slavery discourse. Authors use two distinct techniques to deal with the dilemma of wanting to defend the human qualities of Africans and their belief in the authority of accounts from Africa. They either link any negative accounts to the corrupting effects of slavery and the slave trade or they argue that Europeans behaved in a similar way at the same stage of history.

This second strategy informs Ramsay's positive representation of Africans when he writes:

> ... they are capable of forming, and actually have formed, free independent societies; and, though they have not yet attained the refinements and luxuries of Europe, yet have they shewn no small ingenuity in compacting themselves together, and made no mean progress in many of the arts of life. (RE 232)

The quote shows that Ramsay sees the potential for improvement in Africans. It has been pointed out above that Africans are included in a European discourse of history according to which human societies progress through a number of stages of society before they attain "the refinements and luxuries of Europe" (RE 232). Clarkson defends Africans' propensity for gaming on grounds that "the Africans are no more to be censured for their weakness in this respect, than others in the same stage of society" (CE88 44). A belief in Africans' ability to improve is one of the basic tenets of anti-slavery ideology. Seymour Drescher holds that "the great difference between abolitionists and anti-(or perhaps non-) abolitionists ... in the emphasis placed upon the potential for rapid change" (Drescher, *Racism* 420).

The tendency of anti-slavery authors to portray Africans as potential capitalist subjects become visible in the second edition of Clarkson's *Essay*. He is anxious to maintain that, despite the idyllic situation in Africa, the principles of the market are universal ones and work for Africans as well. Clarkson describes the practice of producing canoes in the inland forests at great distances from the sea:

> Now, if we consider the prodigious length of way which many of these canoes go, and the opportunities that are afforded them; if we consider that regular markets are established through the interior parts of the country to the distance of twelve hundred miles from the water-side; that the same taste for European commodities prevails, and the same inducements are held out to kidnap the unwary, throughout the whole of this extensive space as upon the sea-shore, we may very easily conceive how great a proportion the kidnapped people must make of the number annually transported into slavery. (CE_88 37)

In another place, Clarkson describes how "The gaudy trappings of European art, not only caught their attention, but excited their curiosity: they dazzled the eyes and bewitched the senses, not only of those, to whom they were given, but of those, to whom they were shewn" (CE 44). While this certainly constructs naïve Africans, it is also aimed at making the Other manageable. It seems easy to control these natives by literally holding out a few beads of glass to them.

In *Letters*, Clarkson is equally eager to represent Africans as industrious. Not only does he repeat the practice of inland boat-building (cf. CL 60), he also contrasts the cultivation of the African soil by a free peasantry to the drudgery of the colonial slave:

> In Africa every native is the cultivator of his own little farm, and the crop that follows is the reward of his labour. To place him beyond the reach of want, more land awaits him as his own, if more should be judged necessary, and this to an extent equal to the summit of his wishes. (CL 73)

In another work, Clarkson explicitly proposes "that the Africans, by proper encouragement can be brought into habits of labour: and secondly, that free labour can be made the medium through which the productions of their country may be collected ..." (Clarkson, *Impolicy* 5).

The role of African societies in the discourse on slavery is an interesting one since it is linked to a distinct historical view of human progress through universalistic stages. Accordingly, anti-slavery authors often compare African societies in terms of the earlier stages of European society. The state of nature has an important function in negotiating basic concepts of the human. It is an explicit aim of Thomas Clarkson's *Letters* to provide a "just idea of the state of society in which the natives live" (CL vi). This is in line with the notion of a universal civilising progress referred to above. Clarkson's analysis thus attributes a distinct historical stage to African societies, which is linked to an optimistic outlook on the progress of civilisation in Africa. Clarkson reports that a friend encouraged him to publish his letters since "I think you will prove the natives to have attained a step in the scale of civilization, far beyond what any people imagine" (CL vi).

In *Letters*, Clarkson generally presents African societies in quite a positive way. He writes of the kingdom of Cayor that the king is an absolute monarch and the country is divided into administrative units. He writes of various social orders, the largest of which he refers to as "the people", of whom he writes:

> Among these there is no distinction in point of rights ... There are old and young, rich and poor. The old have no other advantage than that which is given them by age. That, which their years give them, is experience, and experience recommends to favor and respect. As to the rich, who have slaves and cattle of their own, they are not considered as forming another class. That they have advantages, however, there is no doubt, but then these advantages are the immediate consequences of their wealth, and not of any extraordinary right... (CL 44)

Clarkson clearly constructs what he sees as a fundamentally egalitarian society but also defends the privileges of the rich as an immediate consequence of their rights. His description of African villages is quite idyllic: people live in round houses of straw and the kings have a bigger house in the centre of the village. In the middle of the village, there is "a free space be left open for what is called the Publick Place of the village, a place where all publick consultations are held, and all matters of controversy settled" (CL 49). The land is allocated according to everyone's need:

> Each family has occupied that, which it thought would answer its purpose best, or that which it pitched upon the first. There are no disputes with respect to land. If a man has not enough, he may take more, and as much more as he pleases. There are thousands of acres unsettled, so that he has only to choose a spot, which is not occupied by another. (CL 52)

The vastness of the continent allows this kind of egalitarian approach to land ownership, which also resembles a period in European history when the land was not yet settled.

The description of the agrarian society in Clarkson's *Letters* resembles his historical narratives of the dark ages, both in Greek history as well as in medieval Europe. Clarkson explicitly compares the practice of kidnapping individuals for slavery in Africa to "the Grecians in their primitive state" (CE 9):

> The writings of Homer are sufficient of themselves to establish this account. They shew it to have been a common practice at so early a period as that of the Trojan war; and abound with many lively descriptions of it; which, had they been as groundless as they are beautiful, would have frequently spared the sigh of the reader of sensibility and reflection. (CE 9f)

Then again, the same author juxtaposes the Greeks and the European Dark Ages,

> The political state of Greece, in its early history, was the same as that of Europe, when divided, by the feudal system, into an infinite number of small and independent kingdoms. There was the same matter therefore for contention, and the same call for all the hands that could be mustered: the Grecians, in short, in heroick, were in the same situation in these respects as the feudal barons in the Gothick times. (CE 38)

Therefore, Clarkson's description of the political situation of the island of Bisseche in distinctly feudal terms gives evidence to this author's belief in the Africans' potential for improvement:

> This island is in the possession of a certain Seignior or Lord, who is called Bequio. This Seignior holds it of Brac, and gives him a certain number of oxen annually, besides certain articles of merchandize, for the tenure. (CL 19)

Wilberforce draws on similar comparisons in stating that when the Phoenicians first introduced "the first rudiments of civilisation, above all, the art of alphabetical writing" to the Greeks, they were "in a far ruder state than most of the African nations in the present day. They are said to have been cannibals, and to have been ignorant even of the use of fire" (WL 75). The same author applies a universal notion of human progress through distinct stages when he suggests that "the slavery of Africa appeared, in truth, to be a species of feudal or rather of patriarchal vassalage" (WL 91). Both Clarkson's and Wilberforce's historical analyses thus juxtapose the emergence of modern and classical civilisation out of a similarly dark age and imply that the same ought to be expected from Africans once the Europeans stop the slave trade and start exerting their civilising influence.

This description of African societies in terms of earlier episodes of a European master narrative of the progress of civilisation is not without ambiguity. Clarkson describes the king of Dahomey as an absolute ruler, having unlimited power over the lives and properties of his subjects (cf. CE88 39). The account gains a comical quality when the author goes on, "The prince, as if he imitated some of the Roman Emperors, gives largesses to his people on certain days" (CE88 39). In *Letters*, he praises the organisation of African states:

> we find them in their own country under a regular form of government, with divisions and subdivisions of officers, so that a large tract is put into a situation to be governed with ease, and edicts, that are to travel to a considerable extent, to be soon promulgated and obeyed.
> We see also a certain system of jurisprudence instituted... (CL 77)

Despite the positive account of the strict organisational structure of the African kingdom, Clarkson acknowledges that, especially in the case of witchcraft, the African jurisprudence is a weak one. This, however, perfectly fits the historical analysis of African states resembling earlier stages of European history. The author reminds the reader of "how short a time it is, since our own ancestors had recourse to the boiling water and burning plough-share for the same purpose" (CL 77). The teleology of such an analysis of African societies, placing them alongside earlier stages of European societies, puts an enormous amount of discursive power in the hands of those in a colonial centre defining itself as being at the epitome of civilisation.

This kind of representation, of course, contains the Eurocentric idea that the only "channel through which alone ... Africa might have hoped to receive the blessing of religious and moral light" (WL 41) is from intercourse with European nations. This notion conveniently invited European intervention on behalf of "that benighted land" (WL 45), which has so far only received "the feeble light of Mahometanism" (WL 31). Wilberforce generally paints a negative picture of Islam, which he describes as "hostile to all improvement" (WF 79). He argues for the Africans' potential for improvement when he calls it "remarkable, that, barbarous as were the first Mahometan settlers of interior Africa ... yet ... there were many centuries ago great and populous cities, provinces not ill cultivated, and a considerable degree of social order and civilization" (WL 79f).

Africa, thus, has to face the "incursions" of both the slave-trade of the Europeans and the Moors. This makes the Muslim intruders a kind of doppelgänger of the Europeans. Their "feeble light" seems to pose a competing concept of gaining influence on the 'dark continent'. In their claim for ending the slave trade, anti-slavery authors also suggest new forms of a distinctly European intercourse with sub-Saharan Africa. Pro-slavery authors, on the other hand, used the long existence and antiquity of the slave trade to argue that the Portuguese, for example, only diverted an existing trade from the East to the West (cf. FA 89).

Clarkson seems eager to represent the Africans as not having been 'corrupted' by Muslim influence when he writes that "the bulk of the people ... know little about the religion of the country, and, a few external rites excepted, are little of Mahometans but by name" (CL 47). He also sees the Moors as intruders into Africa (cf. CL 20) and contrasts them to the native Africans when he writes:

> The name, by which the Moors have been always known to them [i.e. the Africans], is Nars, in the same manner as they have been known by the appellation of Moors to us. Such a man belongs to the Nar nation. Now this word is not only now expressive of the national name of these barbarians, but has become a word in the language of the Negroes, in consequence of the infamous conduct of the former to convey to the hearer the united characters of a liar and of a thief. (CL 23)

The passage contrasts Africans and Moors, even allowing the first a moral judgement over the latter. Clarkson's description of "wise and virtuous Almammy" (CL 81) has to be understood within a same context:

> This prince began his reign by opposing the ravages of the Moors, who in the time of his timid predecessor, were often suffered with impunity to make incursions into the country for the purpose of getting slaves. (CL 31)

In the conclusion of the text, this African ruler is very much represented in terms of a noble savage when Clarkson even calls him an "illustrious example ... to the sovereigns of Europe" (CL 81). It has been argued that the concept of the noble savage, which is primarily applied to representations of American Indians, first emerged in the work of the Frenchman, Marc Lescarbot, whose reason for calling them noble was because they hunted, which was a prerogative of the nobility in France (cf. Trigger 136). Bruce Trigger argues that primitive humans were increasingly seen in negative terms during the 18th century due to "Enlightenment progressivism, growing racism, and finally Darwinian evolution" (Trigger 136). These schools of thought led to a view of early humans as the antithesis of European achievements. The representation of Africans in the discourse of slavery mirrors this ambivalence. It has been shown above that Africans were often constructed as representing earlier stages of European history. In anti-slavery texts, this is combined with an optimistic outlook on human progress which emphasised the potential for (rapid) improvement, once the impediment of slavery was removed. On the other hand, Clarkson uses Africans as a sort of mirror to offer the European reader a critical view of their own society. He writes:

> Notwithstanding the ignorance and barbarity with which we often charge them, they are not devoid of virtues. To the European master the African exhibits a noble lesson in the mild and gentle treatment of his slave. To the sovereigns of Europe the wise and virtuous Almammy sets a no less illustrious example in extirpating the commerce in the human race; and when we consider this amiable man as having been trained up in a land of slavery ... he is certainly more to be respected than any of the sovereigns of Europe, inasmuch as he has made a much nobler sacrifice than they, and has done more for the causes of humanity, justice, liberty, and religion. (CL 80f)

In *Appeal*, Wilberforce still contrasts the colonial slave with the 'noble savage' Africans in their own country:

> He will find that the Negroes, who while yet in Africa were represented to be industrious, generous, eminent for truth, seldom chargeable with licentiousness, distinguished for their domestic affections, and capable at times of acts of heroic magnanimity, are described as being in the West Indies the very opposite in all particulars; selfish, indolent, deceitful, ungrateful, — and above all, in whatever respects the intercourse between the sexes, incurably licentious. (WA 32)

Wilberforce cites the authority of Golberry and Park to assert that "there never was any uncivilised people of whose dispositions we have received a more amiable character than that which is given of the native Africans by Park and Golberry" (WA 64).

Clarkson, on the other hand, offers a more negative representation of the African's state when it serves his argument that in earlier times the slaveholders might have excused their severity with the fact that the majority of colonial slaves were,

> ... African-born or strangers, and that cargoes were constantly pouring in, one after the other, consisting of the same sort of beings; or of stubborn ferocious people, never accustomed to work, whose spirits it was necessary to break, and whose necks to force down to the yoke; and that this could only be effected by the whip, the chain, the iron collar, and other instruments of the kind. (CT 57)

The ambiguity of these quotes suggests that anti-slavery authors employed quite a fluid concept of the "African", which could be adapted according to various argumentative needs. Africans could thus be represented as noble savages, potential capitalist subjects or romanticised peasants representing earlier stages of history.

5.2.3 Pro-slavery: Locus Horribilis

Pro-slavery authors understandably paint a more negative picture of the situation in Africa. This is not surprising given the prevalent pro-slavery argument that the slave trade was actually a blessing for the Africans since their situation in the European colonies would actually be much improved in comparison to Africa.

Explicit representations of cannibalistic practices are a feature of pro-slavery texts while this is largely absent in anti-slavery ones. One of the more striking examples of this can be found in *Fugitive Thoughts* when the anonymous author writes about Calabar and Bonny:

> These are frequently at war with their neighbors, the Creeks and the Andony-men, and when they take prisoners, they sacrifice them, cut them up, cook them, eat them, and drink the broth that is made of them in public boilers; nay more, they even drink their blood, and will not sell them to the ships for any price. (AF 37)

Gilbert Francklyn also explicitly cites instances of cannibalism (cf. FA 115); he uses the image of cannibalism to back up his overall argument that the slave trade is an ancient practice in Africa and adds:

> Similar causes of war must have been frequent among the Africans, long before the Europeans visited them, and would certainly continue, if no European was ever to approach their coast again. The only difference would be, in that case,

> they would as heretofore murther and eat their prisoners of war, instead of selling them. (FA 121)

Thus, the slave trade is presented as actually being an act of humanity towards the Africans. The same author cites William Snelgrave's account of savage rituals and cannibalism in the interior of Africa to prove that,

> it appears, that, in the course of a very few years merely from their intercourse with the Europeans, this infamous custom [i.e. cannibalism] was not only put an entire stop to, upon the coast, but even held in abhorrence. The same author says, p. 488, 'That the people of Whidaw were so civilized by commerce, that it was a pleasure to deal with them' (FA 123f)

Francklyn again argues that the slave trade has been instrumental in repressing the savage practices of Africans:

> ... the inhabitants of the West Coast have been so far civilized, by their intercourse with the Europeans, that they have entirely (and the people within land, in a great measure) desisted from the abominable practice of immolating and eating their own prisoners. (FA 154)

Similarly, pro-slavery descriptions of the prevailing climate in Africa seem to be calculated to create the image of a *locus terribilis*. Francklyn writes that:

> At this time of the year, for several weeks together, animal food, of all kinds, can scarcely be kept from putrefaction, for three hours after it is killed; and even the fish of the rivers is reckoned unwholesome ... After the rains cease, and the waters of the river, which overflow the country for several hundred miles, subside, the quantities of slime, putrid fish, frogs, and other vermin left on the ground, fill the air with exhalations little short of being pestilential. (FA 133f)

This negative image of Africa and Africans certainly serves the basic argument stated by the anonymous author of *Answer* that "not one individual, (fairly purchased not stolen) ever yet returned or wished to return to their own country; nor would any one of them accept their freedom on such terms" (AA 35). Mercator draws on a more demographic argument to argue in favour of the continuation of the slave trade. He compares Africans to rabbits in an enclosed space (cf. ML 22ff) to show that:

> It is evident that mankind (like any other race of animals) cannot exist beyond the number, for which food is provided by the hand of nature, unless they add to the natural productions of the earth by labour and cultivation; and that, if they increase in a greater degree than the labour so applied furnishes additional means of subsistence, the surplus of the population must either emigrate to some other country or starve. (ML 20f)

Although earlier pro-slavery authors use a more overtly racist argumentation, this tendency seems to disappear in later authors. The anonymous author of *Fugitive Thoughts* quite bluntly puts the Africans' humanity up for discussion when he asks:

> What right have we over blacks? What right have negroes on the coast to make large race of apes, pound corn and draw water for them, whilst they look upon them as a species of human beings? (AF 28)

This kind of argument is less present in the other texts and as the debate about the slave trade progresses, Gilbert Francklyn, for example, acknowledges that:

> The acquaintance we have since had with these people shews us, that they are *not quite so brutish and ignorant*[6] as that author [i.e. Benjamin of Tudela] represents them; (FA 93)

Despite the superficial rehabilitation of Africans, there is, of course, much less urgency to claim Africans for humanity, and while the author claims that the brutish description of Africans has been corrected in the meantime, he nonetheless grants the textual space for the quotation of Tudela. Also, "not quite so brutish and ignorant" remains a rather tame defence of African qualities—"not quite so" implies that they actually are brutish and ignorant, albeit not to the degree one would initially suspect.

In 1807, Mercator fundamentally acknowledges the African's humanity, as evidenced in his demographic argument above.

---

[6] My emphasis.

Nonetheless, he makes sure that some of the fundamentally negative representation of Africans remains when he quotes Park, who writes:

> it was not possible for me to behold the wonderful fertility of the soil, the vast herds of cattle, &c. without lamenting, that a country, so abundantly gifted and favoured by nature, should remain in its present savage and neglected state. (ML 21)

5.2.4 Conclusion

While it would be simplistic to view pro-slavery texts as universally representing the state in Africa in a hyper-negative way while anti-slavery texts do not. This overall tendency exists due to the respective argumentative needs of each side. However, pro-slavery authors like Francklyn also acknowledge that Africans are "not quite as brutish". Interestingly also, anti-slavery authors grant relatively a lot of textual space to the hyper-negative representation of Africans either in quoting their opponents or in outlining the devastating effects of the slave trade. What both sides of the discourse seem to agree on is that Africans live in a state of nature. The respective interpretations of this, however, are quite different ones. While anti-slavery authors more or less take a romantic stance towards this, pro-slavery authors highlight the more negative aspects of "the first situation of man". On the other hand, granting Africans an essentially shared humanity seems to have served the argumentative needs of anti-slavery discourse better. A fundamental humanity was important for a discourse of reform and progress. However, the anti-slavery attempts of including Africans within the category of humanity via such a discourse also asserts a distinction between civilised and non-civilised people.

5.3 Africans as Slaves

The most important feature of the image of the African slave is that it contrasts with what authors seem to perceive as a fully realised human subject. In his essay, "The Question of Cultural Identity", Stuart Hall describes a distinct "Enlightenment subject" defined by the ability to think logically and rationally and based on "a conception of the human person as a fully centred, unified individual, endowed with the capacities of reason, consciousness and action, . . ." (Hall, *Cultural Identity* 275). This concept of humanity can also be found in Article 1 of the UN's 1948 Declaration of Universal Human Rights, stating that "All human beings . . . are endowed with reason and conscience . . ." (UN). This definition, however, is a problematic one, since it makes also possible an exception from humanity of those who are not "endowed with reason and conscience". This raises fundamental questions about who ought to have the power to decide and, consequently, about the nature of the relationship between (state-) power and the individual subject. In his groundbreaking work, *Homo Sacer: Sovereign Power and Bare Life*, Giorgio Agamben holds that a separation of human existence into bare life—*zoe*—and political existence—*bios*—is the "fundamental categorical pair of Western politics" (8) and that "in the 'politicization' of bare life . . . the humanity of living man is decided" (ibid.). For Agamben, political relations are negotiated between inclusion and exclusion in a "process, by which, at the threshold of the modern era, natural life begins to be included in the mechanism and calculations of State power" (3). Thus, Agamben speaks of a "paradox of sovereignty" (ibid. 15ff), which has a certain analogy with Bhabha's concept of colonial mimicry. They both put the (colonial-) subject in a paradoxical position, in a "zone of indistinction between outside and inside" (181) to use Agamben's words, or, to quote Homi Bhabha, constructing a colonial subject that is "almost the same but not quite" (Bhabha, *Culture* 122).

The Africans in the discourse on slavery are very much caught in such a dilemma. In particular, anti-slavery authors at the same time grant and deny a fundamental humanity to Africans. The denial is very much achieved through a distinct representation of Africans as wretched slaves. At the same time, however, claiming Africans' fundamental humanity is a basic tenet of the abolitionist utopia of reform.

Anti-slavery discourse constructs a conceptual difference between slavery in traditional societies and European antiquity and chattel slavery in European colonies in modern times. Both pro- and anti-slavery authors discuss at quite some length those passages of the Bible that mention slaves. While anti-slavery authors have to acknowledge the long existence of slavery, they emphasise the conceptual difference between traditional and modern servitude. They portray the first as a more benevolent form of personal servitude within the context of earlier stages of human societies. The chattel slavery in European colonies, however, is described as being fundamentally at odds with the basic conception of the human as an autonomous individual. Thus, the problematic nature of slavery is constructed within a context of the project of modernity as such. Therefore, glaring descriptions of the inhumanities and the horrors of colonial slavery are one of their principal arguments.

Pro-slavery authors, on the other hand, explicitly try to represent colonial slavery as precisely the kind of benevolent servitude with which their opponents describe the situation of slaves in Greco-Roman antiquity. In doing so, they attempt to emphasise the long existence of slavery, thus pointing to the historical continuity of human bondage from biblical times to European modernity.

Pro-slavery authors, of course, have a vested interest in constructing Africans as essentially lazy and stubborn and thus unfit for any other form of control but that of the whip. James Tobin, for example, is obviously aware that bluntly denying the Africans humanity will not go down too well with his audience. However, he points to the fact that freed slaves in the West Indies are disgusted with labour and, therefore, "generally turn hucksters . . . or domestic servants; or, which is worse . . . set up destructive negro gaming houses; and not a few, becoming arrant vagabonds, maintain themselves entirely by cheating and pilfering" (Tobin 116f). He paints a similarly negative picture of the "black cairibs of St. Vincent":

> notwithstanding their long intercourse and near connection, both with the French and English, they have every appearance of being totally averse to the least civilization, and to be absolutely removed from it, in every respect, as their African fore-fathers. (122)

A central theme of the passage seems to be development. While Ramsay never tires of arguing that Africans, if given the opportunity to do so, would develop into obedient subjects within a European system of wage labour. Tobin is equally eager to prove that they would not. He does actually suggest that the Africans' laziness is part of their nature; it is part of the point he tries to make, namely that Ramsay is mistaken in his assumption that if the Africans were set free, they would do more work through being motivated by self-interest and the concept of delayed gratification.

5.3.1 Quashi: The Character of the Slave

The narrative of Quashi, the slave, can illustrate the contesting images of African character since both Ramsay's *Essay* and the anonymous Gentlemen's *Answer* contain their own version of the story of the slave, Quashi (cf. RE 249ff, AA 92), who "was brought up in the family with his master, as his play-fellow, from his childhood" and, therefore, was connected to him by "the most delicate, yet most strong, and seemingly indissoluble tie, that could bind master and slave together" (249). The story tells of how Quashi has risen to the rank of overseer when his master takes over the plantation and has grown to manhood without undergoing a single whipping and, therefore, takes pride in the smoothness of his skin. The main conflict of the narrative is that Quashi has "done something contrary to the discipline of the plantation" (250) and wants to "save the glossy honours of his skin" (251). The story mentions that it is common among slaves "who expect to be punished for their own fault, or their master's caprice, to go to some friend of their master's, and beg him to carry them home, and mediate for them" (250f). It is in order to seek out this mediation that Quashi hides "among his master's negroe huts" (251). Ramsay emphasises the honourable character of Quashi by pointing out that "his fellow slaves had too much honour, and too great a regard for him, to betray to their master the place of his retreat" and that "it is hardly possible in any case, to get one slave to inform against another, so much more honour have they than Europeans of low condition" (251). To cut a long story short, Quashi is detected by his master before he can find help and tries to run away. His master follows him and just when he is about to seize Quashi, they stumble, fall to the ground and start to wrestle. After some struggle, Quashi gets firmly seated "on his master's breast, now panting and out of breath, and with his weight, his thighs, and one hand, secured him motionless" (252). The story climaxes when Quashi, drawing out a knife, addresses his master, tells him that he is innocent and says:

> 'Yet you have condemned me to a punishment, of which I must ever have borne the disgraceful marks; thus only can I avoid them.' With these words, he drew the knife with all his strength across his own throat, and fell down dead without a groan, on his master, bathing him in his blood. (252f)

It is truly remarkable that suicide serves to express the nobleness of the Africans. While Ramsay referred to Quashi by his obviously African first name throughout the narrative, he now explicitly calls him a man for the first time, lamenting that

> ... had this man been properly educated; had he been taught his importance as a member of society.... can any man suppose him incapable of making a progress in the knowledge of religion, in the researches of reason, or the works of art. (253)

Ramsay concludes by stating that "This is a truly mournful instance of a nobleness and grandeur of mind in a negroe" (253). The essence of this short narrative is that Quashi, whose character retains many elements of the original noble savage, has adopted the rules of honour and discipline governing colonial society to such a degree that he does not see any other escape from the situation than to direct his aggression against himself.

In contrast to that, the anonymous "Gentlemen of St. Christopher" explain that Ramsay's account of the slave Quashi's suicide "is dressed out in fine glaring colours, but unfortunately is not agreeable to truth" (AA 92) and offer their own much more mundane version. In Ramsay's story, the whole chain of events leading to Quashi's suicide is triggered by his doing "something contrary to the discipline of the plantation" (RE 250). The anonymous authors attempt to present Quashi's character in a negative light and explain that "he was pursued for inveigling a female slave from another estate" (AA 92). They follow a similar aim when they conclude their narrative by pointing to "the glossy honours of his skin" (AA 92), which is the reason for Quashi's flight from the plantation in Ramsay's *Essay*, "had before that suffered for repeated insolence and transgressions" (AA 92). Ramsay tries to present the whole episode as an outstanding example of an African's high spirit and nobleness. The authors, however, attempt to portray Quashi's suicide in a more profane light, and even try to give it a comical spin when the pursuing master is "entangled in some pease [before] he could dash the old razor out of his hand" (AA 92). Substituting Quashi's knife for an old razor also aims at taking the heroism out of the story. They also do not allow Quashi to fall "dead without a groan on his master, bathing him in his blood" (RE 253). In their version Quashi's exodus is less dramatic as he only "half executed his threats; he lived several days, long enough to acknowledge and lament his passion" (AA 92). One can see how the anonymous pro-slavery authors clearly construct a counter-image of Quashi which is stripped of any heroic and noble traits and challenge the representation of African slaves in terms of being noble savages. On the other hand, one should also remember that Ramsay's narrative also kills off the character of the noble savage and expresses his explicit dismay at the waste of this "man" not having been made the object of reform through proper education.

5.3.2 The Body of the Enslaved

Perhaps the most striking feature of the representation of Africans in the discourse on slavery is the intense descriptions of the bodily aspects of the "horrors of slavery". In her 1824 claim for immediate emancipation, Elisabeth Heyrick describes what she perceives as the enormities of the West Indian system in the following words:

> What horrible crime could have instigated man to sentence his fellow man, to a punishment so tremendous ? — to doom his brother to undergo the protracted torture of a THOUSAND LASHES? — to have his quivering flesh mangled and torn from his living body ? — and to labour through life under the galling and ignominious weight of chains! (HI 22)

The anti-slavery argument, in particular, has a clear interest in emphasising the wretched situation of the African slave, which is mainly achieved through a vivid visual imagery of the Africans' bodily suffering. The body of the modern human in the discourse of slavery is one which has clear boundaries. It appears that both suffering and discipline are enacted at these boundaries. Foucault also remarked on the fact that at the threshold of the early and late modern periods, the natural bodies of humans are "becoming the target for new mechanisms of power [and] offered to new forms of knowledge" (Foucault, *Discipline* 155).

Transgressions

Anti-slavery discourse readily accepts forms of discipline that stop at the threshold of the body, such as the beatings of soldiers and sailors. However, the cruelty of the West Indian slave system is constructed precisely on the grounds that its punishments do not stop at the boundaries of the African's body. For example, the colonial whippings are described by anti-slavery authors as fundamentally different from the corporal punishments in the military which are portrayed as strongly regulated. Ramsay writes about the use of the cart-whip:

> This instrument, in the hands of a skilful driver, cuts out flakes of skin and flesh with every stroke; and the wretch, in this mangled condition, is turned out to work in dry or wet weather, which last, now and then, brings on the cramp, and ends his sufferings and slavery together. (RE 74f)

Clarkson describes the use of the whip on plantations in quite similar terms: "This instrument erases the skin, and cuts out small portions of the flesh at almost every stroke" (CE 144f). It is clearly the violation of African bodies which makes this sort of punishment inhumane and cruel; thus, African bodies play an important role in the anti-slavery argument. A central feature of these suffering bodies is that they have fluid boundaries, which contrasts them with the humanist notion of the human as a clearly defined individual. For example, Clarkson's description of the Middle Passage contains various transgressions of boundaries:

> Being stowed then in the manner thus described, they soon begin to experience the effects, which might naturally be presumed to arise from their situation. In consequence of the pestilential breath of so many confined in so small a space, they become sickly, and from the vicissitude of heat and cold, of heat when confined below, and of cold when suddenly brought up for air, a flux is generated. Whenever this disorder attacks them, no pen can be adequate to the task of describing their situation. (CE88 93)

In another place, Clarkson has the Africans "mangled alternately with the whip and knife, have been left in that horrid situation, till they have expired" (CE 130). Also, when Clarkson's *Essay* offers a glance into the body of a slave ship the reader sees a mass of people whose bodies almost seem to merge with each other:

> The first scene that presents itself, is a cluster of unhappy people, who, overcome by excessive heat and stench, have fainted away.
> The next that occurs, is that of one of them endeavouring to press forward to the light, to catch a mouthful of wholesome air, but hindered by the partner of his chains, who is lying dead at his feet, and whom he has not sufficient

> strength to drag after him.
> The third is conspicuous in the instance of those, who are just on the point of fainting, and who are wallowing in the blood and mucus of the intestines, with which the floor is covered. (CE 88 93)

The image of the confined space, the representation of the Africans as "a cluster" rather than individuals and their being connected by chains deny individuality and autonomy. The chain promotes an image of Africans as lacking the fundamental human autonomy of free individual movement. The reference to the smell constitutes a further violation of hegemonic notions of keeping bodies separate. Finally, there are various bodily fluids which mix with the human bodies, who literally "wallow" in them. The OED's definition of "wallowing" also mentions "... sensual enjoyment or indifference to defilement" (OED, 'wallow, v.'). This contrasts the African slave with morally disciplined modern European subjects, who uphold clear-cut boundaries of their bodies also by adhering to ritualised forms of cleanliness.

Clarkson's description of the *speculum oris* equally violates the boundaries of African bodies (cf. CE 88_88). He portrays the forced transgression of boundaries in order to make slaves eat as a deviant form of discipline. Thus, Clarkson constructs African bodies that are fluid in their boundaries—food is forced into them, their excretion is unregulated by the subject, and they are violated by the "smart of the whip" or mangled with "cutlasses". The human wretches that are constructed in this way clearly stand in contrast to modern subjects. A further aspect of the description of African bodies is that they are variously violated by the effect of European technology. Clarkson writes of the Dutch colonists at the Cape shooting at the indigenous population:

> the balls discharged by them will sometimes, as I have been assured, go through the bodies of six, seven, or eight of the enemy at a time, especially as these latter know no better than to keep close together in a body (CE 52)

He creates a similar image of projectiles piercing tightly packed bodies of African mutineers on board a slave ship when the sailors fire "a volley together into the thickest of the croud of slaves" (CE88 96). He also reports an incident on an African river where the slave traders fire their guns at natives attacking a village:

> we fired our guns loaden with grape shot, and a volley of small arms among them, which effectually checked their ardour, and obliged them to retire to a distance from the shore; from whence a few round cannon shot soon removed them into the woods. (CE 100)

Also, William Wilberforce's account of a fugitive slave being shot in a colony exhibits a similar imagery:

> two white men fired several times at him with the guns loaded with shot, and the Negroes pelted him with stones. He was at length dragged out of the pool in a dying condition, for he had not only received several bruises from the stones, but his breast was so pierced with the shot, that it was like a cullender.[7] (WL 158f)

Other transgressions of the Africans bodies include cutting their bodies:

> No excuse or intreaty will avail; he must punish them for an example, and he must punish them, not with a stick, nor with a whip, but with a cutlass. Thus it happens, that these unhappy slaves, if they are taken, are either sent away mangled in a barbarous manner, or are killed upon the spot. (CE 152f)

Ramsay reports "instances of slitting of ears, breaking of limbs, so as to make amputation necessary, beating out of eyes, and castration;" (RE 86). William Wilberforce writes of an incident in which a West Indian militia man "made after [a] woman, and, without the least provocation on her part, plunged his bayonet into her, and, as one of the accounts states, very coolly and deliberately stabbed her several times in the breast "(WL 162).

These representations of African bodies thus follow several aims. On the one hand, they want to create what Brycchan Carey

---

[7] That is, a kind of sieve.

has aptly described as sentimental suffering (cf. Carey, *Sensibility*) but, on the other hand, they also create an image of slaves with quite fluid bodies which can easily be penetrated by Europeans, clearly putting them in a position of power. It is a similar way to which the African continent is stereotypically penetrated by the European explorer (cf. WL 23). These bodies are at odds with what authors seem to perceive as the norm for modern, capitalist and European subjects.

Medieval nature of punishments

The focus on the bodily suffering of the slave plays an important role in the construction of an image of slavery as a form of illegitimately severe discipline in order to extract labour from a workforce. David Davis argues that "the anti-slavery movement mirrored the needs and tensions of a society increasingly absorbed with problems of labour discipline" (Davis, *Hegemony* 806). Thus, the image of the slave is constructed against two significant others: the feudal servant and the modern wage labourer. While the first is portrayed as part of a benevolent system regulated by the decency of a romantically idealised feudal lord, the situation of the latter is equally idealised as a Smithian free agent, selling their labour to the highest bidder. The colonial slaves are neither and the bodily dimension of their suffering is a vital part of the argument.

It appears that both suffering and discipline are enacted at the boundaries of the body. The fluidity of the suffering African bodies, which has been described above, is at odds with a concept of a discipline that stops at the boundaries of the body. The contrast with the modern subject is further enhanced by giving the Africans' suffering a distinctly medieval tinge through the images of the chain and the dungeon. Ramsay, for example, describes the common punishments of slaves on plantations:

> The ordinary punishments of slaves, for the common crimes of neglect, absence from work, eating the sugar cane, theft, are cart whipping, beating with a stick, sometimes to the breaking of bones, the chain, an iron crook about the

neck, a large iron pudding or ring about the ancle, and confinement in the dungeon. (RE 85f)

The author explicitly used the term "dungeon" instead of "prison". Foucault argues that the panoptic principles introduced by Jeremy Bentham distinguish the modern prison from the "principle of the dungeon" (Foucault, *Discipline* 200). The anti-slavery author, Ramsay, uses precisely this image of the dungeon to criticise the system of slavery. Also, Clarkson comments on the medieval nature of the slave system when he comments on the mistaken notion that the West Indian creoles were a

> ... stubborn ferocious people, never accustomed to work, whose spirits it was necessary to break, and whose necks to force down to the yoke; and that this could only be effected by the whip, the chain, the iron collar, and other instruments of the kind. But now no such plea can be offered. (CT 57)

A further characteristic of the pre-modern representation of the slave system is that the aim of the punishments inflicted is not one of reform but corresponds to what Foucault describes as the spectacle of the scaffold featuring "the branded, dismembered, burnt, annihilated body of the tortured criminal" (Foucault, *Discipline* 254) in that it is driven by passion rather than cool reason and the wish for reform. Clarkson's reference to "inhuman marks of passion, despotism, and caprice" (CE 152) brings up a further characteristic of (late-) modern discipline; it compartmentalises, separates and distances the executor of discipline from its object. Clarkson further criticises the arbitrary nature of the West Indian system, writing that the slave is "never safe from the sallies of passion and caprice" (CL 75).

The pro-slavery response to this critique of the West-Indian slave system was a rather weak one. They seem to be rather powerless on a fundamental level and once more deal with it by various evasive manoeuvres. The anonymous authors of St. Christopher, for example, blame Ramsay for drawing together all the cruelties every perpetrated in order to create a negative image of the planters and argue that if the same were done about England—"the most humane and best civilized nation of the world" (AA 38)—a similar picture would emerge. Fundamentally, however, the anonymous authors also acknowledge that the cruel treatment is unacceptable. Their proposal is a stronger regulation of the treatment of slaves instead of abolition (cf. AA 40).

Tobin censures Ramsay for holding out the treatment of the French slaves as an example. Not only does he censor the French for indulging in too much intimacy with their slaves (cf. TC 47fn), he also cites a French source to point out that the slaves in the French colonies are utterly miserable (cf. TC 39f). This author seems to be aware that a change of paradigm in terms of discipline is inevitable when he writes:

> Fifteen or twenty strokes with a whip is reckoned a pretty smart infliction; and these are administered on that fleshy part of the body best adapted to bear them. Whoever has often attended a military parade, may have had an opportunity of seeing two, three, or five hundred lashes given to a poor culprit, on a much more sensible part, with a regular professor attending, to tell by the pulse, how much torture human nature is capable of bearing, without expiring. Corporal punishment is of late much disused in the West Indies, and confinement adopted in its place. (TC 47f)

Thus, Tobin tries to portray the administration of punishment in the colonies as a similarly regulated process as the discipline in the British armed forces. Furthermore, he deliberately invokes a medical discourse in his mentioning the attendance of "a regular professor". Francklyn does something similar when he describes the practice of branding slaves in ridiculously euphemistic terms:

> This practice, which prevails in Jamaica, and, I believe in that British island only, is neither cruel nor unnecessary. A silver brand with the initial letters of the purchaser's name, or his plantation mark, is heated enough to raise the scarf-skin, and applied to the fleshy part of the breast or shoulder, previously rubbed with spirits of wine. the place is immediately dressed with sweet oil. The operation is momentary. The pain cannot be half so considerable as a young lady must feel on having her ears bored. The mark serves to enable

every person, who should meet a new Negro, who has strayed from the plantation he belongs to, and is able to tell his master's name, to send or conduct him home. (FA 176)

The author's use of the term "operation", his reference to rubbing with spirits and dressing with sweet oil and his comparison to the piercing of "British ears" draw on the special discourse of medicine. One can see how pro-slavery authors try to find channels in the hegemonic discourse in order to make the transgression of bodily boundaries acceptable.

"...the animal machine"

Another feature of the discourse on slavery is that it frequently positions Africans in relation to animals. Ramsay refers to Africans as "that still more useful, though neglected animal, called a negroe slave" (RE 138) and Clarkson laments that "they are totally considered as cattle, or beasts of labour" (CE 136). Wilberforce writes about slaves as follows: "Depressed therefore nearly to a level with the brute creation, the negro Slaves instinctively adapt themselves to their level, and are immersed in merely animal pursuits" (WL 246). This ties in with the OED's definition of animal: "Contemptuously or humorously for: a human being who is no better than a brute, or whose animal nature has the ascendancy over his reason; a mere animal." (OED, 'animal')

These passages achieve their effect on the reader by an implicit contradiction to what Cary Wolfe calls "the fundamental anthropological dogma associated with humanism . . . that 'the human' is achieved by escaping or repressing not just its animal origins in nature, . . . but more generally by transcending the bonds of materiality and embodiment altogether" (Wolfe, *Posthumanism* xv). This humanist dogma prompts Wolfe's critique of the trans-human strands of post-humanist thought in the tradition of theorists like Nick Bostrom and Hans Moravec (cf. Harfield, *Humanism* 271). Transhumanists continue the paradigms of classical humanism by dreaming of the "overcoming of biological limitations" in the light of "recent biotechnogical advancements" (ibid.) in a rather positivistic sense. One of the better known cultural formations of this being the figure of the cyborg. In contrast to this, Wolfe's posthumanism "opposes the fantasies of disembodiment and autonomy, inherited from humanism itself" (Wolfe, *Posthumanism* xv).

The discourse on slavery clearly stands in a humanist tradition, in that it acknowledges the classical dualism of mind and body which forms the basis of the anthropological dogma referred to above. The location of the African within the larger humanism of the discussion of slavery will be discussed in greater depth in a subsequent chapter. For now, I would just like to point out the location of the enslaved bodies within a binary concept of the mind and what James Ramsay referred to as "the animal machine" (RE 137). Ramsay also implies such a dichotomy when he writes that the West Indian system "obliges them to labour for the support of their bodies, on a day set apart for the improvement of their souls" (RE x) or when he voices the wish that West Indian planters were "careful of the bodies, and tender of the souls of these our fellow-creatures, thus submitted to our power, thus abandoned to our humanity" (RE xvi).

In their attempts to shock readers into the realisation of the inhumane nature of slavery, anti-slavery writers frequently take over the alleged conception of their opponent of slaves as mere animals. Also, the general images used to describe the Africans' miserable situation frequently draw on animal comparisons such as in the expression "the yoke of slavery" (RE 273). Clarkson, for example, writes of the situation during the Middle Passage, "I cannot compare the scene on board this vessel, to any other than that of a pen of sheep" (CE88 92). Clarkson also constructs the cruelty of the sale of the slaves in the colonies based on "the iniquity of valuing a part of the rational creation in so debased a light, and of scrambling for human flesh and blood" (CE88 102f). The author clearly wants to make his readers share his outrage at the fact that human beings are reduced to mere flesh and blood. Also, Wilberforce writes about the treatment of slaves during the Middle Passage, "still food and exercise will be deemed necessary to present the animal in good condition at the place of sale" (WL 100).

In this case, the injustice of slavery is constituted by reducing the slave to a mere animal, which also has its repercussions on the distinct mode of disciplining slaves merely through bodily intervention. Ramsay writes:

> Again, when it is considered, how much the negroes are immersed in sense, how their intellectual powers are wholly employed in the service of the body, and that, respecting them, we have access to the first only by methods that make impression on the other; when he resolves the difficulty of managing, by argument alone, a few slaves living and having their connections among hundreds of their equals, who are restrained only by the whip, every hope of governing them, without certain degree of discipline, subsides; (RE 173f)

What the author laments is that due to their degraded situation, "we" have access to their intellectual powers only through the body as opposed to reason. Also, Clarkson similarly distinguishes between fully realised humans and the slave when he asks:

> For what is it that awakens the abilities of men, and distinguishes them from the common herd? Is it not often the amiable hope of becoming serviceable to individuals, or the state? Is it not often the hope of riches, or of power? Is it not frequently the hope of temporary honours, or a lasting fame? (CE 165)

The humanism of anti-slavery arguments like Clarkson's when he writes: "If the reader should observe here, that cattle are better protected in this country than slaves in the colonies, his observation will be just," (CE 135) clearly distinguishes between humans and animals and presents the whole of creation in a hierarchical order of being.

Ramsay writes that "The inanimate and brute creation was fitted for and submitted to man's dominion; but man himself was left independent of every personal claim in his fellows" (RE 233). Clarkson similarly explains the right of humans to rule over animals:

> ... the right to empire over brutes, is natural, and not adventitious, like the right to empire over men. There are ... many and evident signs of the inferiority of their nature ... their liberty can be bought and sold, because, being void of reason, they cannot be accountable for their actions. (CE 71)

It is hardly surprising that pro-slavery writers are not as anxious to maintain the same clear-cut division between human and animal but rather try to blur the distinction or argue that this is beside the point. The anonymous author of *Fugitive Thoughts*, the most openly racist text of the corpus, asks,

> What right have we over blacks? What right have negroes on the coast to make the large race of apes, pound corn and draw water for them, whilst they look upon them as a species of human beings? (AF 28)

In this passage, the author actually blurs the distinction between humans and non-humans, making it a question of perception rather than an absolute category. This kind of argument is made later in the text when he remarks that:

> The naturalists discover a reasoning faculty in the brute creation, and the botanists have from them learned the virtues of many medicinal herbs; by the puncture of a bat in Egypt, a man in a high fever was relieved, and from that accident phlebotomy took its rife; the stag, when almost run blind in the chace, seeks the swamp, and with the sharp point of a stag bleeds his eyes. Many other instances may be mentioned, wherein instinct in animals keeps pace with human reason, the huge sagacious elephant kneels to pigmy man, and employs his mighty strength at command; the wonderful docility of horses, dogs, pigs, and even ferocious animals may be seen every day at places of public exhibition. (AF 58)

Generally speaking, however, the anti-slavery claim for African humanity seems to be in line with the hegemonic ideology of that day. While there is a tendency to downplay the importance of the question, most pro-slavery authors had to acknowledge, albeit grudgingly at times, the Africans' basic humanity. James Tobin, at least superficially, acknowledges this when he argues the whole discussion of the inferiority of the slaves is beside the point since "it has never been pretended, that the ... slaves of modern times ... are, any way inferior to their masters, except in strength, policy, or good fortune" (TC 141).

5.3.3   Wretches

Despite this, also anti-slavery discourse is characterised by various strategies of subtly dehumanising Africans, which will be analysed in this chapter. An investigation of James Ramsay's text will serve as a case study in order to unveil the dehumanising tendencies which are often obscured by superficial claims for their humanity. Ramsay by no means offers his readers an image of Africans as fully human. He calls them "a wretched race of mortals," (RE 108) "despised beings, who have found no friend, helper, or protector," (RE 109) "wretches, whom the crimes and avarice of selfish men have placed in our power," (RE xiii) "such unpitied, and despised objects as our slaves in general are," (RE xv) "human wretches" (RE 145) and "creatures, whose only motive of action is present feeling, who have no reputation to support, no lasting interest to care for" (RE 171).

Although Ramsay quotes Exodus xxvi: 16 on the title page of his *Essay* "God hath made of one Blood all Nations of the Earth" (RE i), he also points out the fact that slavery has "sunk human nature down to the lowest depth of wretchedness [and] hunger, mistrust, oppression, ignorance, produce in the slaves worthlessness, and crimes;" (RE 103). This ambivalent representation of Africans is especially evident when Ramsay writes that "there is no difference between the intellects of whites and blacks, but such as circumstances and education naturally produce" (RE 203). It is truly remarkable how the text at the same time claims and denies African humanity sometimes even within the space of only one sentence. What Ramsay actually does is to rationalise human difference and thus put it at the service of gaining power over those who are different by subjecting them to a discourse of reform and improvement. The implication of this argument is that those humans who are not impeded by slavery, such as the allegedly free British worker, are very much made responsible for their own situation in life. This makes one understand why Ramsay suggests such drastic measures for getting rid of "the nuisance" of British "vagabond beggars". He suggests:

> Let every vagabond be considered as the property of the public. Let a day be fixed, by proclamation, for apprehending them throughout the kingdom. Let their service be sold for seven years to such as have employment for them (RE 41).

The suggestions are very much in line with Foucault's description of the reactions of European states to spreading poverty in the 17th and 18th centuries under the term "the great confinement" (Rabinow 131) in *Madness and Civilization*.

Thus, Ramsay's promotion of Africans' fundamental humanity, based on a rejection of racism, also has to be seen in a context of gaining power over them. He argues that "before we proceed to claim the rights of society, and of a common religion for Africans, we must first put them in possession of that humanity, which is pertinaciously disputed with them" (RE 197). Besides creating a dichotomy between "us" and "them", the passage clearly assigns the power to define humanity to "us", implying that "we" can just as easily take humanity away again. This kind of contrast is referred to by Bhabha when he explains that "the discourse of mimicry is constructed around an ambivalence" and describes it as "the desire for a reformed, recognisable Other, as a subject of a difference that is almost the same, but not quite" (Bhabha 122). Through a representation of Africans as potentially human but not quite, Ramsay attempts to encapsulate them in a discourse of discipline and reform.

In this respect, it seems highly significant that Ramsay's text represents Africans as "wretches" 30 times. The OED defines "wretch" as "someone who is sunk deep in distress" and mentions an interesting obsolete meaning of "one driven out of or away from his native country, a banished person; an exile" (OED, 'wretch'). Ramsay's use of the word points in a similar direction, as can be seen from the following selection of concordance lines of various forms of the lemma "wretch*" in his 1784 *Essay*:

Selection of six concordance lines KWIC – "*wretch*" Ramsay, 1784	
RE 25	of their slaves sunk gradually down to the lowest degree of **wretchedness** and misery.
RE 74f	flakes of skin and flesh with every stroke; and the **wretch**, in this mangled condition, is turned out to work
RE 86fn	had it then performed by a cooper's adze, and the **wretch** was left to bleed to death, without attention, or dressing.
RE 86fn	and then it was amputated by a surgeon, and the maimed **wretch** lived some years.
RE 103	sunk human nature down to the lowest depth of **wretchedness**. Hunger, mistrust, oppression, ignorance,
RE 108	In these we behold a **wretched** race of mortals, who are considered as mere machines

Fig. 14: Africans as wretches – KWIC

The concordance output is revealing in two respects. Firstly, the concept of wretchedness is clearly connected with an image of present inferiority: the "wretches" in the examples are "sunk down to the lowest degree of wretchedness" (RE 25), or "sunk down to the lowest depth of wretchedness" (RE 103). Furthermore, "wretchedness" seems to have a strong bodily dimension, since the wretches' bodies, the boundaries of their bodies, or some sort of bodily suffering are present in quite a few of the selected concordance lines: "lacerated carcass" (RE 64), "flakes of flesh and skin ... mangled condition" (RE 74f), "left to bleed to death" (RE 86), "amputated ... maimed" (RE 86fn). This emphasis on what Ramsay calls "the animal machine" (RE 137) very much represents Africans as the sort of bare life which Agamben sees as central to the creation of state sovereignty through a transformation into political beings (cf. Agamben 4). In other words, Ramsay's text portrays the body and its sufferings as something that ought to be overcome in the process of civilising and humanising the "wretches" he writes about. These examples leave no doubt about the fundamental Otherness of Africans. Ramsay's representation claims humanity for Africans only to make them objects of a discourse of reform and improvement.

5.4 Managing the African — Humanity, Rebellion and Reform

5.4.1 The Africans' Humanity

Apart from its connections to British imperialism (cf. Drescher, *Capitalism* 165), the discourse on slavery is very much a discussion of the modern subject. As has been shown above, the discussion of slavery in late 18th and early 19th century Britain was at heart a negotiation of the fair means of extracting labour from a workforce by contrasting the modern capitalist subject to the slave (cf. Davis, *Hegemony* 168). As noted, the discourse on slavery temporally coincides with what Hobsbawm referred to as the "Age of Revolution". The French and industrial revolutions show how the fundamental concepts of the human also changed on a tangible political level at the threshold between the early and late modern periods. Foucault even went so far as to remark, "before the end of the 18th century man did not exist" (qtd. in Harfield, *Humanism* 266). While Britain did not go through any actual political revolution at that time, unlike France, it certainly saw its fair share of social change as a major site of the Industrial Revolution. The enormous support that the abolitionist movement saw, especially in the manufacturing towns of the north, backs up Davis's theory that abolitionism "mirrored the needs and tensions of a society increasingly absorbed with problems of labour discipline" (Davis, *Hegemony* 171).

British anti-slavery texts contrast the slave to both British peasants and metropolitan wage labourers. To consolidate this contrast, the first are portrayed in a highly romanticised way while the latter are argued to be in a better situation than the colonial slave merely due to the possession of a quite abstract form of personal freedom. James Ramsay clearly stands in the tradition of Adam Smith when he explains that the superiority of the British labourer over the colonial slave "is balanced on the side of the workman by his being free to refuse or accept the condition" (RE 10). Thomas Clarkson almost sees the negative representations of the peasant in pro-slavery texts as an insult when he writes in *Essay*:

> If the representations of the receivers be true, it is evident that those of the most approved writers, who have placed a considerable share of happiness in the cottage, have been mistaken in their opinion; and that those of the rich, who have been heard to sigh, and envy the felicity of the peasant, have been treacherous to their own sensations. (CE 219f)

Wilberforce makes a similar point in his 1807 *Letter on the Abolition of the Slave Trade*:

> When from the West Indies themselves I have heard the same assertion, that the negro Slaves are happier than our labouring poor, let me be forgiven for declaring, that such an opinion, formed not by transient visitors, but by those to whom a Negro sale, working under the whip, public and severe floggings of decent females, private punishments, and all the other sad particulars of negro humiliation are thoroughly known, has, I own, created in mv mind a reflection of a different character. (WL 201f)

All three authors invalidate any comparison of the conditions of slaves and labourers by sliding into the discussion of abstract concepts of freedom or, in the last case, a personal attack against the moral character of West Indian planters. It is, therefore, clear that for the abolitionists, any unfavourable comparison of British workers and slaves was unacceptable. Thus, the image of the slave served as a standard for defining Britain as free soil and at the same time justified domestic working conditions (cf. Davis, *Hegemony* 168). The argumentative need to contrast the free and the slave worlds, however, had a dehumanising effect on the representation of the colonial slaves as "wretches" in anti-slavery rhetoric. Wilberforce describes slaves in his *Letter*:

> Sunk as the Slaves at present are, we are assured they do not feel into what a depth they have been depressed. We are told that they are not shocked, as we are for them, by the circumstances of a Negro sale, or by the other degrading particulars of their treatment; the spirit of the man is extinct, or rather dormant within them. (WL 236)

The representation of the slaves in this quote shows that they were certainly not seen as fully human in their present state, as "the spirit of man is extinct" (WL 236) in them. Furthermore, Wilberforce's "Africans" clearly lack self-awareness, since they need Europeans to feel the appropriate shock about their circumstances for them. It is an interesting detail that the author seems to correct himself when he describes the spirit of man as "dormant" rather than "extinct". The adjective "dormant" implies the possibility of waking up or of being awakened, while being "extinct" certainly denotes a more irreversible absence of a quality. The specific mode of paternalistically denying full humanity to Africans in the discourse on slavery was, therefore, not a static one, but rather one that strongly relied on the potential for rapid improvement. Drescher argues that:

> it was precisely because the abolitionists linked negative characteristics so causally and so completely to the African slave trade and to colonial slavery that they could assure their contemporaries of a more rapid civilizing of blacks than of any other "backward" people on the globe. (Drescher, Racism 420)

Based on this, Drescher reasons that the failure of this utopia of the Africans' rapid improvement being achieved then became instrumental for the rise of scientific racism. The theme of the Africans' humanity is also present in Thomas Clarkson's *Essay*, in which he writes about Africans:

> Had the Africans been made for slavery, or to become the property of any society of men, it is clear, . . . that they must have been created devoid of reason: but this is contrary to fact. It is clear also, that there must have been, many and evident signs of the inferiority of their nature, and that this society of men must have had a natural right to their dominion: but this is equally false. (CE 214)

As can be expected from a writer in the period of the Enlightenment, reason is the primary definer of humanity. Clarkson does indeed argue that there are no signs of inferiority in Africans, which would theoretically justify their absolute domination by a "society of men" (CE 214). However, his reasoning does not question the fundamental concept of a binary distinction between dominator and dominated based on a prescribed set of criteria. Thus, Clarkson does not fundamentally criticise the domination of those who are of "an inferior nature", be it due to the non-possession of reason or other "evident signs of inferiority" (CE 214).

Citing exemplary commitments of humanism such as its opposition to cruelty against animals or the discrimination of disabled people, Wolfe blames "the philosophical and theoretical frameworks, used by humanism [for grounding] discrimination against non-human animals and disabled in the first place" (Wolfe, *Posthumanism* xvii). In her work on the posthuman, Braidotti criticises the humanistic practice of merely extending the boundaries of an existing binary distinction (Braidotti, *Posthuman* 79) in the attempt to fight discrimination. She writes that this "noble gesture . . . is inherently flawed, on two scores" firstly, because it "confirms the binary distinction" and secondly because it "denies specificity" (Braidotti *Posthuman* 79). Therefore, Braidotti stresses the importance of reasserting "the concept of difference as both central and non-essentialistic" (Braidotti, *Posthuman* 100). Unfortunately, none of this can be said of the image of Africans created in the discourse on slavery, which envisions post-slavery Africans very much as reformed Enlightenment subjects. What the discourse on slavery proposed, was not even the extension of an existing boundary but rather a utopia of reform and improvement to assimilate the former slaves into a Eurocentric ideal of the human.

The highly problematic nature of the underlying concept of the human can also be seen in the very presumption of the attempts of various anti-slavery authors to prove the humanity of Africans. Thomas Clarkson's use of Philis Wheatley's poetry for this end is a good example of this:

> From Hymn to the Morning
> Aurora Hail! and all the thousand dies,
> That deck thy progress through the vaulted skies!
> The morn awakes, and wide extends her rays,
> On ev'ry leaf the gentle zephyr plays.
> Harmonious lays the feathered race resume,
> Dart the bright eye, and shake the painted plume.
> -- -- &c &c.
> Lest it should be doubted whether these Poems are genuine we shall transcribe the names of those, who signed a certificate of their authenticity.
> His Excellency Thomas Hutchinson, Governor.
> The Honorable Andrew Oliver, Lieutenant Governor. . . . (CE 173f)

Thomas Clarkson concludes his assessment of Philis Wheatley's humanity in the following way,

> Such is the poetry which we produce as a proof of our assertions. How far it has succeeded, the reader may by this time have determined in his own mind. We shall therefore only beg leave to accompany it with this observation, that if the authoress was designed for slavery, (as the argument must confess) the greater part of the inhabitants of Britain must lose their claim to freedom. (CE 174f)

An additional reason why I believe the underlying concept of the human to be problematic is that it is highly charged in terms of power relations. Throughout Clarkson's assessment, there is a lingering threat of exclusion from humanity, both against Wheatley, whose humanity he proves, and against "the inhabitants of Britain", who, for the sake of Clarkson's argument, might also "lose their claim to freedom" (CE 175) should they fail to produce such poetry as Wheatley. In the quote, humanity is not something that comes naturally, but has to be earned and approved by an external authority. Perhaps unwillingly, Clarkson thus claims the deciding power over humanity for the colonial centre, the strategic location of which is still enhanced by citing the names of respectable persons who vouch for the poem's authenticity, which the author would presumably not have done in the case of a white British or American author. Furthermore, the nature of the poem shows that the humanity which Clarkson claims for Africans is by no means a truly universal one, but one very much informed by a European frame of reference. The imagery of the poem contains clear references to classical European antiquity in its use of the terms "Aurora" and "zephyr". Therefore, I dare raise the question of whether Clarkson's use of Wheatley's poetry can actually be described as an attempt to cite an authentic African voice and not as an instance of colonial mimicry. To quote Bhabha, I would suggest that the use of Wheatley's poetry in this context be indeed seen as part of "a complex strategy of reform, regulation and discipline, which appropriates the Other as it visualizes power" (Bhabha, *Culture* 122). Wheatley, thus, serves Clarkson's need to produce a "reformed, recognizable other, as a subject of difference that is almost the same, but not quite." (Bhabha, *Culture* 122)

One has to bear in mind that the conception of the human in humanism was never free from the influence of political interest. Braidotti describes the humanistic human as "neither an ideal nor an objective statistical average or middle ground. It rather spells out a systematised standard of recognisability—of Sameness—by which all others can be assessed, regulated and allotted to a designated social location" (Braidotti, *Posthuman* 26). This is why theorists like Harfield, Braidotti and Wolfe advocate the transgression of the classical human in the form of the post-human. The quotes above further illustrate the importance of a post-colonial reading of the texts of the European Enlightenment and humanism. Braidotti states:

> Post-colonial theory developed this insight into the notion that ideals of reason, secular tolerance, equality under the Law and democratic rule, need not, be and indeed historically have not been, mutually exclusive with European practices of violent domination, exclusion and systematic and instrumental use of terror. (Braidotti, *Posthuman* 46)

The inherent Eurocentrism of late 18th- and early 19th-century colonial philanthropism is also reflected by the universalistic concept of the history of human progress which pro- and anti-slavery writers typically employ. It has been shown above that in his 1786 *Essay*, Clarkson proposes a version of early human history outlining three distinct stages which all human societies have to go through, "a first stage of dissociation and independence" (CE 56ff), "a state of independent society" (CE 59) and finally a "state of subordinate society" (CE 660). One need only recall Hobbes' and Rousseau's contrasting ideas about the original situation of man to see that questions about man's state of nature were a central concern of the European Enlightenment. Thomas Clarkson writes about debt slaves in Africa: "the Africans are no more to be censured for their weakness in this respect, than others in the same stage of society" (CE 43f). To propose universal stages of society, however, is to deny specificity by subjecting all human societies to a teleological concept of progress leading to one universal endpoint. The claim of knowing the endpoint of human development, again, puts an enormous amount of discursive power into the hands of a colonial centre, with the additional advantage of defining metropolitan subjects as "the most free, enlightened, and happy people that ever existed upon earth" (WL 42). Wilberforce and the other abolitionists blame slavery for denying the Africans the many blessings of a connection with Europeans, keeping them in "their present state of unexampled darkness and degradation" (WA 75):

> instead of producing any such effect as might be hoped for from a commercial connection between a less and a more civilized people; instead of imparting to the former the superior knowledge and improvements of the latter; instead of awakening the dormant powers of the human mind, of calling forth new exertions of industry, and thus leading to a constant progression of new wants,

desires, and tastes; to the acquisition of property, to the acquisition of capital, ... (WL 85)

Wilberforce, thus, explicitly describes the endpoint of history as a capitalist utopia inhabited by Smithian *homines oeconomici*. In his 1823 *Thoughts on the Necessity of Improving the Condition of the Slaves in the British Colonies*, Thomas Clarkson perhaps expresses the degree to which Africans were made the objects of a Eurocentric capitalism in the most explicit way:

> In fact, the Negro character is malleable at the European will. There is, as I have observed before, a singular pliability in the constitutional temper of the Negroes, and they have besides a quick sense of their own interest, which influences their conduct. (CT 42)

5.4.2 Suicide or Death

Clarkson attributes the different courses of individual action to different national characters:

> Those of the leeward coast are in general pusillanimous, and in cases of this kind are content to revenge their injuries upon themselves, by seeking their own deaths. Those, on the other hand, of the Windward Coast, consisting of a nation of hunters, and trained to war, are bold and intrepid, and on all occasions attempt to punish their enslavers at the hazard of their own lives. (CE88 94)

Clarkson's *Essay* contains several instances of rebelling slaves. The author explicitly advocates the African's right to rebellion (cf. CE 153f), even asking the readers if they would not act in the same way under similar circumstances (cf. CE 241). Clarkson's references to the gallantry of the leaders of a mutiny aboard a slave ship (cf. CE88 96) gives the act of rebellion a distinctly positive tinge. However, his *Essay* only contains instances of unsuccessful uprisings, which end in the death of the slaves. Clarkson reports "upon a certain vessel [which] had procured a hundred and ninety slaves from the Windward coast" (CE88 94) and where the slaves rise against the crew. At first, they are successful and even manage to make themselves the "masters of the vessel" (CE88 95). Eventually, however, they are "deprived of their gallant leaders, and unable to continue their exertions" (CE88 96) and have to retreat. The crew of the slave ship then manages to fire "a volley ... into the thickest of the croud of slaves" (CE88 96). The shock of this is "too severe for them to stand, and they retreated accordingly where they could" (CE88 96). Thus, the insurrection of the slaves ends:

> Most of the slaves, on examination, were found to be in a wounded state, and some of them so mangled, that scarcely any other prospect remained, than that they would either die, or become a burthen upon their hands. All these were immediately ordered to leap into the sea. Some of them, who had no connections on board, waited not a moment, but received and obeyed the summons with joy. The rest staid only to embrace their relations and friends, and then, without any hesitation, and with marks of chearfulness in their face, but mixt with disdain when they cast their eyes on the receivers, they leapt into the sea, and terminated their existence there. (CE88 96)

Thus, the slaves gain a sort of final victory over their oppressors through their noble suicide. A similar trope can be found in Clarkson's description of the *Zong* incident, when he describes that ten of the slaves about to be jettisoned, "did not wait to be hand-cuffed, but bravely leaped into the sea, and shared the fate of their companions" (CE 131fn). In this way, Clarkson's text manages to "kill off" quite a substantial number of rebellious slaves. By this, Clarkson probably tries to mitigate the fear of slave rebellions. Either the Africans are killed in the act of rebellion or they direct the aggression against themselves, committing suicide. However, this raises the question of whether Clarkson's text actually allows any autonomous agency for Africans. The Africans who survive are the wretched, despondent objects of a slavery, which "depressed their minds; ... numbed their faculties; and, by preventing those sparks of genius from blazing forth, which had otherwise been conspicuous; ... gave them the appearance of being endued with inferiour capacities than the rest of mankind" (CE 22).

The discourse on emancipation, in particular, had an interest in rendering the Africans harmless. Clarkson writes that the settlement in Sierra Leone was a success despite the fact that "They must have contracted as mortal a hatred of the whites from their sufferings on board ship by fetters, whips, and suffocation in the hold, as the West Indian from those severities which are attached to their bondage upon shore" (CT 20).

5.4.3 Rebellion

The emphasis on the more threatening aspects of African slaves, of course, changed over the period of 50 years, which my text corpus covers. While the abolition debate was more concerned about a discussion of Africans' fundamental humanity, the emancipation debate was, of course, at heart an attempt to assuage the fears of potential uprisings.

Ramsay, for example, dedicates a full chapter of his *Essay* to the vindication of the "natural capacity of African slaves" (197). In this fourth chapter of *Essay*, entitled "Natural Capacity of Slaves vindicated" (197), Ramsay sets out to defend the Africans' and Europeans' common humanity, arguing that "before we proceed to claim the rights of society, and of a common religion for Africans, we must first put them in possession of that humanity, which is pertinaciously disputed with them" (197).

While early abolitionist texts are, thus, more concerned with the question of African humanity, the texts after the Haitian Revolution are increasingly concerned with the theme of the slave rebellion. Wilberforce's *Letter* repeatedly refers to "the lesson which the Island of St. Domingo has taught" (WL 321), but explicit descriptions of bodily suffering are largely absent from the emancipation debate. Authors do refer to the injustice and cruelty of working slaves under the whip; the explicit descriptions of the violated bodies are, however, absent. The representation of inhumane treatment is not so much aimed at arousing the sentimental affections of the reader as at seeking to brand West Indian slavery as a system of control at odds with the fundamental conception of humans underlying a capitalist wage labour:

> It is idle and insulting to talk of improving the condition of these poor beings, as rational and moral agents, while they are treated in a manner which precludes self-government, and annihilates all human motives but such as we impose on a maniac, or on a hardened and incorrigible convict. (WA 16)

Also, Clarkson strikes a similar chord when he suggests:

> There must be new laws again more akin to the principle of reward than of punishment, of privilege than of privation, and which shall have a tendency to raise or elevate their condition, so as to fit them by degrees to sustain the rank of free men. (CT 6)

Clarkson's *Thoughts* already betrays its preoccupation with the issue of safety already in its title when he promises the reader his thoughts on "the practicability, the safety and the advantages" (CT i) of emancipation. Also, 31 of the 60 pages of this text consist of 6 or 7 instances of peaceful emancipations of whole bodies of Africans (cf. CT 16–48).

Elizabeth Heyrick chooses another form of dealing with the threat of slave rebellions. She is relatively outspoken in her support of rebellion:

> As long as a human being is bought and sold,—regarded as goods and chattels,—compelled to labour without wages,—branded, chained, and flogged at the caprice of his owner; he will, of necessity, as long as the feeling of pain, the sense of degradation and injury remain, he will, unless he have the spirit of a Christian martyr, be vindictive and revengeful. (HI 13)

However, the argument suggests that emancipation would make the causes and motivations of taking revenge disappear. The passage constructs Africans as being driven by the same motives as all human beings, thus making them manageable.

The pro-slavery argument is straightforward in conjuring up the "horrors of St. Domingo" (ML 16) and the image of the literally unleashed cruelty of the rebels. Bridges, for example, challenges the advocates of emancipation to "look on St. Domingo; that fostered child of your disordered fancy: where are your boasted results of emancipation to be traced, but in the appalling features of a barbarous revolt?" (BV 7).

The fact that the discourse on abolition was fraught with excessive cruelties and enormities, of course, put the pro-slavery argument in a position to represent the potential backlash from the former slaves in equally drastic terms. The prior representation of Africans as wretches, as has been shown above, allowed them to argue that former slaves would, of course, act with the according inhumanity towards their former enslavers. It has been argued that the whole image of the zombie hordes still haunting 21st-century popular culture had its origin in the representation of the Haitian revolutionaries as equally fanatical hordes (cf. Lauro 98).

5.5 Africans in Terms of Gender—African Women

The assessment of the pronouns and nouns in the text corpus, which was done in one of the preceding chapters, showed that generally, "Africans" are mainly plural and male in both pro- and anti-slavery texts. However, an appraisal of the image of Africans would not be complete without an analysis of the representation of African women. The following section will look at the function that explicitly female Africans have in the discussion of slavery.

One of the more common instances in which female Africans appear, especially in anti-slavery texts, is when authors want to enhance their descriptions of suffering Africans. This kind of use seems to be informed by the notion that suffering women invite even more empathy than suffering men, drawing on prevalent gender stereotypes of women as the fairer, gentler and weaker sex.

Ramsay states "We cannot pass over in silence the usual treatment of pregnant women and nurses" and remarks that pregnant women are usually kept at work during "the last months of their pregnancy, and hence suffer many an abortion" (RE 88).

Clarkson reports an incident on a slave ship in which "an African girl ... was chained by the neck to the main mast of the vessel between the decks" (CE88 88f) and later in the same text tells of an unsold woman who was ordered to be thrown overboard by "the tyrant of the ship" (CE88 103). Wilberforce relates the story of a West India militiaman who kills a pregnant woman when "without the least provocation on her part, plunged his bayonet into her, and, as one of the accounts states, very coolly and deliberately stabbed her several times in the breast" (WL 162).

One of the stock scenes of sentimental suffering in anti-slavery is the moment when the slaves are sold in the colonies and families are torn apart. Clarkson describes how

> ... the wife is separated from her husband, or the mother from her son: and if these cruel instances of separation should happen; if relations, when they find themselves about to be parted, should cling together; or if filial, conjugal, or parental affection, should detain them but a moment longer in each other's arms, than these second receivers should think sufficient, the lash instantly severs them from their embraces. (CE 133)

Wilberforce writes of "the anguish of husbands torn from their wives, wives from their husbands, and parents from their children; (101) the pangs arising from the consideration, that they are separated for ever from their country" (WL 100f).

The same author uses female suffering to make his point about "the cruel, and, at least in the case of the female sex, highly indecent punishments inflicted in public, and in the face of day" (WA 16). Also, Heyrick uses female suffering for argumentative purposes when she criticises the colonial law "which authorizes a female negro to be stripped in the presence of her father, husband or son, and flogged with a cart whip!" (HI 20).

Sexual intercourse, in general, can be seen as a further instance of transgressing Africans' bodily boundaries in line with what has been written above on this topic. A predominantly female form of this is the exposure to sexual violence. In his paper on pro-slavery representation of female Jamaican slaves, Henrice Altink points out that:

> As female purity was considered priceless in the metropolitan society of the day, the sexual abuse of female slaves was an excellent means for abolitionists to demonstrate that slavery reduced slaves to a less than human condition and that it corrupted slaveholders because it prevented them from living up to the metropolitan norm of masculine restraint. (Altink 272)

Both Ramsay and Wilberforce criticise the use of unmarried men as managers of plantations:

> married managers ... have numberless ... advantages over single men, in point of character, faithfulness, and application; yet planters have determined it to be better to employ perhaps a dissipated, careless, unfeeling young man, or a grovelling, lascivious, old batchelor (each with his half score of black or mulattoe pilfering harlots, who, at their will, select for him, from among the slaves, the objects of his favour or hatred) rather than allow a married woman to be entertained on the plantation. (RE 83f)
> The fact is perfectly notorious, that it has been the general policy to employ instead of married managers and overseers, single young men as the immediate superintendents of the gangs; and hence it too naturally follows, that they who, from their being the depositories of the master's authority, ought to be the protectors of the purity of the young females, too often become their corrupters. (WA 21)

Ramsay draws the reader's attention to the fact that "that Mulattoe girls, during the flower of their age, are universally sacrificed to the lust of white men; in some instances, to that of their own fathers" (RE 232).

Tobin counters the accusation of sexual violence by shifting the discussion to the French colonies, when he accuses the French of such a "family intimacy between the French planters and their slaves [which] produces such a number of Mulattoes, Meztizes, and other shades of complexion, that their owners cannot find employment for half their mixed breed about their houses" (TC 37 fn).

On the other hand, the accusation of sexual violence towards female slaves is countered by pro-slavery authors' allegations of female slaves' hyper-sexuality (cf. Altink 272). The anonymous author of *Observations* generally observes that Africans would see the concept of marriage as an infraction upon their human rights (cf. AO 32). In particular, the author of *Fugitive Thoughts* represents Africans in general as "being the most lascivious of all human beings" (AF 15). He writes of women in particular:

> Negresses are by constitution lascivious, their dances express it by indecent gesticulations. Many of those women being confined to the conversation of one man only, cannot have their desires satisfied. Therefore it often happens, when their warm wishes are afloat, that on seeing accidentaly an object, and a favourable opportunity, they throw off all restraint, and if he will not gratify their desires, full of revenge and rage at the disappointment, they fly to their husband, accuse the man of an attempt, and slavery is his slightest punishment; there are no actions for crim. con. in that country, the law enforced by Potiphar against Joseph is still observed. (AF 30)

The basic image of the African woman as sexually active can also be found in anti-slavery texts, although not to the same extent as in pro-slavery ones. Clarkson, for example, cites the example of African kings sending out their wives as seductresses:

> These wives are strictly commanded to go out, and to attempt to seduce the young and the unwary. Every person so seduced and found out (and it is the business of the seductress to betray) forfeits his liberty, and becomes the property of the prince. (CE88 41)

Generally, however, a portrayal of African women as fundamentally virtuous was more in line with the overall anti-slavery utopia. Wilberforce, for example, cites Mungo Park, praising the "the conjugal fidelity of the women" (WL 67). The author repeatedly writes of the "licentious intercourse between the sexes" (WA 28) as one of the evils of the slave system, contrasting it with the image of the African in a state of nature. Wilberforce quotes the West Indian planters themselves to the effect that polygamy is "the grand obstacle to the production and rearing of children" (WL 124). In this respect, female Africans play an important part in the anti-slavery utopia in which the colonies self-sufficiently "breed" their slaves. In this utopia, the image of the sexually active African woman is also present, for example, when Wilberforce writes that Africans are "perhaps, the most prolific of all the human species" (WL 67). In these instances, however, the discourse on demography sanitises the lascivious nature of the intercourse. Wilberforce criticises the practice of importing more male slaves than female ones:

> What then can shew more clearly, that the planters do not, even yet, set themselves in earnest to produce an increase by breeding, than that, under an exaggerated impression of the effects of importing a too small proportion of females, and with a probability, at least, of abolition before their eyes, they suffer it to continue the interest of the Slave merchant, in preference to bring over males. (WL 119)

This shows a distinct view of slave populations as the object of demographic considerations. Anti-slavery authors considered it as completely legitimate to engineer populations to the needs of the West Indian plantation economy. During the abolition debate, the only change that authors propose is the breeding of a workforce rather than importing one from Africa. In *Mighty Experiment*, Drescher points out that in the period of abolition and emancipation, the West Indies became a laboratory for social theories and emphasises the importance of the science of demography (cf. Drescher, *Experiment* 4–7). Demographics as a science of analysing and ordering human multiplicities is certainly a central concern of the anti-slavery argument. Clarkson writes:

> Ten thousand people under fair advantages, and in a soil congenial to their constitutions, and where the means of subsistence are easy, should produce in a century 160,000. This is the proportion in which the Americans increased; and the Africans in their own country increase in the same, if not a greater proportion. Now as the climate of the colonies is as favourable to their health as that of their own country, the causes of the prodigious decrease in the one, and increase in the other, will be more conspicuous. (CE 236fn)

The attempt to manage the "licentious intercourse between the sexes" (WA 28) is part of the larger discourse of reform that the Africans are subjected to and which clearly wants to regulate the mingling of both white and black bodies.

5.6 Africans in Terms of ~~Race~~

Before beginning an analysis of the racial dimension of the discourse on slavery, I would like to outline a very brief working definition of the term '~~race~~'. My approach to the concept is mainly informed by George Mosse's seminal work, *Towards the Final Solution*. In line with what Mosse writes about the history of European racism, I see racism as a system of essentialist social and moral classification closely linked to aesthetics. At heart, racism is about the construction of essential difference which, in the case of Africans, is based on complexion. Thus, the pernicious nature of racist logic lies in the fact that it constructs an essential and ethnocentric superiority of one group over another based on aesthetic judgements.

My analysis starts with a quantitative appreciation of the use of expressions in referring to Africans which derive their meaning based on Africans complexions. In the late 18th and early19th centuries the term "negroe" certainly did not have the negative connotations it has today. Nonetheless, the signification of the term is based on the Africans' blackness rather than their geographical origin, unlike the more neutral and geographically defined term "African(s)".

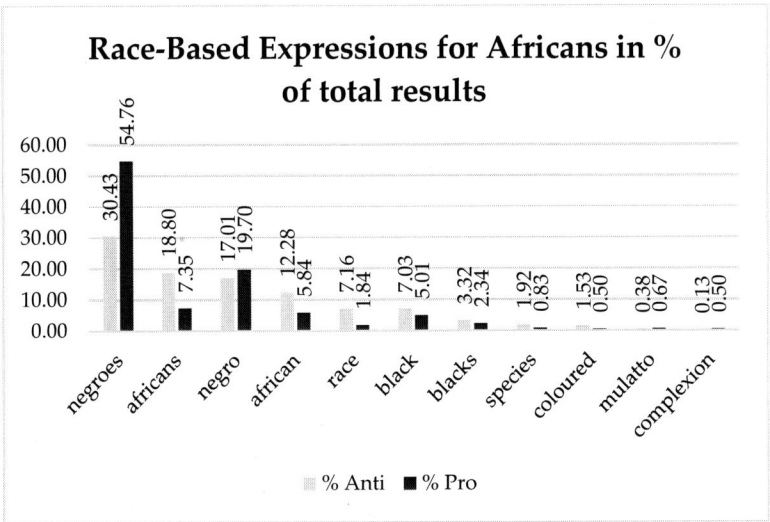

Fig. 15: Racialized expressions for Africans[8]

The table above shows that anti-slavery authors do indeed use a less race-based representation of Africans. There is a remarkable difference between the frequencies in the use of the word "African". It has to be noted that the textual basis for the bar chart above is only segments coded "Africans" which are outside the quotes. Thus, the extensive direct quotes in some of the pro-slavery texts do not distort the result since the statistics only consider those parts of texts in which authors do not quote other sources.

---

[8] The table shows the frequencies of a selection of terms implying a race-based representation of Africans. The percentages are of the total frequencies of all the terms in the query.

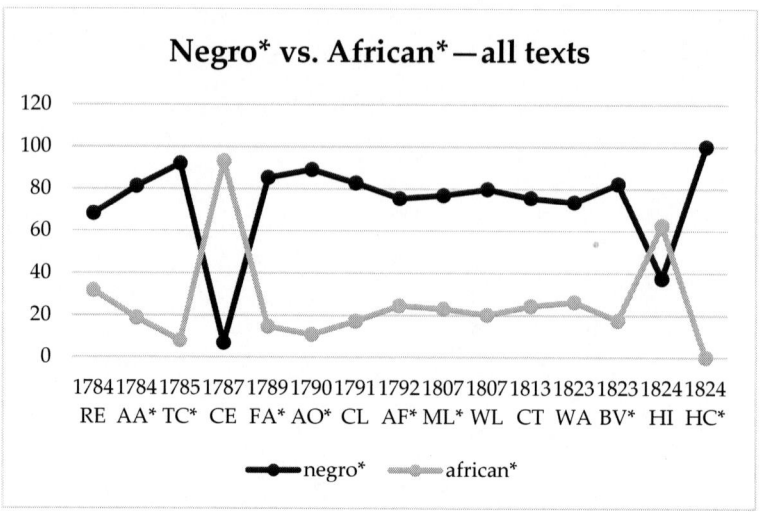

Fig. 16: 'Negroes' vs. 'Africans' [9]

The line graph above shows that it is primarily two texts which are responsible for the overall difference between the pro- and anti-slavery use of 'Africans' vs. 'negroes' for the representation of Africans. Clarkson's 1787 *Essay* and Heyrick's 1824 *Immediate Emancipation* show a significantly different distribution in the uses of the terms 'negro*' and 'african*'. The possible reasons behind this tendency will be analysed below.

In the prologue to the 1985 edition of *Toward the Final Solution*, Mosse states: "during the eighteenth century ... Europeans could [still] entertain enlightened and even utopian views of non-Europeans" (ix). He, furthermore, writes about the situation in the 18th century that, "at first the realization that different races existed did not lead to racism, [however] the fine line between the perception of racial differences and racism was only too easily bridged" (x). Despite the undoubtedly utopian views, especially of anti-slavery writers, one has to bear in mind, that the discourse on slavery is, of course, a fundamentally racialised one. It is at heart a discussion of

---

[9]   Table showing instances of "negro*" vs. "african*" in percent. Proslavery texts are marked with an asterisk*.

the slave trade and subsequent slavery of black African slaves. There is no denying the historical fact that millions of black Africans were enslaved and transported across the Atlantic by white Europeans. This is also evident at the lexical level, when one considers that after "slave/s" the most frequent term for referring to the objects of the discourse is as "negro/es" and not the more geographically determined "African/s", which only comes in third place.

The fact that Ramsay's *Essay*, which is the first major anti-slavery text that extensively deals with the question of ~~race~~, supports Kitson's argument that the emphasis put on the question of race by anti-slavery authors was not justified by the pro-slavery argument (cf. Kitson, *Reflections* 11). Ramsay seems to feel the need to oppose an alleged pro-slavery argument when he writes:

> Suppose different races, and that they vary in point of excellence; yet, in what chapter of nature's law is it declared, that one quarter of the globe shall breed slaves for the rest? (RE 233)

The anonymous "Gentlemen of St. Christopher" bluntly reject the use of the racial argument when they reply: "We cannot name the chapter, but it is so declared in the code of their national laws and practice." (AA 91) and also James Tobin argued that the difference of slaves was a social rather than a racial one (TC 141f). I have suggested above that the notion of slavery as being contrary to the humanity of its objects is a central element of the anti-slavery argument. Because of this, anti-slavery logic always sees the mere act of justifying the existence of slavery as a denial of the slaves' and thus the Africans' fundamental humanity.

5.6.1 *Whiteness, Light, Darkness, Blackness*

The implications of notions of light and whiteness versus darkness and blackness for racist conceptions of mankind and especially Africans are quite obvious and have often been commented on in the scholarly debate on racism (cf. for example Mosse). The very term

"En*light*enment" stands in contrast to the Africans visible blackness. Ramsay, for example, goes to quite some lengths to refute any inference from the African's exterior blackness to any racially defined intellectual inferiority.

As this is of central importance for making modern notions of both intellectual and material progress valid for black Africans it is certainly worthwhile analysing the images of colour and light which can be found in the texts.

		KWIC – "light" – all texts
Document	Para	Preview
AA	52	inted in 1772, throws the clearest LIGHT upon the subject of slavery, that
AA	106	is country will appear in its true LIGHT.' Establishment of Clergy and the
BV	27	ssing the divine image. The bright LIGHT of Christianity is obscured and su
CE	84	the subject, have been brought to LIGHT. Nor has it received less support
CE	254	truth of the position in a clearer LIGHT. At the same time I must confess,
CE	22	now seeing the matter in its true LIGHT, that their congratulations had pr
FA	59	ous man would consider in the same LIGHT as bearing false witness; and he h
HC	65	Gospel, our own conscience, or the LIGHT of truth. This city is a burden to
HI	57	nces of the times, — to increasing LIGHT and civilization? It is absurd to
HI	71	rforce, and a Buxton. If the clear LIGHT, the full information, they have s
RE	97	mplexioned people might throw some LIGHT on the blackness of the African. T
RE	166	e should never appear in any other LIGHT among them than that of their inst
WL	22	cling in defiance, of the clearest LIGHT, not only in opposition to our own
WL	53	e blessings of religious and moral LIGHT, and social improvement, are preci
WL	121	ll, are moral improvement, and the LIGHT of religious truth, and the hope f

WA	59	eligious darkness into the blessed LIGHT of Christianity ? But even selfint
WA	72	can possibly exhibit in a stronger LIGHT the extreme force of the prejudice
WA	72	e hope, "full of immortality," the LIGHT of heavenly truth, and all the con

Fig. 17: 'Light' – KWIC

This selection of the use of the term "light" shows that many of the authors very much subscribe to the symbolism of "En*light*enment". In the concordance lines, "light" stands for knowledge, recognition and rational understanding via the visual channel and also has a dimension of religious revelation. The grand narrative of en*light*enment about man's progress from medieval darkness to modern and enlightened society certainly introduced an emphasis on the visual as such (cf. Oxford. *Short World History*). The implications of this for humans with darker complexions was, unfortunately, a pernicious one. Mosse therefore correctly describes 18th-century enlightenment as the cradle of modern racism (*Solution*, 1). The table below shows various uses of the term "darkness":

	KWIC – "dark" and "darkness" – all texts	
Document	Para	KWIC
AA	30	igin of slavery may be involved in DARKNESS, yet in that most ancient book the
BV	22	some particulars worse than pagan DARKNESS and depravity, hundreds of thousan
BV	43	e meaning, when addressed to their DARK comprehensions, you observe that
CE	69	d zone for any time, are become as DARK coloured as our native Indians of
CE	69	generations, they would become as DARK in complexion." <footnote 1, p.20
FA	109	tle [83] influence, indeed, in the DARK and ignorant ages preceding the Re
HC	55	phere, and the protracted reign of DARKNESS, vice, and barbarism. Having acc
HI	64	ntrenchments of the very powers of DARKNESS, in which courage would be more av

HI	70	t darkness come upon them." Mental DARKNESS, and spiritual night, steal fast u
RE	133	as bending down the soul in utter DARKNESS, the more effectually to enslave t
RE	62	h and neglect, while all around is DARKNESS and doubt. Yet on no account is t
RE	95	observed that their blood is of a DARK red. This may be accounted for fro
TC	143	the law was exerted, to sift this DARK business to the bottom, but withou
TC	152	women, and the rapid increase of a DARK and contaminated breed, are evils
WL	54	state and happiness of Africa. The DARKNESS of Paganism were a very inefficien
WL	79	of their ever emerging out of this DARK and barbarous state. The most resp
WL	93	ern regions, till then immersed in DARKNESS and barbarism; and they sprung up
WA	60	r [32] native land, and in all the DARKNESS and abominations of paganism, with
WA	71	ourse between the sexes, and Pagan DARKNESS, are nearly universal among them;
WA	105	their present state of unexampled DARKNESS and degradation! While efforts ar

Fig. 18: 'Darkness' – KWIC

As can be seen, "dark" and "darkness" stand for ignorance, doubt, paganism and a miserable situation in the text. This shows that most authors subscribe to a Christian imagery of light and darkness, in which light stands for positive values such as salvation, while darkness has negative connotations and frequently denotes paganism. The fact that many of the concordance lines combine darkness and barbarity suggests that the religious image of salvation informs the whole concept of civilisation and human progress as well.

THE IMAGE OF AFRICANS 319

	KWIC – "black" and "white" – all texts	
Document	Para	KWIC
AA	65	mbrace it; but that can be done by BLACK labourers only.---"French slaves a
AA	75	addition to the consumption of the WHITE inhabitants." Here a distinction i
AA	98	kin never blisters, while vagabond WHITE sailors blister whenever the sun r
AA	104	hether a house has been built by a BLACK or white workman.—Whatever discove
AO	76	<49> great encouragement to induce WHITE families to settle in that island;
AF	55	olitioners pretend to feel for the BLACK race, let them view an embarkation
AF	78	the negroes have not feelings like WHITE men, and are as sensible of pain;
AF	78	scales infinitely smaller than in WHITE men, the pores and soporific vesse
AF	87	ands to redress all grievances the BLACK slaves are subject to from the sev
BV	18	o any length which may degrade the WHITE population of these Western isles,
BV	18	n whose ruin you aspire to raise a BLACK republic, similar to that of your
CE	71	of this notion, these unfortunate BLACK people, refused to go to the new m
CE	37	sume, that the purest <footnote 1> WHITE is as far removed from the primiti
CE	76	om the darkest black to the purest WHITE must have actually been accomplish
CE	76	otus relates, that the Colchi were BLACK, and that they had crisped hair. T
CT	8	ro-evidence is invalid against the WHITE oppressor, and so long as human na
CT	15	trocity in the sight of a thousand BLACK spectators, and no harm will happe
CT	35	rious and honest people from their WHITE neighbours. A few years afterwards
CT	60	, had succeeded also in making the BLACK labourers return to the plantation
FA	124	untries. These are the Negroes, or BLACK slaves, the posterity of Ham." Suc
FA	7	These people, who had never seen a WHITE man before (so could not have made

FA	51	ysical reason, why the Negroes are BLACK, and have curled wool on their hea
FA	82	. This change of manners among the WHITE inhabitants of the West Indies, is
HI	50	h restrain and punish crime in the WHITE population, would still restrain a
HI	50	l restrain and punish crime in the BLACK population. The danger arising fro
RE	187	severity, and which the white and BLACK overseers stand over them to see e
RE	260	an annual supply of slaves. As the WHITE inhabitants are numerous, slavery
RE	75	rity or brutality. Speaking of the WHITE or superior race, he goes on to af
RE	92	ses, prominent chins, woolly hair, BLACK skins; to which the curious anatom
TC	93	l of their proprietors, and that a WHITE man is not accountable for the mur
TC	154	are lazy, sensual, and cruel. The BLACK cairibs of St. Vincent are the des
WL	5	ond all comparison the bulk of the BLACK population. What then can shew mor
WL	87	charging the bulk of the resident WHITE population of the West Indies with
WL	118	are protected by law equally with WHITE men, in their lives and property;
WL	167	is, from its very small number of WHITE inhabitants, and its peculiar situ
WA	38	ves is never [14] admitted against WHITE men, the difficulty of legally est
WA	49	f the coloured women; and that the WHITE men who form connections with them
WA	65	on of slavery, after preparing the BLACK population for the enjoyment of it
WA	67	e necessary end of maintaining the BLACK population, to adopt effectual mea

Fig. 19: 'Black and white' – KWIC

The concordances show that white and black are very much used to construct identity. The discourse on slavery does indeed separate mankind into a black and a white part. Skin colour is unquestionably an important dividing line and means of categorisation of humans. The recurrent use of expressions like "white inhabitants/population" and "black inhabitants/population" suggests the importance of the concepts for the construction of identities, especially in the West Indies.

		Frequent Collocations "white" and "black" – nouns 1R – all texts					
	collocations "white" – 1R				collocations "black" 1R		
Rank	Freq	MI	item	Rank	Freq	MI	item
1	25	6.45799	man	1	11	8.17663	population
2	22	6.22727	men	2	7	8.37255	traders
3	19	6.04203	people	3	7	3.29076	slaves
4	17	7.27831	inhabitants	4	6	9.88712	trader
5	8	7.84127	servants	5	5	8.17931	skin
6	5	8.04071	savages	6	5	4.44308	people
7	5	6.39016	race	7	3	10.24969	regiments
8	4	6.39016	population	8	3	6.90730	labourers
9	4	6.99530	labourers	9	2	8.07977	troops
10	3	4.81115	persons	10	2	2.38861	slave
11	3	5.10796	person	11	2	8.88712	skins
12	3	7.11530	man's	12	2	5.39527	race
13	2	4.68561	sugar	13	2	6.77165	princes
14	2	6.14505	servant	14	2	7.51789	overseers
15	2	7.97512	sailors	15	2	7.22416	overseer
16	2	4.05758	masters	16	2	3.09488	men
17	2	5.80520	families	17	2	3.14117	man
18	2	4.22618	children	18	2	4.51789	inhabitants
19				19	2	5.46086	evidence
20				20	2	5.67767	colour

Fig. 20: 'Black and white' – collocations

All of these collocations (with the exception of "white sugar" and "black colour") show that both white and black frequently appear in such combinations as describe human beings. This gives evidence to what has been said above about the importance of racial concepts in order to create human identity. What is striking is the much higher frequency of "man/men" in combination with white than with black. On the other hand, only "black" collocates with slave/s while "white" does not. Another interesting fact is that in all the texts only "black skin/s" are worth mentioning (7x), while the combination "white skins" only appears once. This indicates that "white skins" are perceived as the norm by these authors.

It is also worth noting that the term "whiteness" is not used at all in the text whereas the authors use the term of "blackness" 12 times. Since the suffix -ness refers to "a state or condition" (OED), this can well be seen as evidencing that being black is considered as being a special state and condition while "white" rather refers to the norm, which does not make it necessary to point out the existence of "whiteness".

After these introductory observations, the rest of the present chapter will deal with the concept of race in each text individually.

5.6.2 Anti-slavery

The issue of race certainly seems to be an important topic already in Ramsay's *Essay*. In the first section of the chapter, entitled "Objection to African Capacity, drawn from Philosophy, considered", Ramsay refutes David Hume's notorious footnote from his essay on national character (cf. Hume 236), in which he suggests that Africans are inferior to Europeans since "there never arose a man of genius among negroes" (qtd. in RE 198). Ramsay draws a historical comparison between Hume's view of the uncivilised Africans and the Roman image of the Britons as uncivilised and also notes the fact that Charlemagne still presented it as a remarkable thing that the Britons "that though their country lay far north, yet it had produced several great men" (RE 199). In section two, he deals with the difference of Africans, making it clear that linking appearance and genius, as he calls it (RE 212), is ridiculous since "on this supposition, hereditary indefeasible right in Kings would not only be a subject of ridicule, but of grave discussion. We need only to distinguish accurately the stamp of royalty to put ourselves under the best possible government" (RE 212f).

Although he clearly opposes legitimising slavery on the grounds of appearance, he also writes that "West Indian children, educated in England, improve not only in complexion, but in elegance of features: an alteration arising, perhaps, equally from change of climate, of diet, and of education" (RE 212). The notion of improvement in the quote puts whiteness over blackness. He starts his third section on anatomy by quoting a "gentleman, justly celebrated for his accuracy in the course of his anatomical researches, [who] has discovered a surprizing difference between European and African skulls. This suggested to him the idea of drawing out a series of heads in this gradation: European, African, monkey, dog" (RE 219). The section deals with skull forms and other scientific anatomic observations of the time. In accordance with contemporary science, Ramsay allows that skull forms vary and that differently sized brains could result in different degrees of intelligence and capacities. Yet, his conception of head forms is a dynamic one, since he concludes:

> Suppose then an African, in his savage state, to have less brains, and in consequence less reason, yet still a sufficiency for his situation; the question then is, whether his head, his brains, and his reason, would not expand in the successive generations of civilized life. (RE 225)

He also emphasises that there is not "any essential difference between the European and African in mental powers" (RE 229). However, this also has to be seen in the context of power relations. A static concept of exclusion based on racial differences is certainly a less powerful model than a dynamic system of exclusion based on the individual's conformity with social norms. Ramsay describes the desired effect of the improvement of the Africans' situation as follows:

> A new rank of citizens, placed between the black and white races ...They would naturally attach themselves to the white race, as the more honourable relation, and so become a barrier against the designs of the black. (RE 289)

Apart from the implied degradation of Africans as the less honourable relation, the author's hope that the "new rank of citizens ... would attach themselves to the white race" (RE 289) hints at a wish for conformity to norms set by a white middle class.

One has to be clear about the fact that Ramsay, and, for that part, most other anti-slavery authors by no means reject or seek to downplay the existence of different races, he writes:

> ... the characteristics of negroes shew themselves chiefly about the face, where nature has fixed both the national attributes and the discriminating features of individuals, as if intended to distinguish them from other families, and bind them in the social tie with their brethren. (RE 203f)

Although Ramsay's text does not take the step to combine the concepts of racial difference and aesthetics to form a stringent system of social and moral classification, we can find two main elements of modern racism in his *Essay*: a strong belief in the function of the visual—"national attributes and discriminating features" (RE 203f), and the idea that outer appearance functions as a distinguisher of various social and ethnical groups.

It also has to be mentioned that the hypothetical validity of ranking humans according to ~~race~~ is allowed ample space in Ramsay's text so much so that at least the 21st-century reader sometimes almost forgets that Ramsay is only supposing. We often find passages like "For argument's sake, suppose negroes of a different and even of an inferior race," (RE 232), "Suppose different races, and that they vary in point of excellence; yet, in what chapter of nature's law is it declared that one quarter of the globe shall breed slaves for the rest?" (RE 233). Mosse explains that the fine difference between the mere perception of different human types and the development of racism was "only too easily bridged, as happened, for instance, when racism polluted the relationship between imperial masters and native populations" (Mosse, *Solution* x). The difference between pro- and anti-slavery texts cannot be defined along the line of the existence or non-existence of what could anachronistically be described as racist concepts. I, therefore, agree with Seymour Drescher when he sees the "the emphasis placed upon the potential for rapid change." (Drescher, *Racism* 420) as the main difference between pro- and anti-slavery authors.

Ramsay's mentioning of the "social tie" (RE 233) indicates that his perception of social class is also informed by aesthetic judgements. For example, it is his opinion that,

> ... children of the lowest peasants ... are seldom found to take a high station in literature, as in elegance of form. The middle ranks of life, that supply conveniences to soften, not luxuries to drown nature, are most favourable to elegance of form and acuteness of understanding. (RE 227f)

Thus the author's defence of the "middle ranks of life" is based on a fundamental belief in the connection between aesthetics, social status and, in the final consequence, the quality of the individual. This is a key feature of modern racism in that it clearly sets "a certain standard of beauty which ... lent itself to the creation of stereotypes" (Mosse, *Solution* xi) according to Mosse. The last quote shows that in Ramsay's case, the aesthetic standard is very much a white, British and middle-class one. In connection with what has been said above about the negotiation of a just claim to a middle-class identity, it is interesting to note that Mosse points out that "racism rushed to the support of respectability [which] the middle class used ... as a weapon against the so-called loose life of the aristocracy and the lower classes" (Mosse, Solution viiif). Ramsay combines his claim for African humanity with successfully presenting a powerfully persuasive, capitalist utopia of cultural and aesthetic improvement not only of Africans but of humanity as a whole, which the pro-slavery authors could do little to counter.

The concept of ~~race~~ in anti-slavery texts is of course also informed by the need to create Others, who nonetheless possess the fundamental humanity necessary to make them accessible to the disciplines of the colonial and capitalist projects. Thomas Clarkson deems the topic of ~~race~~ sufficiently important to dedicate a whole chapter to what he calls "the second argument, by which it is attempted to be proved that the Africans are an inferiour link of the chain of nature, and are designed for slavery," (CE 178). The author states that this alleged argument "is drawn from colour, and from those other marks, which distinguish them from the inhabitants of Europe" (CE 178). Just like his predecessor, Ramsay, Clarkson implies that the argument has been introduced by someone else. However, he hides the actual agent behind a passive construction. In *Letters*, Clarkson similarly alleges that it is the pro-slavery lobby who introduced the question of race, although he also obscures the actual origin of the argument:

> It has been constantly handed about, and this with some share of success, that the natives of Africa have not the same faculties as other men; by which it is insinuated, that they were born, or at least are fit only for slaves. (CL 77)

After a long section in which he weighs various scriptural explanations of the variety in human appearance, Clarkson concludes that if the scriptures are true mankind comes "from the same original" (CE 183f) and also argues that there is only one species of humans on more biological grounds when he states:

> The mulattoe is as capable of continuing his own species as his father; a clear and irrefragable proof, that the scripture account of the creation is true, and that 'God, who hath made the world, hath made of one blood all the nations of men that dwell on all the face of the earth.' (CE 187f)

In a skilfully constructed argument, Clarkson also hypothetically allows the existence of different species of humans and asks:

> Now what must we justly conclude from such a supposition? Must we conclude that one species is inferiour to another, and that the inferiority depends upon their colour, or their features, or their form?-No-We must now consult

the analogy of nature, and the conclusion will be this: 'that as she tempered the bodies of the different species of men in a different degree, to enable them to endure the respective climates of their habitation, so she gave them a variety of colour and appearance with a like benevolent design.' (CE 183f)

Clarkson's text challenges the whole racial argument when he questions the fundamental validity of basing social subjugation on difference in form or colour:

> For if you admit the form of men as a justification of slavery, you may subjugate your own brother: if features, then you must quarrel with all the world: if colour, where are you to stop? (CE 185)

In *Essay*, Clarkson tries to find a sort of compromise when he states that the original colour of mankind was a kind of "dark olive" and that "the purest white is as far removed from the primitive colour as the deepest black" (CE 190). Apart from the implied association of whiteness with purity and blackness with depth, another problematic aspect about Clarkson's view of race is that he is over-enthusiastic about the potential for rapid change. The author fundamentally holds the impact of environmental factors responsible when he writes that "when the black inhabitants of Africa are transplanted to colder, or the white inhabitants of Europe to hotter climates, their children, born there, are of a different colour from themselves; that is, lighter in the first, and darker in the second instance" (CE 201), he gets the timeframe of potential change radically wrong. Behind this stands the author's undoubtedly benevolent intention of questioning the essential nature of race relacing it with a more dynamic concept. The same intention can be suspected in the following passage:

> Neither is this variation in the children from the colour of their parents improbable. The children of the blackest Africans are born white. In this state they continue for about a month, when they change to a pale yellow. In process of time they become brown. (CE 203)

The author's intention of constructing a notion of ~~race~~ which is non-essential is certainly a positive one. However, his project is unfortunately flawed. Clarkson's underlying wish for rapidly changing complexions is, of course, unrealistic. However, it shows that the author is indeed torn between rejecting the importance of bodily difference altogether, as in the quote above, and the hope for the eventual disappearance of different complexions due to climatic influence. As this kind of utopia for radical racial change was, of course bound to fail, I would argue that it was perhaps unwillingly instrumental in the emergence of a scientific racism as an alternative model of explanation. When the utopian Africans of anti-slavery discourse failed ot improve according to Eurocentric expectations of progress, the imperial projects of the later 19th century resorted to earlier, more essential, patterns of explanation.

Similar to Clarkson, Wilberforce also states that the argument of race had its origin with the pro-slavery side:

> The advocates for the Slave Trade originally took very high ground; contending, that the Negroes were an inferior race of beings, It is obvious, that, if this were once acknowledged, they might be supposed, no less than their fellow brutes, to have been comprised within the original grant of all inferior creatures to the use and service of man. (WL 54)

Wilberforce, however, names the origin of the negative stereotypes about Africans. He cites the notoriously racist accounts by Bryan Edwards and Edward Long as the sources of the negative perception of Africans in the colonies. Wilberforce dedicates a whole section of his Letter (WL 54–74) to the argument that "negroes" are an "inferior race" (WL 54).

Wilberforce tries to answer the question of how someone like Edward Long, whom Wilberforce calls a "commonly respectable author", writes "of the race of Negroes in such terms, as they who have read the more recent accounts of Africa will peruse with astonishment" (WL 57). On the one hand, Wilberforce sees the negative representation as a result of the prejudices and bias created by the

West Indian slave system. Accordingly, the author blames the West Indians for having a false consciousness:

> It is not that the Barbadian (I say it seriously and with sincerity) is less humane, in general, than the inhabitants of other countries; but Negro Slaves are not comprised within the scale of his humanity; or, to be more accurate, they do not assume, in his estimate of things, the rate and value of human beings. (WL 161)

After writing in similar terms of Bryan Edwards—Wilberforce counters with the accounts of Park and Golberry writing about African natives in more positive terms.

However, Wilberforce does not ascribe negative accounts of West Indian slaves purely to perception; he also holds the slave system responsible for what he calls the *actual* "degradation of the negro race" (WL 127) when he writes that

> ... the various moral defects of the negro system appear to me often to be almost entirely caused, and always to be extremely augmented, by the Negroes, as a race, being sunk into the lowest state of degradation. (WL 127)

Later on, the author again writes that "the low estimate of the Negro race" must have a tendency "to keep them in their present abject and depressed condition" (WL 153). Despite his consciousness of the perceptual nature of the alleged inferiority of Wilberforce thus acknowledges the fact that West Indian slavery was, of course, a race-based form of oppression and that the concept of race was a tangible one in the running of the West Indian slave systems. In accordance with this, Wilberforce emphasises the pernicious influence of the concept of race when he contrasts West Indian slavery with slavery among the ancients:

> the Slaves among the ancients were in general of the same complexion, features, and form, with their masters ... the West Indian Slave, on the Contrary, his colour, his features, his form, his language, his employment, all tend on the one hand to extinguish sympathy, and on the other, to shut him up as it were close and bound in his dreary dungeon, without a ray of light, without a chance of escape, the victim at once of degradation and despair. (WL 130)

Thus, Wilberforce only challenges race as the reason behind the inferiority not the inferiority of Africans per se. Wilberforce's text also allows ~~race~~ to exist as a viable category—while he does not advocate the discrimination and degradation of Africans based on their race, he allows for race to exist both as a category of perception and of group identity. In *Appeal*, the author returns to the discussion of perception and real difference and states that, especially in "vulgar minds" (WA 10),

> the personal peculiarities of the Negro race could scarcely fail, by diminishing sympathy, to produce impressions, not merely of contempt, but even of disgust and aversion. But how strongly are these impressions sure to be confirmed and augmented, when to all the effects of bodily distinctions are superadded all those arising from the want of civilization and knowledge, and still more, all the hateful vices that slavery never fails to engender or to aggravate. (WA 10)

The passage is informed by the underlying assumption that a different appearance indeed diminishes sympathy and creates aversion and disgust. What Wilberforce mainly criticises in his texts, however, is that viewing the Africans' degradation as an essential one would be an obstacle to improvement of "the negro race". Just like Clarkson, therefore, Wilberforce opposes the essentialist notion that "the indolence of the Negro race was utterly incurable, and that without the driving whip they never would willingly engage in agricultural labour" (WL 67) and uses Park's account to suggest that "the Africans, when prompted by any adequate motives, would work diligently and perseveringly both in agricultural and manufacturing labours." (WA 67).

It becomes clear that a static categorisation would be detrimental for the eventual aim of the anti-slavery utopia of the African's improvement and inclusion in the system of wage labour. The anti-racism of Wilberforce is, therefore, informed by the desire of constructing Africans as suitable "raw-material" for the project of improvement.

In *Thoughts,* Clarkson argues along similar lines as Wilberforce when he writes of the disdain in which the West Indian masters hold their slaves:

> The West Indian master looks down upon his slave with disdain. He has besides a certain antipathy against him. He hates the sight of his features, and of his colour; nay, he marks with distinctive opprobrium the very blood in his veins, attaching different names and more or less infamy to those who have it in them, according to the quantity which they have of it in consequence of their pedigree, or of their greater or less degree of consanguinity with the whites. (CT 6)

Clarkson also makes Africans fundamental humanity a cornerstone of the anti-slavery project of subjecting Africans to capitalist and European means of discipline and reform:

> Every man who is born into the world, whether he be white or whether he be black, is born, according to Christian notions, a free agent and an accountable creature. This is the Scriptural law of his nature as a human bring. (CT 10)

One has to bear in mind that although anti-slavery authors generally reject the notion of the Africans being an "inferior link of the chain of nature" (CE 164), the general tendency of ordering the whole creation in a hierarchical chain is indeed very much present in the discourse on slavery in general. The epistemology of the concept of the great chain of being was described at length by Arthur Lovejoy in his work of the same name (cf. Lovejoy, *Chain*). Lovejoy refers to the importance of the concept, calling the phrase "one of the most famous in the vocabulry of Occidental philosophy, science and reflective poetry" (Lovejoy, *Chain* xxiii). Clarkson speaks of peoples who have "advanced more or less in the scale of social life" (CE 169) in *Essay* and shows "the natives to have attained a step in the scale of civilization" (CL vi) in *Letters.* Also, Wilberforce frequently uses the concept of the scale of being when he writes of "the poor calumniated Hottentots, who were long regarded as among the lowest in the scale of being" (WL 68) or when he discusses how "any being is considered as possessing a higher or a lower place in the scale of existence" (WL 132). That the idea describes a divine order becomes evident when this author explains that God "has a right to assign to all his creatures their several places in the scale of being" (WL 318). The main difference between pro- and anti-slavery texts in this regard is that while the first do not propose any utopia of reform, Wilberforce and the other anti-slavery writers see the Africans' "extreme degradation in the intellectual and moral scale of being" (WA 10) as something negative and ultimately propose to "raise them in the social scale" (WA 11).

In *Thoughts*, Clarkson again argues for the arbitrariness of using skin colour as a distinguishing mark between master and slave when he writes that in classical antiquity, the difference in complexion did not "as it now does, a most marked distinction between the master and the slave, so as to increase this stigma and to perpetuate antipathies between them" (CT 16). Despite this, Clarkson does also allow for skin colour to be a valid mark of national identity when he refers to Africans living "under the unnatural government of the whites" (CT 20).

Heyrick's text refers to white and black populations of the West Indies only once in order to mention that:

> Were slavery in the British colonies extinguished, the same laws which restrain and punish crime in the white population, would still restrain and punish crime in the black population. (HI 13)

Although she speaks of two populations in her text, *Immediate not Gradual Abolition* does try to break with the prevalent race-based representations of Africans. This also shows in Heyrick's use of the term "Africans" rather than "negroes", which has been referred to in the beginning of this chapter. In this respect she picks up on Clarkson's similar tendency in *Essay*. In both cases the motivation for this is accusing pro-slavery writers of racism while at the same time explicitly representing Africans by means of geographical origin rather than skin colour and by repeatedly referring to them as "fellow creatures" (HI 11, 23) "human beings" (HI 13) or "fellow man" (HI 22).

5.6.3 Pro-slavery

Kitson comments on the over-emphasis of the race issue in abolitionist writings. He holds that the importance attributed to the discussion of racial issues by writers like Ramsey and Clarkson is not justified by the arguments of their opponents because "actual public racialist justifications of slavery and the slave trade in the period 1780–1815 were comparatively rare." (Kitson, *Reflections* 11). I do not fully agree with this. Although some pro-slavery authors indeed seemed to be at a bit of a loss at how to deal with the question of Africans' racial inferiority the pro-slavery argument as a whole does, of course, have a vested interest in casting Africans as essentially different and thus inferior.

Pro-slavery authors follow a dual approach in dealing with the question of race. On the one hand, they seem to be aware of a hegemonic notion of human equality when they argue that the whole question of race is beside the point. The anonymous "Gentlemen of St. Christopher" for example, call Ramsay's chapter:

> Objection to African capacity drawn from form ... mere fighting with shadows, which like the last is inconclusive, and nothing to the purpose, let it be determined in whatever manner the Essayist may most approve of. (AA 88)

Also, in answer to Ramsay's question, "in what chapter of nature's law is it declared that one quarter of the globe shall breed slaves for the rest," (RE 233) they argue that the question of race is not an issue, pointing out that "We cannot name the chapter, but it is so declared in the code of their national laws and practice".

However, they remark in the same place:

> As to negro abilities there may have been some few instances, but in general We repeat that they are miserably stupid. White servants will hang pictures, lay tables, and fold cloths strait, not one negro in a thousand, though bred a

carpenter and assisted with his square and rule, can do it, after many years practice. (AA 91)

Also, other passages make little secret of what they really think, and try to mock Ramsay's argument, "The 'finding a sensible, sober negro to be surety for another's good behaviour' has been often attempted, but always in vain" (AA 94) and point out the "indolence, ignorance, and prepossession of the slaves" as the reason for the "inefficacy of [Ramsay"s] public attempts to instruct slaves" (AA 84).

The "Gentlemen of St. Christopher" also seek to reject the influence of environmental factors when they state that "The sun certainly does not make them [black], though he supposes it" (AA 88). The "Gentlemen" also do not fail to highlight Ramsay's assumptions about the initial whiteness of African children. However, their attempt to maintain an essential difference between whites and blacks does not only pertain to outer appearance. Their argument again hinges on the Africans' alleged ability to perform basic household tasks, such as laying tables or folding cloth (cf. AA 27). They argue against Ramsay's utopia of reform and improvement that

> their improvement and conversion cannot take place, till they are furnished with such abilities and endowments of the mind, as they have not at present and in all probability never may till the day of judgment ... (AA 27)

Later in the text, the Gentlemen again point out that Ramsay's plan for improvement and conversion is entirely futile and Africans need to be kept under severe discipline and are essentially not fit to become capitalist subjects, since

> those who are made free ... injure society [and] either turn hucksters, or carry on a regular system of thievery with their late brethren: Scarce one labours in any way for the community, none for the plantations, or in any respect for the real advantage of society. (AA 71f)

The passages show that upholding an essential difference between races is central to the argument of the "Gentlemen of St. Christopher", since their whole attack against Ramsay's "plan for their improvement and conversion" (AA 27) rests on the Africans' alleged inability to improve. One can see how maintaining an essential difference is a cornerstone of the pro-slavery argument against the anti-slavery utopia of reform and for maintaining the status quo.

The anonymous author of *Fugitive Thoughts* argues even more bluntly for the essential difference of Africans:

> It is asked if the negroes have not feelings like white men, and are as sensible of pain; this is denied by the best informed writers and most learned anatomists; they say the cutis or scarf skins, is formed of scales infinitely smaller than in white men, the pores and sudorific vessels in proportion, numerous, which exude moisture, and keep the skin constantly in a state of pliability, whilst a white man's scales having a larger surface, become, parched and rise in blisters, when exposed to the sun, besides, the vessels and fibres that convey sensation, are of a grosser texture in the blacks, they mind not in travelling through their thorny woods, if a branch should strike one, into their flesh an inch deep; without any seeming concern they will cut it out, and rub the wound with sand by way of styptic, some nations score their children's flesh with a knife, from below the navel to the shoulder, in three lines, which they think necessary to salvation, others cut the skin on their forehead and cheeks. The wool upon their heads protects them from a coup de soleil frequent and fatal to Europeans, many have died suddenly of a stroke of the sun, or the effect, it has on the brain in very hot weather, but should a person recover, a paralytic affection generally remains. (AF 27f)

The author creates an image of Africans as a more crude type of human based on bodily differences and their insensitivity to pain. Also, the reference to the "wool upon their heads" (AF 28) instead of "hair" implicitly compares them to animals.

An important authority for both pro- and anti-slavery writers is Edward Long's *History of Jamaica* with its infamous comparison of "Hottentots" and orang-utans. Bridges defends Long's notoriously negative description of Africans when he writes:

> If you will turn to the 356th page of Long's second volume, you will find that author labouring in the science of comparative anatomy, to prove, what in his days was a very popular subject of controversy, that, as in the inanimate and inferior parts of the creation, so even up to man, there are conjoining links in the great chain of nature, the lowest of which, in the human species, seems to be the Hottentot. (BV 17f)

The author also attempts to blur the distinction between humans and brute creation, quoting Long:

> He endeavours to prove, also, that the highest of what we esteem the brute creation, the oran-outang, is endowed with sense and reason, little inferior to that barbarous race. His former position is probably correct; and the latter, for aught we can prove to the contrary, may be so too. (BV 18)

While Bridges does not descend into racist arguments himself, he still suffers Long's racist slur to stand uncorrected in his text under the semblance of objectivity. Tobin, Cursory Remarks

Tobin's approach to Ramsay's argumentation is a slightly more subtle one. He seems to have felt the need to conform to Ramsay's fundamental assumptions, at least to a certain degree, in order to be taken seriously in the discourse. Therefore, he superficially agrees with Ramsay on the issue of race, writing about Ramsay's chapter on this topic that it "is entirely employed in endeavouring to restore the negroes to that equality with the whites, from which many very ingenious philosophers have lately attempted to degrade them" (TC 40), which conveniently leaves the outcome of the question open and presents both options as equally plausible. Tobin probably refers to such Enlightenment thinkers as David Hume whose description of "Negroes" ... [as] naturally inferior to the Whites" (Hume 236) has gained some notoriety. Again, this author does this under the semblance of scientific objectivity. Tobin clearly distances himself from the whole argument in not providing an outright opinion on the topic. However, the mentioning of the philosophers' ingenuity in the passage, does tacitly suggest the plausibility of their ideas. It has already been mentioned above, that Tobin seeks to minimise the importance of Africans' race and humanity to the discussion as a whole and wants to steer the discussion into another direction:

> I cannot indeed consider the merits of this famous controversy of much consequence, even to the open and avowed advocates for slavery (if any such there are) as it has never been pretended, that the slaves either of the Jews, Greeks, or Romans of old, or the European and Asiatic slaves of modern times, were, or are, any way inferior to their masters, except in strength, policy, or good fortune. (TC 141f)

While Tobin's text is characterised by strategies to divert attention away from those racist ideas which he expected not to go down well with the wider public, a more subtle racism can, however, be clearly observed. This is especially characterised by a concern about racial purity. In a footnote, he discusses Africans in Britain and complains about the "strange partiality shewn for them by the lower orders of women, and the rapid increase of a dark and contaminated breed" (TC 118). The use of the deprecating terms "contaminated" and "breed" reveal the author's true convictions. In another place, Tobin expresses his dismay at the mixing of the races in the French colonies:

> ... and in the French islands, the promiscuous commerce with coloured women is carried to such an indecent height, that in a planter's house, the white wife is frequently the person of least consequence in the family. (TC 29)

The same author also presents it as a scandalous situation that in the French colonies, he has "frequently seen, the whip of a French overseer laid over a pair of naked shoulders much whiter than his own" (TC 37). He expresses a similar concern, pointing out "The lower ranks in Spain are avowedly debased, by their long intercourse with the Moors; and the Portuguese still much more, from the importation of negroes among them." (TC 118)

Gilbert Francklyn, on the one hand, tries to construct slavery as a social rather than a racial concept when he refers to slaves in an expressly non-racial way, calling them "those people, who are placed by the Providence of God in a servile condition" (FA 164):

> That it is in some particular instances such as it ought not to be, there is no doubt: but where is the country where the weak are not oppressed by the strong? Much would that person merit who could effectually prevent it; till that is done, the man who depends on another's will or caprice for his daily subsistance, whether he be white or black, is in such a state of servitude as may justly be called slavery. (FA 164)

However, he also hints at the futility of including Africans in a system of wage labour due to a more essential difference when he points out that "he must know little of the generality of Negro, or any other slaves, who will suppose they will work without compulsion." (FA 165)

Francklyn clearly opposes Clarkson's notion of rapidly changing human complexions when exposed to a different climate:

> That the offspring of the first Portuguese, by black women, and their continuing from father to son, to mix with the black inhabitants of the country, have, for many generations past, become undistinguishable from the Negroes, there can be no doubt; for they are Negroes in every sense. But that white people will ever become black, by living within the torrid zone, or their offspring deviate from the complexion of their forefathers, there is not the slightest ground to imagine.
> Many young ladies, descendants of some of the first settlers in the islands, and now in England for their education, are of as fair and delicate complexion as any women in Europe. (FA 218f)

While Clarkson adheres to a dynamic, changeable concept of race, Francklyn is eager to assert that race is static and that complexion does not change over time. What neither, however, takes into account (cf. Clarkson's statement on the Jews) is that sexual interrelations between the races could be mainly responsible for the change of complexion. Both seem to be unable to re-think the separateness of races. This leads Clarkson to downplay the space of time needed for human adaption, and to negate the possibility of "interbreeding" which, in historical times, is certainly the main reason for any changes of complexion.

In their attempt to maintain the colonial status-quo, pro-slavery texts clearly want to create a distance between 'us' and 'them'.

Quite in contrast to anti-slavery texts, they had no interst in actively claiming Africans for humanity. Therefore they seem to prefer to leave the whoe question of racial inferiority open, having their respective arguments ready for both cases. If Africans were indeed inferior, the severity of slavery is justified by the need to discipline the savage African. If Africans are humans, pro-slavery authros argue for the social nature of slavery just like Tobin does when he writes that "it has never pretended that . . . slaves . . . are in anyway inferior to their masters except in strength, policy or good fortune" (TC 141f).

I suppose that anti-slavery authors, on the other hand, so willingly blame the pro-slavery advocates for racialised justifications of slavery because it fitted their fundamental argument that slavery has a dehumanising effect. Their whole argument hinges on the presupposition that slavery constitutes a form of in-human treatment. Quite obviously, the pro-slavery lobby did not agree with that (cf. Tobin). The anti-slavery argument at the same time made the inclusion of the subject in a capitalist system of wage labour the very emblem of humanity.

6 Conclusion

I suggest that, despite some elements that can be perceived as racist from a 21st century perspective, anti-slavery discourse attempted to establish a universal, non-race-based conception of mankind and to universalise the control mechanisms of an emerging capitalism. As Braidotti argues, this kind of humanism constituted a "civilizational ideal, [and] fuelled the imperial destinies of nineteenth-century Germany, France and, supremely, Great Britain" (Braidotti 15). Similarly, Foucault writes of the "blackmail of enlightenment", which constituted "a privileged domain for analysis" (Rabinow 43).

My analysis of the historical dimension of the discourse of slavery has shown that there are basically three elements of the European historical master narrative which are of central importance. Firstly, texts intensively discuss the original situation of mankind. At the risk of oversimplifying, it can be said that pro-slavery authors adhere to a more Hobbesian view of the earliest ages, while the notion of the noble savage living harmoniously in a state of nature is favoured by anti-slavery writers. Secondly, Greco-Roman antiquity was not only an important source of civilisation within the Eurocentric master-narrative but also faced authors with the problem of incorporating the existence of slavery in both ancient Greece and Rome into their analyses. Pro-slavery authors pointed to slavery in antiquity as a justifying fact, while anti-slavery authors tried to prove that the slavery of the ancients was conceptually different from modern chattel slavery. Furthermore, it has to be noted that the discourse on slavery features a highly teleological conception of history and of universal progress. The image of Africans is therefore negotiated against the background of a highly Eurocentric historical master-narrative that posits Greco-Roman antiquity as a single source of civilisation. In this context, I have pointed to the interesting image of Islamic civilisation as a rival model. Another discursive event that enters the discussion of slavery is the fall of the Roman Empire; especially within the context of the recent American Independence, texts draw comparisons between the British and the Roman Empires and negotiate the relationship between colonial centre and margin.

Thirdly, the feudal past was another important image which was used to build arguments for or against slavery. While pro-slavery authors of course emphasise the hard lot of the feudal peasant, anti-slavery authors tend to create a more romanticised image of the relationship of a benevolent feudal lord and a happy peasant. Anti-slavery texts in particular strongly draw on a master narrative of a transition from medieval servitude to modern freedom in order to create an impetus for ending slavery as a pre-modern practice.

The statistical appraisal of the text corpus has shown that Africans in both pro-and anti-slavery texts are present primarily in the plural, which suggests that the discourse of slavery is a discussion of human multiplicities rather than individuals. The analysis of the pronouns referring to Africans led to a similar result, the most frequent pronoun being the plural third person possessive pronoun "their", which also indicates that the Africans in the texts are very much defined by the European authors who construct "their" identity based on the "property" they ascribe to them. My investigation of the most frequent adjectives showed a clear emphasis on constructing an ethnically-based identity for Africans and, especially in anti-slavery texts, a tendency to belittle Africans and victimise them.

The authors' knowledge of Africa is an exclusively indirect one; thus, the image of Africa and its inhabitants is very much a projection of their respective beliefs. As the authors are faced with a limited basis of primary sources, the images of Africa are the result of a different interpretation of the same texts, as has been shown with the case of Mungo Park. On the one hand, the anti-slavery image of Africans is dominated by the corruption of natural harmony through a pernicious European influence. On the other hand, African societies are portrayed as similar to European ones at earlier stages of history, which is both part of a romanticised view of a feudal and agrarian past and a highly teleological concept of history. The Islamic influence in parts of Africa is constructed as a kind of doppelgänger of the European colonial incursions. While earlier texts frequently depict Africans as noble savages, this seems to decline over the years and is almost absent in the emancipation debate, which primarily focuses on Africans as the objects of colonial reform.

Pro-slavery writers had, of course, an interest in portraying Africa and its inhabitants in a more negative way. This is mainly because of the standard argument that the slave trade was actually a blessing for the Africans in taking them to the European colonies. Accordingly, African societies are portrayed as slave-holding ones in order to vindicate the European merchants by arguing that the actual enslavement is done in and by their native societies. Explicit instances of cannibalism are only to be found in pro-slavery texts. Anti-slavery texts either portray Africans in their state of nature as noble savages or attribute any negative accounts to the corrupting influence of the slave trade.

By far the most prominent way of representing Africans in this discourse is, of course, as slaves. The image of the slave contrasts strongly to the fully realised humans of European modernity. Thus, Africans are subjected to the discourse and mechanisms of Eurocentrism. The discourse puts the slave in an ambiguous situation between exclusion from humanity and the desire for a reformed and recognisable Other (cf. Bhabha, *Culture* 122) which informs anti-slavery utopias of reform. Pro-slavery authors, on the other hand, attempt to decry their opponents' dreams of reform as visionary by pointing to a more essential difference in Africans. The image of the slave is constructed against two significant comparisons: the feudal peasant and the capitalist wage labourer. The treatment of the slaves has at times a distinctly pre-modern tinge in that it corresponds to what Foucault calls the "principle of the dungeon"

(Foucault, *Discipline* 200) and "the spectacle of the scaffold" (Foucault, *Discipline* 254)

Another central feature of the slave is their vivid suffering, which is constructed primarily as a massive transgression of boundaries, making the body of the slave fluid and penetrable. I have argued that this, apart from certainly fulfilling sensationalist aims, served the end of also making African bodies penetrable to various European discourses. The texts literally transgress the bodily boundaries of their objects. The bodily dimension of the image of the slave is strongly linked to assertions of the inhumanity of slavery, which are, in turn, strongly informed by the dogma of classical humanism that "'the human' is achieved by repressing its animal origins in nature" (Wolfe, *Posthumanism* xv). Thus, Africans are represented as a very distinct form, as wretches who are placed in a zone of non-distinction between the inhuman state of the slave and a discourse of discipline and reform.

Thus, the discourse of slavery was a negotiation of the modern subject against the Other of the African slave. The superiority of the modern wage labourer was constructed based on relatively abstract notions of freedom, which conveniently defined Britain as free soil. Unfortunately, this had the side-effect of casting Africans as not fully human. Furthermore, when Africans did not conform to the anti-slavery utopias of rapid reform and improvement, this became instrumental for racist tendencies to emerge in the 19th century and justified the unequal power relations of imperialism.

The discourse of slavery is, therefore, built around a binary distinction between human and slave. The example of Clarkson benevolently proving Philis Wheatley to be human based on the merits of her poetry shows that this kind of extending an existing boundary to include others is problematic. In this case, it creates a mimetic Other, over whom Europe has discursive power. Especially in anti-slavery texts, Africans are routinely represented as "wretches", which arouses the audience's compassion but also subtly puts Africans in a limbo between inclusion and exclusion from humanity, the deciding power over which clearly resides with the colonial centre, even in the anti-slavery utopia.

When it comes to the theme of slave rebellion, the texts employ several strategies for rendering Africans harmless. The texts from the emancipation debate argue that freeing the slaves is the only way to ensure the safety of the colonies. The abolitionist compositions, in particular, frequently direct the aggression of the Africans against themselves, as is evidenced by the recurring theme of suicide.

It has been pointed out that the Africans in these texts are primarily plural and male. However, female Africans serve two functions in the discourse. On the one hand, they enhance descriptions of sentimental suffering, also in the form of sexualised violence. Sexuality, and thus women, play an important role in the context of demographic considerations, especially of anti-slavery writers, who tend to represent African women as sexually virtuous as part of a representation as noble savages, while pro-slavery authors often refer to African women's hyper-sexuality.

Surprisingly, there is little statistical difference between pro- and anti-slavery texts in terms of their use of race-based expressions in order to represent Africans. With the explicit exceptions of Clarkson's *Essay* and Heyrick's *Immediate Emancipation*, all the texts favour ethnically defined expressions such as "negroes" over the more geographically determined term "Africans". The reason for the relatively large presence of the issue of race in anti-slavery texts lies in the fundamental anti-slavery logic that only non-humans could justly be reduced to the state of slavery. Thus, they implicitly blame their opponents for racism, even if this is not justified by so many instances of outright racism in pro-slavery texts, as Kitson suggests (cf. Kitson, *Reflexions* 11). Therefore, pro-slavery texts primarily deal with the issue in terms of refuting their opponents' attacks. However, the pro-slavery argument did not have an interest in defending Africans from racist attacks, but of course could make their point for maintaining the status quo by tacitly letting notions of the slaves' essential inferiority stand. The anti-slavery texts on the other side had an interest in subjecting Africans to their universalist utopia of progress and reform. The ethnic dimension of pro- and anti-slavery discourse thus primarily differs in the potential that the authors see for rapid change. While the first favours an essentially different African whose inherent laziness cannot be reformed, the anti-slavery utopias of reform call for a more dynamic concept of difference. In terms of racism, it has to be said that the humanitarian aims of anti-slavery stand very much in the tradition of the European enlightenment. This however, was not only highly charged in terms of establishing a Eurocentric universalism, but also created a distinct imagery which favoured whiteness over blackness.

Bibliography

Abbreviations

AA – Anonymous, *Answer*
AF – Anonymous, Fugitive Thoughts
AO – Anonymous, *Observations*
CE – Clarkson, *Essay* (1st ed., 1786)
CE88 – Clarkson, *Essay* (2nd ed., 1788)
BV – Bridges, *Voice*
CL – Clarkson, *Letters*
CT – Clarkson, *Thoughts*
FA – Francklyn, *Answer*
HC – Hampden, *Commentary*
HI – Heyrick, *Immediate Abolition*
ML – Mercator, *Letters*
RE – Ramsay, *Essay*
TC – Tobin, *Cursory Remarks*
WA – Wilberforce, *Appeal*
WL – Wilberforce, *Letter*

Primary Sources

African Merchant. *A Treatise upon the Trade from Great-Britain to Africa; Humbly recommended to the Attention of Government.* London: R. Baldwin, 1772. *Google Book Search*. Web. 16 July 2012.

Anon. *An Answer to the Reverend James Ramsay's Essay, on the Treatment and Conversion of Slaves, in the British Sugar Colonies. By some Gentlemen of St. Christopher.* Basseterre, 1784. *Google Book Search*. Web. 15 May 2011. (Abbreviated: AA)

Anon. *Fugitive Thoughts on the African Slave Trade, Interspersed with Cursory Remarks on the Manners, Customs and Commerce of the African and American Indians.* Liverpool, 1792. *Recovered Histories.* Web. 17 August 2008. (Abbreviated: AF)

Anon. *Observations on the Project for abolishing the Slave Trade, and on the Reasonableness of Attempting some Practicable Mode of Relieving the Negroes.* London, 1790. *Recovered Histories.* Web. 20 January 2009. (Abbreviated: AO)

Anon. *Number I. Abridgement of the Minutes of the Evidence, taken before a Committee of the Whole House to Whom it was Referred to Consider of the Slave trade, 1789.* N.p., n.d. *Google Book Search.* Web. 4 April 2016.

Bentham, Jeremy. *The Panopticon Writings.* London: Verso, 1995. Print.

Bridges, George Wilson. *A Voice from Jamaica; in Reply to William Wilberforce, Esq. M.P.* 2nd ed. London, 1823. *Google Book Search.* Web. 29 July 2016. (Abbreviated: BV)

---. *The Annals of Jamaica.* Vol. 2. London, 1828. *Google Book Search.* Web. 29 July 2016.

Burke, Edmund. *The Works of the Right Hon. Edmund Burke with a Biographical and Critical Introduction by Henry Rogers and Portrait after Sir Joshua Reynolds.* London, 1837. *Google Book Search.* Web. 14 June 2016.

Clarkson, Thomas. *An Essay on the Slavery and Commerce of the Human Species, Particularly the African, Translated from a Latin Dissertation, which was Honoured with the First Prize in the University of Cambridge, for the Year 1785, With Additions.* London, 1786. *Recovered Histories.* Web. 8 February 2010. (Abbreviated: CE)

---. *An Essay on the Slavery and Commerce of the Human Species, Particularly the African, Translated from a Latin Dissertation, which was Honoured with the First Prize in the University of Cambridge, for the Year 1785*. The Second Edition, Revised and Considerably Enlarged. London, 1788. *Recovered Histories*. Web. 8 February 2010. (Abbreviated: CE88)

---. "Thoughts on the Necessity of Improving the Condition of the Slaves in the British Colonies, With a View to their Ultimate Emancipation; and on the Practicability, the Safety, and the Advantages of the Latter Measure." London, 1823. *Slavery, Abolition, and Emancipation: Writings in the British Romantic Period. Vol. 3. The Emancipation Debate*. Ed. Debbie Lee. London: Pickering and Chatto, 1999. 85–144. Print. (Abbreviated: CT)

---. *The History of the Rise, Progress, and Accomplishment of the Abolition of the African Slave Trade by the British Parliament*. 2 vols. London, 1808. *Google Book Search*. Web. 24 November 2015.

---. *An Essay on the Impolicy of the African Slave Trade: In Two Parts*. 1788. Freeport and New York: Books for Libraries Press, 1971. Print.

---. "Slave Ship". *Wikipedia*. Web. 24 November 2015.

Conrad, Joseph. *Heart of Darkness*. London: Penguin, 1994. Print.

Francklyn, Gilbert. *An Answer to the Rev. Mr. Clarkson's Essay on the Slavery and Commerce of the Human Species, particularly the African; In a Series of Letters, from a Gentleman in Jamaica, to his Friend in London: Wherein Many of the Mistakes and Misrepresentations of Mr. Clarkson are pointed out, Both with Regard to the Manner in which that Commerce is carried on in Africa, and the Treatment of the Slaves in the West Indies. Shewing, at the Same Time, The Antiquity, Universality, and Lawfulness of Slavery as as [sic!] ever having been one of the States and Conditions of Mankind.* London: Logographic Press, 1789. *Google Book Search*. Web. 4 April 2016 (Abbreviated: FA)

---. *Observations, Occasioned by the Attempts Made in England to Effect the Abolition of the Slave Trade; Shewing the Manner in which Negroes are Treated in the British Colonies in the West-Indies: and also some Particular Remarks on a Letter Addressed to the Treasurer of the Society For Effecting such Abolition, from the Rev. Robert Boucher Nicholls, Dean of Middleham.* Kingston and London, 1789. *Google Book Search.* Web. 4 April 2016.

Gibbon, Edward. *The History of the Decline and Fall of the Roman Empire.* New York: Harper and Brothers, 1841. *Google Book Search.* Web. 18 July 2012.

Hampden, John. *A Commentary on Mr. Clarkson's pamphlet entitled "Thoughts on the necessity of improving the conditions of the Slaves in the British colonies, with a view to their ultimate emancipation".* London: J. Ridgway, 1824. (68p). Print. (Abbreviated: HC)

Hegel, Georg Wilhelm Friedrich. *Lectures on the Philosophy of History.* Trans. J. Sibree. London, 1861. *Google Book Search.* Web. 17 November 2015.

Heyrick, Elizabeth. *Immediate, not gradual Abolition: or an Inquiry into the Shortest, Safest, and Most Effectual Means of Getting Rid of West Indian Slavery.* London, 1824. *Google Book Search.* Web. 25 April 2009.

Hobbes, Thomas. *Leviathan, or the Matter, Forme, & Power of a Common-Wealth Ecclesiasitcall and Civill.* London: 1651. *Google Book Search.* Web. 19 October 2015.

House of Commons. "Motion Respecting the Trial and Condemnation of Missionary Smith at Demerara." 11 June 1824. *Historic Hansard: 1803–2005.* Web. 7 June 2016.

Hume, David. *The Philosophical Works of David Hume.* Vol. 3. Edinburgh, 1826. *Google Book Search.* Web. 31 July 2017.

Long, Edward. *The History of Jamaica.* London, 1774. *Google Book Search.* Web.

Mercator (John Gladstone). *Letters Concerning the Abolition of the Slave-Trade and Other West-India Affairs*. London: 1807. *Bayerische Staatsbibliothek Online Resource*. Web. 25 August 2010. (Abbreviated: ML)

Ramsay, James. *An Essay on the treatment and conversion of African slaves in the British sugar colonies*. London: J. Philips, 1784. *Google Book Search*. Web. 17 January 2010. (Abbr. RE)

Rousseau, Jean Jacques. "A Dissertation on the Origin and Foundation of the Inequality of Mankind." *The Miscellaneous Works of Mr. J. J. Rousseau*. Vol 1. London: 1767. 135–314. *Google Book Search*. Web. 19 October 2015.

Smith, Adam. *An Inquiry into the Nature and Causes of the Wealth of Nations*. 11th ed, 2002. *The Project Gutenberg*. Web. 5 Sept 2006.

Tobin, James. *Cursory Remarks Upon the Reverend Mr. Ramsay's Essay on the Treatment and Conversion of African Slaves in the Sugar Colonies*. 1785. *Cornell University Library Digital Collection*. Print. (Abbr. TC)

Tevelyan, George. *English Social History. A Survey of Six Centuries. Chaucer to Queen Victoria*. London: Longman, 1947. Print.

Wilberforce, Robert I., and Samuel Wilberforce. *The Life of William Wilberforce. In Five Volumes*. Vol. 1. London, 1838. *Google Book Search*. Web. 6 June 2015.

Wilberforce, William. *A Letter on the Abolition of the Slave Trade: Addressed to the Freeholders and Other Inhabitants of Yorkshire*. London: T. Cadell and J. Hatchard, 1807. *Google Book Search*. Web. 17 June 2008. (Abbr. WL)

---. *An Appeal to the Religion, Justice, and Humanity of the Inhabitants of the British Empire, on Behalf of the Negro Slaves in the West Indies*. London, 1823. *Google Book Search*. Web. 17 June 2008. (Abbr. WA)

---. *Substance of the Speeches of William Wilberforce, Esq. on the Clause in the East-India Bill for Promoting the Religious Instruction and Moral Improvement of the natives of the British Dominions in India, On the 22d of June, and the 1st and 12th of July, 1813.* N.p. 1814 [?]. archive.org. Web. 7 June 2016.

Secondary Sources.

Adolphs, Svenja. *Introducing Electronic Text Analysis. A Practical Guide for Language and Literary Studies.* New York: Routledge, 2006. Print.

Agamben, Giorgio. *Homo Sacer: Sovereign Power and Bare Life.* Stanford: University Press, 1998. Print.

Anon. "Gilbert Francklyn: Profile and Legacies Summary ????-1799." *Legacies of British Slave-ownership.* UCL, 2016. Web. https://www.ucl.ac.uk/lbs/person/view/2146632169 3 April 2016.

Altink, Henrice. "Deviant and Dangerous: Proslavery Representations of Jamaican Slave Women's Sexuality, c. 1780–1834." *Slavery and Abolition.* 26.2 (2005): 271–288. Print.

Ashcroft, Bill, Gareth Griffiths and Helen Tiffin. *Post-Colonial Studies: The Key Concepts.* 2nd ed. London and New York: Routledge, 2007. Print.

Bender, Thomas. Introduction. *The Antislavery Debate: Capitalism and Abolitionism as a Problem in Historical Interpretation.* Ed. Thomas Bender. Berkeley, Los Angeles and London: University of California Press, 1992. 1–13. Print.

Bhabha, Homi. "Of Mimicry and Man: The Ambivalence of Colonial Discourse." *October* 28 (1984): 125–133. *JSTOR.* Web. 31 March 2010.

---. *The Location of Culture.* 1994. London and New York: Routledge Classics, 2004. Print.

Braidotti, Rosi. *The Posthuman.* Cambridge: Polity Press, 2013. Print.

Brennan, Jim. "George Wilson Bridges: Profile and Legacies Summary." *Legacies of British Slave-ownership*. UCL, 2016. Web. https://www.ucl.ac.uk/lbs/person/view/11365 29 July 2016.

Brogan, Hugh. "Clarkson, Thomas (1760–1846), Slavery Abolitionist." *Oxford Dictionary of National Biography*. Online ed., May 2011. Oxford: University Press, 2004. Web. 4 September 2012.

Carey, Brycchan. *British Abolitionism and the Rhetoric of Sensibility: Writing, Sentiment and Slavery, 1760–1807*. Houndsmill and New York: Palgrave Macmillan, 2005. Print.

Curtin, Philip D. *The Image of Africa: British Ideas and Action, 1780–1850*. 2 vols. Madison: University of Wisconsin Press, 1964. Print.

Davis, David Brion. *Slavery and Human Progress*. Oxford: University Press, 1984. Print.

---. "Reflections on Abolitionism and Ideological Hegemony." *The Antislavery Debate: Capitalism and Abolitionism as a Problem in Historical Interpretation*. Ed. Thomas Bender. Berkeley, Los Angeles and London: University of California Press, 1992. 161–199. Print.

---. "Reflections on Abolitionism and Ideological Hegemony." *The American Historical Review* 92.4 (1987): 797–812. *Jstor*. Web. 3 March 2009.

---. *The Problem of Slavery in the Age of Revolution 1770–1823*. Ithaca and London: Cornell University Press, 1975. Print.

---. "Slavery and 'Progress'." *Antislavery, Religion, and Reform: Essays in Memory of Roger Anstey*. Eds. Christine Bolt, and Seymour Drescher. Folkestone, Kent: Dawson Archon, 1980. 335–366. Print.

Drescher, Seymour. *The Mighty Experiment: Free Labour versus Slavery in British Emancipation*. Oxford: University Press, 2002. Print.

---. *Capitalism and Antislavery: British Mobilization in Comparative Perspective*. New York and Oxford: Oxford University Press, 1987. Print.

---. "Cart Whip and Billy Roller: Antislavery and Reform Symbolism in Industrializing Britain." *Journal of Social History* 15.1 (1981): 3–24. *Jstor*. Web. 22 August 2011.

---."The Ending of the Slave Trade and the Evolution of European Scientific Racism," *Social Science History* 14.3 (1990): 415–450. *Jstor*. Web. 13 March 2009.

Elias, Norbert. *Über den Prozeß der Zivilisation. Soziologische und psychogenetische Untersuchungen. Erster Band. Wandlungen des Verhaltens in den weltlichen Oberschichten des Abendlandes*. 1st ed. Frankfurt am Main: Suhrkamp, 1997. Print.

Faulkner, Carol. "The Roots of Evil: Free Produce and Radical Antislavery, 1820–1860." *Journal of the Early Republic* 27.3 (2007): 377–405. *Jstor*. Web. 12 August 2016.

Ferguson, Moira. "Elizabeth Heyrick and Cruelty to Animals: Gender, Class, Nationalism."*The Centennial Review* 37.2 (1993): 325–354. *Jstor*. Web. 12 August 2016.

Foucault, Michel. *Discipline and Punish. The Birth of the Prison*. 2nd Vintage Books Edition. New York: Random House, 1995. Print.

Gramsci, Antonio. *Selections from the Prison Notebooks*. Eds. Quintin Hoare and Geoffrey Nowell Smith. New York: International Publishers, 1971. Print.

Grundy, Isobel. "Elizabeth [née Coltman] Elizabeth (1769–1831), Slavery Abolitionist and Philanthropist." *Oxford Dictionary of National Biography*. Online ed., Jan 2010. Oxford: University Press, 2004. Web. 4 September 2012.

Hall, Stuart. "The Question of Cultural Identity." *Modernity and Its Futures, Understanding Modern Societies: An Introduction*. Eds. Stuart Hall, David Held and Tony McGrew. Cambridge: Polity Press, 1992. Print.

---."The West and the Rest: Discourse and Power." *Formations of Modernity. Understanding Modern Societies: an Introduction.* Eds. Stuart Hall and Bram Gieben. Cambridge: Polity Press, 1992.

Harfield, Timothy D."Exposing Humanism: Prudence, Ingenium, and the Politics of the Posthuman." *Journal of Historical Sociology* 26.2 (2013): 265–288. *Jstor*. Web. 30 December 2014.

Harmer, Harry. *The Longman Companion to Slavery, Emancipation and Civil Rights.* Harlow: Pearson Education Limited, 2001. Print.

Haskell, Thomas L."Capitalism and the Origins of Humanitarian Sensiblity, Part 1." *The American Historical Review* 90.1 (1985): 547–566. *Jstor*. Web. 21 August 2012.

---."Capitalism and the Origins of the Humanitarian Sensibility, Part 2". *The American Historical Review* 90.3 (1985): 547–566. *Jstor*. Web. 21 August 2012.

Hochschild, Adam. *Bury the Chains: The British Struggle to Abolish Slavery.* Paperback ed. London: Pan Books, 2006. Print.

Hogg, Peter C. *The African Slave Trade and its Suppression: A Classified and Annotated Bibliography of Books, Pamphlets and Periodical Articles.* London: Frank Cass, 1973. Print.

Hurston, Zora Neale. *Tell My Horse. Voodoo and Life Haiti and Jamaica.* Harper Perennial Modern Classics Edition. New York: Harper Perennial, 2009. Print.

Jäger, Siegfried and Florentine Maier. "Theoretical and Methodological Aspects of Foucauldian Critical Discourse Analysis and Dispositive Analysis." *Methods of Critical Discourse Analysis.* Eds. Ruth Wodak and Michael Meyer. 2nd ed. London: Sage, 2009. 34–61. Print.

---. *Kritische Diskursanalyse: Eine Einführung.* 4th Ed. Münster: Unrast-Verlag, 2004. Print.

Kitson, Peter. "'Candid Reflections': The Idea of Race in the Debate over the Slave Trade and Slavery in the Late Eighteenth and Early Nineteenth Century." *Discourses of Slavery and Abolition: Britain and its Colonies, 1760–1838.* Eds. Brycchan Carey, Markman Ellis, and Sara Salih. Houndsmill and New York: Palgrave Macmillan, 2004. 11–25. Print.

Lauro, Sarah and Karen Embry. "A Zombie Manifesto: The Nonhuman Condition in the Era of Advanced Capitalism." *Boundary 2* 35.1 (2008). 85–108. Web.

Lee, Debbie ed. *Slavery, Abolition and Emancipation: Writings in the British Romantic Period. Volume 3. The Emancipation Debate.* London: Pickering and Chatto, 1999. Print.

Lovejoy, Arthur. *The Great Chain of Being: A Study of a History of an Idea.* 1st e-book Ed. New Brundwick and London: Transaction Publishers, 2010. *Google Book Search.* Web. 31 July 2017.

Marx, Karl and Friedrich Engels. *The German Ideology: Part One.* C.J. Arthur ed. New York: International Publishers, 1970. Print.

Matthew, H.C.G. "Gladstone, Sir John, first baronet (1764–1851)." *Oxford Dictionary of National Biography.* Online ed., Jan 2008. Oxford: University Press, 2004. Web. 4 September 2012.

Mautner, Gerlinde. "Checks and Balances: How Corpus Linguistics can Contribute to CDA." *Methods of Critical Discourse Analysis.* Eds. Ruth Wodak and Michael Meyer. 2nd ed. London: Sage, 2009. 122–143. Print.

Mosse, George L. *Towards the Final Solution: A History of European Racism.* Madison: The University of Wisconsin Press, 1985. Print.

Pocock, J.G.A. "Gibbon's Decline and Fall and the World View of the Late Enlightenment." *Eighteenth-Century Studies* 10.3 (1977): 287–303. *Jstor.* Web. 18 July 2012.

Quinault, Roland. "Gladstone and Slavery." *Historical Journal* 52.2 (2009): 363–383. *Jstor.* Web.

Quintanilla, Mark. "Mercantile Communities in the Ceded Islands: the Alexander Bartlet George Campbell Company". *International Social Science Review* 79.1/2 (2004): 14–26. *Jstor*. Web.

Rabinow, Paul ed. *The Foucault Reader*. New York: Pantheon, 1984. Print.

Rycenga, Jennifer. "A Greater Awakening: Women's Intellect as a Factor in Early Abolitionist Movements, 1824." *Journal of Feminist Studies in Religion* 21.2 (2005): 31–59. *Jstor*. Web. 12 August 2016.

Said, Edward. *Culture and Imperialism*. London: Vintage, 1994. Print.

---. *Orientalism*. New York: Vintage, 1979.

---."Blind Imperial Arrogance: Vile Stereotyping of Arabs by the U.S. Ensures Years of Turmoil" <http://www.ems.ucsb.edu/people/rightmire/ling2/Arrogance.htm>. Web. 21 February 2012.

Seabrook, William. *The Magic Island*. New York: Harcourt, Brace and Co, 1929. Print.

Sheridan, Richard. "The Condition of the Slaves on the Sugar Plantations of Sir John Gladstone in the Colony of Demerara, 1812–1849." *New West Indian Guide/Nieuwe West-Indische Gids* 76.3&4 (2002): 243–269. *KITLV*. Web. 1 June 2016.

Shillington, Kevin. *History of Africa*. 3rd ed. Houndmills: Palgrave Macmillan, 2012. Print.

Shyllon, Folarin. *James Ramsay: The Unknown Abolitionist*. Edinburgh: Canongate, 1977. Print.

Small, David. "James Tobin (1736/7–1817)." *Oxford Dictionary of National Biography*. Online ed., Jan 2008. Oxford: University Press, 2004. Web. 4 September 2012.

Theweleit, Klaus. *Männerphantasien 1+2*. 3rd ed. n.p.: Piper, 2000. Print.

Trigger, Bruce. "Review: The Myth of the Noble Savage by Ter Ellington." *The International History Review*. 24.1 (2002): 136–137. *Jstor*. Web. 17 October 2016.

Turley, David. *The Culture of English Anti-slavery: 1780–1860*. London: Routledge, 1991. Print.

van Dijk, Teun. "Multidisciplinary CDA: A Plea for Diversity." *Methods of Critical Discourse Analysis*. Eds. Ruth Wodak and Michael Meyer. 1st ed. London: Sage Publications, 2001. 95–119. Print.

van Dijk, Teun. "Critical Discourse Analysis." *The Handbook of Discourse Analysis*. Eds. Deborah Schiffrin, Deborah Tannen, and Heidi E. Hamilton. Oxford: Blackwell, 2001. Print.

Watt, J. "Ramsay, James (1733–1789)." *Oxford Dictionary of National Biography*. Online ed., Jan 2008. Oxford: University Press, 2004. Web. 4 Sept 2012.

Webb, Marc O. *Cicero's Paradoxa Stoicorum: A New Translation with Philosophical Commentary*. N.p., 1985. Google Search. Web. 14 April 2016.

Williams, Eric. *Capitalism and Slavery*. London: Andre Deutsch, 1964. Print

Wodak, Ruth and Michael Meyer."Critical Discourse Analysis: History, Agenda, Theory and Methodology." *Methods of Critical Discourse Analysis*. Eds. Ruth Wodak and Michael Meyer. 2nd ed. London: Sage Publications, 2009. 1–33. Print.

Wolfe, Cary. *What is Posthumanism*. Minneapolis and London: University of Minnesota Press, 2010. Print.

Wolffe, John. "Wilberforce, William (1759–1833)." *Oxford Dictionary of National Biography*. Online ed., May 2009. Oxford: University Press, 2004. Web. 4 September 2012.

Young, B.W. "Warburton, William (1698–1779), Bishop of Gloucester and Religious Controversialist." *Oxford Dictionary of National Biography*. Online ed., May 2007. Oxford: University Press, 2004. Web. 16 September 2015.

ibidem.eu